Trucker Rhapsody & Other Plays is a sweeping and incisive exploration of what it means to be human in an American landscape of conflict, unrest, and inequality during the past 50+ years. Press-Coffman calls to mind Kushner and Deavere Smith, providing no easy healing but offering the balm of empathy. When she holds a mirror up to nature in these plays, we may not like what we see, but perhaps we won't be so quick to look away.
—**Dr. Judith Sebasta**, Austin Community College

These plays, set in recent historical moments of heightened pressures and conflicting interests, are nonetheless driven by the characters in all their flesh-and-blood humanity, their impulses both grand and trivial. Toni Press-Coffman has a natural instinct for authentic dialogue. Her fully dimensional characters materialize before you, emerging from the page effortlessly. Her skill at weaving divergent threads and points-of-view into one complex, irresolvable but co-arising American experience is unique.
—**Susan Marsden**, Resident Director, Eureka Theatre (Retired)

Toni Press-Coffman is a humane creator of characters struggling to navigate their interwoven lives. Times and spaces overlap as we witness their struggles to form community in a world of disunity.
—**James Reel**, Arts Critic and Journalist

Perhaps Toni Press-Coffman's greatest gift as a writer is to break open her characters (widely diverse, spanning centuries, races, genders, class and politics) to reveal to us their beating hearts. Often meticulously researched, her plays are never burdened by historical detail, but enriched by a context that helps us, her audience, to glimpse the full humanity of her characters. Given voice by a theatrical language that is both heightened and deceptively natural, Press-Coffman's plays pulse with a driving rhythm and flashes of searing imagery.
—**Brad Erickson**, Playwright and Executive Director, Theatre Bay Area

Playwright Toni Press-Coffman challenges her readers and audiences to delve deeply into the lives and worlds of her characters, both based on real people and fictional. Her plays are, ironically, both retrospective and uncannily timely, carrying readers back through the social turbulence of the sixties or into the political tinderbox of the twenty-first century. She explores motifs of the feminist and drug cultures in America and the impact of language and music on changing social structures. Reverie, overlapping time frames and dialogue, and fast moving, juxtaposed scenes give the plays' action a docu-dramatic edge. Her characters' intelligence and passion often belie their youth and circumstances. In these plays, Ms. Press-Coffman raises a plethora of societal, cultural and philosophical questions that her characters seek to answer or ignore at their peril.
—**Jacqueline Leo**, Director, Theatre and Dramaturgy Instructor

The storytelling of Press-Coffman's *Trucker Rhapsody* pulls no punches. Her play, utilizing language and rhythm, evokes the history it tells and challenges the audience to keep watching. Although it's an iconic story that many know, we leave it learning more about the heart of the characters and the day's imprint upon so many lives.
—**Katherine Murphy**, Director

TRUCKER RHAPSODY
&
OTHER PLAYS

TRUCKER RHAPSODY
&
OTHER PLAYS

TONI PRESS-COFFMAN

Wising Up Press

Wising Up Press
P.O. Box 2122
Decatur, GA 30031-2122
www.universaltable.org

Copyright © 2021 by Toni Press-Coffman

All rights reserved. No part of this book may be used or reproduced in any manner whatsoever without written permission, except in the case of brief quotations embodied in critical articles or reviews.

Catalogue-in-Publication data is on file with the Library of Congress.
LCCN: 2021944193

ISBN: 978-1-7376940-9-0

CONTENTS

FOREWORD	1
UNCONDITIONAL WAR	3
TRUCKER RHAPSODY	61
ARMOR	107
STAND	161
UNITED	221
AFTERWORD	284
ACKNOWLEDGMENTS	286
PLAYS BY TONI PRESS-COFFMAN	288
AUTHOR	289

I dedicate this book of plays to my playwriting colleagues, Brad Erickson, Katherine Murphy and Cherylene Lee, who have joined me on playwriting retreats every nine months or so for more than twenty-five years. They have given me the immeasurable gifts of support for my career, a profound understanding of my aesthetic, and feedback all along the way of the creation and revision of my work.

To Glen, my renaissance man of a husband, whose curiosity knows no bounds and whose love I can count on every minute of every day, thank you. You have my heart.

FOREWORD

How do we aptly sum up the turbulence and devastation wrought during the first quarter of the twenty-first century? Should we start with the world pandemic that has claimed hundreds of thousands of lives, shut down economies and separated us from our loved ones, or in some cases, our homelands? Or the civil unrest that happens when the former leader of the United States of America makes it clear that not all states and all people are deserving of concern and funding? Maybe the fear that a simple slogan, Black Lives Matter, creates in those who cannot grasp the concept of privilege? Or do we begin with a riotous crowd, so besotted with a fabrication that they storm the nation's Capitol, looking for, and drawing, blood? We are braced for disaster; our social structures ruptured by a year of masks and fear, we live through our computers and nurture a deep distrust of what we perceive as other. Such times, we think, are unprecedented.

The five plays written by Toni Press-Coffman and presented in this collection, which take place in the US from 1967 to the present, are a blazing reminder that today's struggles, while new to us, are themes that have surfaced before. Civil unrest, racial inequality, integrity in one's work, the law of unintended consequences, a terrorist attack—in these pieces, Press-Coffman recreates real moments in history, yet these are not merely historical plays. Historical plays, or documentary plays, tend to emphasize events, and the facts that surround those events. Press-Coffman's plays humanize the players so that they are not merely action figures, but thoughtful, engaged agents of their deeds. Somehow, she manages to penetrate the motivations of her characters much like a Method actor would prepare for a role—artfully uncovering their inner thoughts and provocations. We understand why one character would want to hurt another, even if the act is criminal. We understand what would make a character turn to drugs. We understand why a character would want to help another character, even though that character might be perceived as having a competing, even dangerous, agenda.

Press-Coffman is a fearless writer who is able to identify with and portray people in the mainstream, people in the margins, people of different races, sexes, ages, and classes. My husband and I read "Trucker Rhapsody" aloud. When we finished we sat in contemplative silence. "She is able to understand, to feel, every character's point of view," said my husband finally. This is no easy feat. Press-Coffman is not judging. She is merely presenting us with human beings who make decisions, take action, all with consequences, some good, some bad.

Reader, in these times of isolation, I urge you to have a play reading with your friends—on Zoom, in a backyard, at an outdoor cafe. Reading these pieces aloud will give you a deeper understanding of events and how they occur, as well as some comfort in the fact that, indeed, we humans have always struggled with our place in the world, with ourselves, and with each other. When you are done reading, you too will feel a little less afraid, a little more uplifted, as she has created a space that includes all of us, with empathy and compassion.

Michele Markarian
Playwright, *Unborn Children of America*

UNCONDITIONAL WAR

CHARACTERS:

LYNDON JOHNSON, President of the United States
LADYBIRD JOHNSON, his wife
AIDE, White, aide to the President, late 20s-30s at the start of the play
MR. YOUNGBLOOD, Black, a Porter, 50s-60s

TONY MOSES, Black, Harlem resident, 16-17 at the start of the play
BUTCH JOHNSON, Black, Harlem resident, 16-17 at the start of the play
LEROY TOWERS, Black, Harlem resident, 17 at the start of the play

WAYNE PEARSON, Black, SNCC (Student Nonviolent Coordinating Committee) Worker, Lexington Mississippi, 21 at the start of the play
VIRGINIA (GINNY) HAWTHORNE, Black, SNCC Worker, Lexington Mississippi, 20 at the start of the play
HARTMAN TURNBOW, Black, resident of Lexington Mississippi, 30s

JASPER PEDERS, White, Berkeley student, 20-21 at the start of the play
DAVID DOUBIAGO, White, former Berkeley student, 21 at the start of the play
HARMONY, White, Jasper's girlfriend after the war, 17

Scene 1: Christmas Eve 1963 in the following locations: Johnson's study in his Texas home; a street in Harlem; a living room in Berkeley; a freedom house in Lexington, Mississippi; a porch in front of an Akron, Ohio home.

Scene 2: March 1965 in the following locations: Johnson's study in his Texas home; a street in Harlem; a freedom house in Lexington, Mississippi; a street in Lexington, Mississippi.

Scene 3: January 1968-May 4, 1970 in the following locations: Johnson's study in his Texas home; a street in Harlem; a living room in Berkeley.

Scene 4: December 1971-January 1972 in the following locations: Johnson's study in his Texas home; a meeting room in Austin, Texas; a living room in Berkeley.

SCENE 1

(Christmas Eve 1963. In the dark, we hear several gunshots. As the lights come up on PRESIDENT LYNDON JOHNSON's study, we hear his recorded voice.)

JOHNSON: My fellow Americans. All I have I would have given gladly not to be standing here today. The greatest leader of our time has been struck down by the foulest deed of our time. Today John Fitzgerald Kennedy lives in the immortal words and works that he left behind. No words are sad enough to express our sense of loss. No words are strong enough to express our determination to continue the forward thrust of America that he began. The dream of conquering the vastness of space—the dream of education for all of our children—the dream of an all-out attack on mental illness—and above all, the dream of equal rights for all Americans, whatever their race or color. On the 20th of January 1961, John F. Kennedy told his countrymen that our national work would not be finished in the first thousand days, nor in the life, of his administration, nor even perhaps in our lifetime on this planet. But, he said, "Let us begin." Today, in this moment of new resolve, I say to all my fellow Americans, let us continue.

(Sometime during the recording's playing, on the stage, JOHNSON pours himself a glass of orange soda. AIDE sits and watches him. JOHNSON lifts his glass.)

JOHNSON: Let me get you a drink—hard, soft—we got everything. (*standing, calling*) Bird!!
AIDE: No thank you.
JOHNSON: How about some of this? You want to join me in a glass of orange crush? Come on now, it's no trouble, it's my pleasure.
AIDE: I'm really not thirsty.
JOHNSON: (*overlap*) I appreciate you coming, I'll tell you that. I'm always happy to have you down here and I promise you, you are going to love a Johnson Christmas. Tonight, you will not be able to believe what you're tasting. Bird sets a fine holiday table.
AIDE: Yes, I remember. Last year—I ate so much, I could hardly stand up.
JOHNSON: (*overlap*) That's right, you were here last Christmas Eve, weren't you? Am I right?
AIDE: Last two, Mr. Johnson.

(JOHNSON gets up and goes to him, sits on the arm of AIDE's chair, and puts

his hand on his shoulder.)

JOHNSON: There's nothing like Christmas on the Pedernales, is there?
AIDE: No, sir.
JOHNSON: Last year was nothing. Last year I was still the Vice-President. (*JOHNSON laughs loudly. His laughter subsides. He moves his face very close to the AIDE's*) This year I am the President, and I need your help. I badly need your help.

(The lights dim on JOHNSON's voice, and come up on:

TONY, LEROY and BUTCH standing on a Harlem Street. Although they are all about the same age, BUTCH is quite a bit bigger than TONY and LEROY. They're listening to music on a transistor radio—"It's All Right" by the Impressions—singing and dancing along. TONY carries a sketchpad, which he taps on with a pencil in time to the music

GINNY and WAYNE in the SNCC office and freedom house in Lexington, Mississippi. They sit at a table with a lamp on it, doing paperwork.

JASPER sits in a Berkeley living room, in a yoga position in front of a lit candle.

(A LOUD GUNSHOT)

LEROY, TONY and BUTCH frolic.

JASPER meditates.

WAYNE and GINNY jump out of their chairs and under the table.)

WAYNE: Holy shit.
GINNY: The light.
WAYNE: What?
GINNY: The light. (*She quickly gets up and bumps her head against the table.*) SHIT. (*She jumps up again and turns off the light so quickly, she knocks it over as she gets back under the table.*)

(Just as she gets down, **ANOTHER SHOT RINGS OUT.** *WAYNE and GINNY stay under the table in black.)*

GINNY: Wayne? (*beat*) Wayne? Where are you?
WAYNE: I'm right here.
GINNY: Jesus, answer me when I talk to you. You scared me.
WAYNE: I'm here. I'm not hit.
GINNY: Wayne?
WAYNE: Shh. I hear 'em coming up to the house.
GINNY: Are you sure?
WAYNE: SHHHHH.

LEROY: (*singing along*)
Say It's All Right
Have A Good Time
Cause It's All Right
Yeah, It's All Right

(*Exhilaration and laughter from Harlem.*)

WAYNE: (*a whisper*) He's at the window.

BUTCH: Leroy, you sing good. Those Impressions got nothin' on you.
LEROY: Shit.
BUTCH: Shit, nothin'. I'm already plannin' on becomin' your manager and makin' you famous, and travelin' all around the world in the finest clothes with the finest women.
TONY: You got big plans.
LEROY: That's good, Butch. You dream that dream, why not?
TONY: You got to make sure that dream's not gonna fool you, lead you around by the nose, then drop you on your ass.
BUTCH: You carryin' that drawin' pad with you everywhere, you got to be dreamin' something.
TONY: This I got control over.
LEROY: Baby, nobody got control over nothin'. That's why my mama say, "leave it in God's hands, Leroy."

(DAVID *enters the room where Jasper is meditating.*)

DAVID: Evening, Jasper.

(*JASPER ignores him.*)

DAVID: You're gone again, Jasper, you're in the land of the light. (*DAVID shakes his head and walks to the stereo, where he puts on a Bob Dylan album. He stands in front of the record as it plays and salutes it.*) Jasper is away again, Bobby. But I—I salute you, my man. (*He moves to JASPER.*) You packed, buddy?

GINNY: Is he still there?
WAYNE: Yes.
GINNY: Is there only one of them?
WAYNE: Yes.
GINNY: Is he coming up to the house?
WAYNE: (*fierce whisper*) You are going to get me killed, Virginia. Shut up.

(*JASPER opens his eyes and gets up, walks over to the record.*)

DAVID: He has returned to the land of the living. Jasper, you packed or what? (*no answer*) We're going to miss our plane. (*no answer*) My mother will pee her pants if we miss the plane, Jasper, and Theresa will be disappointed if we're late, man. Could we not disappoint my little sister?

(*JASPER salutes the record. A beat, then he turns to DAVID. JASPER is a formidable presence, very tall, with a deep, deep voice.*)

JASPER: Dave. (*He waits.*)

(*After a couple beats, DAVID turns to him.*)

JASPER: You don't listen. How many times do I have to tell you the same thing? The most important thing any of us learns to do is—
JASPER/DAVID: (*this is a ritual*) Pay attention. (*They hug each other, laugh.*)
DAVID: 20,000 students at Berkeley, how'd I get hooked up with you, man?
JASPER: How you doing, buddy?
DAVID: Good.
JASPER: There is more than one way to live and, therefore, more than one land to live in.

WAYNE: They're gone.

GINNY: You positive?
WAYNE: Yeah.

DAVID: Jasper? Let's please not miss our plane.

(*JASPER blows out his candle. Black for a second, then:*

WAYNE turns on the lamp and puts it on the table. GINNY comes out from under the table and looks up at Wayne.)

GINNY: They gone?
WAYNE: Yeah, Ginny. They're gone. (*He reaches out to her and she takes his hand. He pulls her to her feet.*)
WAYNE: Merry Christmas, crackers.

(*TONY stands a bit apart from BUTCH and LEROY, sketching. LEROY looks toward the sky.*)

LEROY: Hey, man, it's snowing.
BUTCH: Gonna be a white Christmas, baby.
TONY: There is not another kind of Christmas. White the only kind they is.
LEROY: Look at those flakes. Those are fine, big flakes. We gonna have our own winter wonderland right here uptown. (*singing, making fun*) "In the lane, snow is glistenin." Shit.
BUTCH: I tell you what else I'm gonna do, Leroy. I'm gonna learn to play the piano and I'm gonna accompany you, just like Bobby Tucker play behind Billie Holiday back in the day.
TONY: Where you gonna get a piano, Butch?
LEROY: You ever played a piano?
BUTCH: They got one down at Wiltwyck. I banged on it some down there. They used it to try to reform me. You know, play that beautiful music, get off that shit, start livin' clean. Then again, I am not on shit in the first place so that part of reforming me was easy.
LEROY: Well, we are going to get you a piano. We gonna steal you a big, beautiful piano.
TONY: Sure thing. We do that for you, Butch.
BUTCH: You gonna have to get pretty far out of Harlem for that work.
LEROY: There's one at the Holy Rollers my mama goes to.
BUTCH: You gonna steal the Holy Rollers' piano?

LEROY: My mama'd lay down and die if that piano disappeared. Am I right?

(They laugh. Then, one by one, they sit down on the sidewalk.)

WAYNE: *(touching GINNY, who is shaking)* It's okay, Ginny. Don't cry now.
GINNY: DON'T CRY? *(She clears the table of all the papers, which fall on the floor.)* SHIT.

(BUTCH stands up.)

TONY: Where you going?
BUTCH: It's Christmas tomorrow, baby. I got to wrap up a gift for mama. I told her I found her something and asked her, you don't need me to wrap it up, right? I just give it to you in the bag with a bow on top. She say what kinda present is that? "NO!"
TONY: You crazy, Butch. Course she say no.
LEROY: How 'bout a little Christmas carol before you go?
BUTCH: White Christmas?
TONY: Shit.
BUTCH: Santa Claus is Comin' to Harlem?
LEROY: And we gonna light him up.
TONY: I know one.
LEROY: What you talking about?
TONY: We're Catholic. You know.
LEROY: Your mama never been inside a church, man.

(Long pause. TONY and BUTCH look at LEROY, who takes a small step back, sucks in his breath. He puts his hands up in apology.)

LEROY: Yeah.

(DAVID and JASPER sit together in front of DAVID's childhood home in Akron, Ohio. Golden orange light in the distance.)

DAVID: *(pointing)* Steelworks. My father's in there right now sweating his life out. I keep thinking something's going to fall on him and kill him and mom's going to be left here with four kids to take care of. But then I can sit here and glance that way and think—look at those colors. Gold. Orange. God, that's beautiful.

JASPER: I thank you for inviting me to share in your midwestern holiday celebration.
DAVID: I'm talking to you about my father, Jasper. (*beat*) Jerk.
JASPER: That was a heartfelt appreciation, Dave.
DAVID: Yeah, you're welcome.
JASPER: Your mother's dinner was unparalleled.
DAVID: Unparalleled lasagna?

(*The lights dim everywhere else on the stage as they come up on JOHNSON's ranch. The AIDE sits there alone. JOHNSON enters.*)

JOHNSON: Can't afford a day off, even today. Even tomorrow. How was that dinner, any good?
AIDE: It was delicious.
JOHNSON: I'm gonna get mine now, in a few minutes. (*He pours himself an orange soda.*) Fuck, I miss cigarettes. I haven't had a cigarette in eight years and I still miss smoking every day. Still do miss it. That sucking. Nothing like it. (*He laughs.*) Nothing like that sucking.
AIDE: (*standing*) Will you thank Bird for me?
JOHNSON: You're staying, right? A couple days?
AIDE: Well, I didn't bring any clothes.
JOHNSON: Clothes? Shit, we'll get you clothes. What we'll do is, tomorrow morning before breakfast we'll fly up and get that gorgeous wife of yours and fly her down here with you. I love that woman of yours, you know I do.
AIDE: I don't know, Mr. Johnson.
JOHNSON: What do you mean, you don't know? Sure you know. (*pause*) I can't be alone tonight. I know I won't be able to sleep and I can't face being alone. (*beat, then a laugh*) Who's the President of the United States around here, you or me?
AIDE: You, Mr. Johnson.
JOHNSON: That's right. Now, lots of people are gonna be here tomorrow to celebrate the holiday with their president. (*laugh*) To kiss their president's ass. Which is just fine with me. I want 'em to kiss my ass in Macy's window and say, boy, that sure was sweet. Even Bobby Kennedy. What do you think of that?
AIDE: I think that's a longshot.
JOHNSON: (*a big laugh*) Except I'm the boss now and he'll just have to eat all those bad feelings, because now I've got his pecker in my pocket.

I win, see. (*after a pause*) I know what you're thinking. At what cost? (*fierce*) Well, I know that. But he's dead and it's my turn and I'll tell you something else. I'm going to do what he just talked about doing. He waffled, you and I both know he waffled. He was so wrapped up in that clean cut—I'm from Harvard—I'm smarter than all the rest of the folks in this country—bullshit that he didn't get it done. Well, I may not have gone to Harvard, but there's a saying here in Texas. If you know you're right, just keep coming and no gun can stop you. I am coming and let me tell you something, we're going to pass that goddamn civil rights act and we're going to do it fast or I'm going to bust every one of your asses. (*A pause. He looks out the window.*)

LEROY: (*to Tony*) So?
TONY: Well, I was in the choir, man.
BUTCH: Then sing it to us, Tony.

(*TONY looks at them and shakes his head.*)

BUTCH: Come on, man. Sing it to us.
TONY: It's "O Holy Night".
BUTCH: Sing "O Holy Night" to us.
TONY: Suppose somebody sees me or something?
LEROY: Then if they got something to say about it, we gonna bust their ass. Shit, Butch standing here. Nobody gonna say nothin' with Butch right here.

(*Another beat, then TONY starts to sing.*)

TONY: (*singing*) Oh Holy Night, the stars are . . .
BUTCH: Go on, Tony.
LEROY: Yeah, go on.
TONY: (*singing*)
Oh Holy Night, the starts are brightly shining.
It is the night of our dear Savior's birth.

(*He continues to sing.*)

(*In the freedom house, WAYNE is picking papers up off the floor.*)

GINNY: No. Leave 'em there. (*She stomps across the room, over the papers.*)
WAYNE: (*but laughing*) Stop. Ginny. Stop it.

(*She does. He keeps picking up papers.*)

WAYNE: The maid's off today, you want to help me do this?
GINNY: You never mind. I'll clean up my mess.
WAYNE: Come on, let's get something on the radio.

(*GINNY picks up papers as WAYNE turns on the radio. He gets "Get A Job" first, goes past it.*)

GINNY: I like that.
WAYNE: I'm looking for Christmas music. (*He keeps fidgeting, gets in "O Holy Night."*) Okay?
GINNY: That's gonna make me think about my mama, which I don't want to do. (*beat*) Eligible to vote in Holmes county. What difference does it make how many? They're not coming out.
WAYNE: They are going to come out.
GINNY: Before that Sheriff's goons kill you and me? I gave up my sophomore year of college for this, Wayne, and I'm not registering anybody. I'm spending half my life under this damn table.
WAYNE: What we need is more help.
GINNY: What we need is a different country to live in. Shit, I am hungry. I've been hungry for three weeks, and it'd be different if we were doing what we're getting our stinking 18 dollars a month for, but we're not registering anybody.
WAYNE: We're gonna get some of those white boys from Harvard down here to help us and you're gonna see what a difference it makes.
GINNY: Oh, yeah, I can tell how much help those (*imitating him*) white boys from Harvard are gonna be, Wayne. I can see already how much you're gonna appreciate their help.
WAYNE: Listen to the pretty music, Virginia.

TONY: (*singing, finishing the song*)
  O Night.
  O Holy Night.

(*Silence on the stage for several seconds.*)

BUTCH: Merry Christmas, Tony
LEROY: Yeah, you too. Merry Christmas.
BUTCH: Leroy, Merry Christmas.

(BUTCH exits.)

DAVID: Merry Christmas, Jasper.
JASPER: Yes. Thank you.
DAVID: So. *(pause)* I'm going to Mississippi.
JASPER: *(a beat)* You sign up?
DAVID: Yes. Yesterday.
JASPER: Well done. *(beat)* How are you feeling?
DAVID: Good. *(a laugh)* I'm not scared yet.
JASPER: *(puts and arm around David)* Social experiment.
DAVID: I knew you were going to say that.
JASPER: It is a noble social experiment and holy mission and your courageous decision to participate warrants a reward.
DAVID: You got any?
JASPER: My suitcase is filled with the evil weed and it is calling us.
DAVID: I hear it.
JASPER: I was saving it for your Yuletide offering. But Christmas Eve, close enough.
DAVID: Let's get ripped. *(He and JASPER exit.)*

TONY: You going home?
LEROY: No, baby. I was thinkin' if you know where I can get some stuff I'd buy a little bit.
TONY: You got the money?
LEROY: I got it.
TONY: Come on then. I'll take care of you. *(He puts his arm around LEROY and they start to exit.)* Your Mama finds out I helped you buy junk, she gonna kill me.
LEROY: *(a chuckle)* You right about that.

(TONY and LEROY exit, TONY giving LEROY a friendly punch in the ribs.)

GINNY: I've lost 15 pounds in 7 weeks.
WAYNE: Me too.

GINNY: You think mama would invite me down for some Christmas dinner? Not even for Christmas. She's so scared shitless me working with SNCC's going to get her killed.
WAYNE: Which it might.
GINNY: Which I know it might. Why aren't you home, Wayne?
WAYNE: Your mama. My daddy. He was pissed because I went away to college. He needed me to work that little farm he's got, growing his own cotton crop, and he never does any better than break even. Forget that, you know? Now I got my college degree, but it doesn't make a difference to him. Once I was gone, I was gone.
GINNY: Why won't they stand up for themselves?
WAYNE: You know why. They don't want to spend half their lives under this damn table. Listen, I'll be back in a little while.
GINNY: You're going to leave me here alone? Don't you dare leave me here alone.
WAYNE: I'll be back before you even realize I've been gone.
GINNY: Where are you going?
WAYNE: Virginia, I am going out to get us a Christmas tree. Just a little one.
GINNY: Come on, I don't need a Christmas tree.
WAYNE: We need one.
GINNY: Never mind the Christmas tree. Take me dancing.

(WAYNE laughs.)

GINNY: What's so damn funny?
WAYNE: I'm just gonna waltz you into one of the hotspots in downtown Lexington and nobody's gonna mind. Matter of fact, maybe I'll just call the sheriff and ask him to give us a ride downtown.
GINNY: Okay, so how you gonna pay for this little Christmas tree?
WAYNE: They might not be registering, but they like us. I'm gonna find someone with the Christmas spirit.
GINNY: In that case, bring me back a hamburger.
WAYNE: You'd be surprised. *(He starts out, then turns back to her.)* Tomorrow we're gonna do something fun. I don't know what, but something.
GINNY: You promise?
WAYNE: I promise.
GINNY: You swear to God?
WAYNE: Ginny, I will see you shortly. *(He exits.)*
(GINNY sits down with her paperwork. The lights dim on her, as they come up

on JOHNSON's ranch. JOHNSON is at the window, AIDE's somewhere in the room.)

JOHNSON: A lot of changes have taken place in this hill country. (*beat*) I was born here.
AIDE: Yes, sir. I know.
JOHNSON: And I still live here. I've seen the night illuminated and the kitchens warmed and the homes heated where once the cheerless cold held sway. (*pause*) I fucking lit up the Pedernales and now I'm going to go further. We can pass the Civil Rights Act now. I didn't vote for it in the fifties because we didn't have the votes and there's nothing worse than a dead liberal. If you're going to kill a snake with a hoe, you have to get it with one blow at the head. I am going to kill that snake now and you are going to help me do it. (*going to the door*) BIRD. Bring me something to eat. (*beat*) She in bed or what? (*beat*) BIRD. (*to AIDE*) There she is. (*out the door*) I want some dinner. (*to AIDE*) I think I liked her better when she was skinnier. (*He laughs.*) She's the best woman who ever lived, even with a few extra pounds.
BIRD: (*off*): Do you need soda?
JOHNSON: Got some. (*to AIDE*) How about you? You need any more to eat?
AIDE: I'm stuffed.
JOHNSON: You're skinny as a rail. I used to be too, you know, but with Bird's rum pie. I'll tell you.

(BIRD *enters with a tray. He sits down to eat. She starts to leave.*)

JOHNSON: Where you going? Stay here.
BIRD: I'm tired. I'm going to bed.
JOHNSON: Stay here. Sit down.

(*She sits. He eats.*)

JOHNSON: (*pointing to a portrait in plain view, to AIDE*) You know Sam Rayburn?

AIDE: Of course, Mr. Johnson.
JOHNSON: Why in the name of God did he pick this year to go and die on me? I need him now. (*beat, then to Bird*) What are you doing here? Go to

bed.
BIRD: Good-night, darling. (*to AIDE*) Good-night.
AIDE: Good-night, Mrs. Johnson.

(Bird starts to exit. Johnson goes to her, kisses her deeply.)

JOHNSON: You remember when I kissed you in the Taj Mahal right in front of that prince or sheik or whatever the hell he was? You remember that?
BIRD: Remember? I nearly fainted. Good-night. (*She exits.*)
JOHNSON: (*to AIDE*) How long you been married?
AIDE: I got married last summer, sir.
JOHNSON: Was I there?
AIDE: Yes, sir. You sang, actually. At the reception.
JOHNSON: (*chuckles*) Did I?
AIDE: You certainly did.
JOHNSON: You're kinda old to just be gettin' to the marriage game. How old are you?
AIDE: 35.
JOHNSON: Back in '28 I was teaching those Mexican kids and you were just being born?
AIDE: Yes, sir.
JOHNSON: Isn't that somethin'? You just bein' born and me already teachin' school. (*beat*) They were pathetic, those kids. Everybody around here was poor, but I never saw anything like that kind of poverty. Now I've got the chance to do some real good for those kids, and their own kids, and I'll let you in on a secret. I mean to use it. (*beat*) You want something to eat?

SCENE 2

(Late March 1965. As the lights come up, we hear JOHNSON's recorded voice.)

JOHNSON: Unfortunately, many Americans live on the outskirts of hope. Some because of their poverty and some because of their color and all too many because of both. And this administration, here and now, declares unconditional war on poverty in America. It will not be a short or easy struggle, but the richest nation on earth can afford to win it. We cannot afford to lose it.

(On stage, JOHNSON is laughing. BIRD is sitting near him, and the AIDE is

somewhere in the room.)

(In the freedom house, GINNY and DAVID are on the floor, kissing passionately.)

JOHNSON: So I said you know, George, you can turn that situation around in a minute. Why dontcha just desegregate your schools? Let's you and I go out there in front of those TV cameras right now and announce you've decided to desegregate every school in Alabama. (*imitating Wallace*) Oh, no, Mr. President, I can't do that. The schools have got school boards; they're locally run. I haven't got the political power to do that. I said, don't you shit me, George Wallace. (*He laughs heartily.*) He nearly peed his fuckin' deep South pants.

(WAYNE enters the freedom house, sees GINNY and DAVID kissing.)

WAYNE: For Christ's sake. (*beat, and he takes a deep breath*) I brought Mr. Turnbow. You wouldn't mind registering a voter, would you? (*beat*) They told him the registrar wasn't in and made him wait all morning and then closed for lunch. I brought him over here for something to eat and then we're going to go on back. (*as he turns toward the door*) I'd appreciate you both coming with me because we've got eleven others waiting to see how Mr. Turnbow does and it looks like there might be trouble.
GINNY: Of course we'll go with you.
WAYNE: (*looking behind him*) Come on in, Mr. Turnbow.
DAVID (*to GINNY*): I wish he wouldn't talk to you that way.
GINNY: Not now, David.

(GINNY starts to fix sandwiches as WAYNE and HARTMAN TURNBOW enter. TURNBOW is a farmer, about 30 years old. He wears a soft hat and carries a briefcase.)

(LEROY enters and sits on a stoop, humming to himself.)

TURNBOW: (*to DAVID*) Hartman Turnbow. (*He and DAVID shake hands.*)

DAVID: David Doubiago.
TURNBOW: Funny name there.
DAVID: Italian.
GINNY: David's from Berkeley, Mr. Turnbow. Berkeley, California.

TURNBOW: Good deal.
GINNY: I'm Ginny Hawthorne.
WAYNE: Sandwich, Mr. Turnbow?
TURNBOW: Yes, I'll have it.
DAVID: (*pointing to briefcase*) Let me take that.
TURNBOW: Not too far. That's my gun.

(*DAVID puts the briefcase down. GINNY stares at TURNBOW, who starts to eat.*)

LEROY: (*singing*)
    Daddy's home.
    Daddy's home to stay.

(*BUTCH enters.*)

BUTCH: Hey, Leroy. You seen Tony?
LEROY: Tony'll be right by. How's that job?
BUTCH: It's nothin'. Dishes is dishes. Look, Leroy, you expect me to make you famous, you got to get off this Daddy's Home thing and get behind some new shit. Where's Tony at? Painting?
LEROY: He was doing that painting earlier today.
BUTCH: You see that work?
LEROY: Yeah. I seen it.
BUTCH: Beautiful stuff. He got all that CRE-A-TIV-I-TY, man. I envy that cat.
LEROY: He got—I can't place it. Something inside him, and we don't see it so much. You see that picture he paint of that little boy got killed in Mississippi? What's that little nigger's name?
BUTCH: Emmett Till.
LEROY: He got that picture of that boy all drowned and washed up on the riverbank. Baby, that picture scare me. (*beat*) It sure is beautiful. (*Beat LEROY starts to shake, tries to control it.*)
BUTCH: You don't look so good, baby.
LEROY: I'm a little strung out, but it's gonna be okay.
BUTCH: That where Tony's at right now? Getting you stuff?
LEROY: He'll be right here, don't worry about it.
BUTCH: I'll be back.
LEROY: Don't be like that now.

BUTCH: You were clean a year, Leroy. Now you're back on shit.

(LEROY tries to get up.)

LEROY: I'm gonna get clean again, man.
BUTCH: No, stay there. It's all right. I'm behind you.

(LEROY sits there, starts to shake. Stops. Starts to hum. Holds his arms tight, tries to keep humming, stops. BUTCH sits beside him.)

JOHNSON: I know those sons of bitches are out there breaking things and busting heads and rioting and it just hurts them, but I'll tell you the truth and that's if I were them I'd have been kicking butt a long time ago. These Negroes have been laying down and taking it, they have been taking it, and I know I've wondered when the hell are they going to wake up and punch someone in the face? You do not let people treat you like that and then expect them to give you respect when you ask for it.
BIRD: Of course, that's easier said than done. With the risk it would have been. Well, the risk it still is. Many of them have died trying, haven't they?
JOHNSON: What the hell are you talking about? Who said they didn't die trying for fuck's sake? What I'm saying is these riots are going to kill my programs. They're going to murder the Great Society. Now's a fucking stupid time to be standing up for themselves.
BIRD: You wouldn't respect them other otherwise, would you? Not that I'm advocating violence, but would you, darling?
JOHNSON: *(to AIDE)* Women. *(beat)* We have got to shove these programs through, that's what I'm saying, and I don't care who I have to roll over to do it, including every one of those punks in Harlem.
BIRD: Of course, they're the ones your programs are for.
JOHNSON: *(a roar)* OF COURSE THEY ARE. *(beat)* My programs are for everyone. I'm going to be remembered as the president who did more for the people of the U.S. of A. than any other. That's how I'm going to be remembered. *(beat)* Where is everybody? What time is it?
AIDE: The others thought the meeting was happening in Washington, Mr. Johnson. We can expect some of them to be late.
JOHNSON: I EXPECT NO ONE TO BE LATE. Especially that fucking George Ball because he's gonna sit in my living room, in my own home, and attack my foreign policy. You cannot please these college men. I am making new fucking lives for black people, for old people, for poor people,

for—for everyone—and all he can think to say to me is (*imitating him*) Do you think it's wise to send more troops over there, Mr. President? Jesus H. Christ, how do I know if it's wise? It's what has to be done. I am not going to let a bunch of little, yellow communists beat me and that's all there is to that. (*beat*) It's going to be over before he knows it. Shit, they can't keep up with us.
AIDE: I'm sure George is giving you the best—
JOHNSON: (*murderous*) You're sure what?
BIRD: That George is asking questions like that out of concern for your Great Society.
JOHNSON: HE'S A PUSSY.

(*BIRD takes a big breath and stands.*)

BIRD: (*to AIDE, with a smile*) Excuse me. (*She starts to exit.*)
JOHNSON: Bird?

(*She stops, turns and waits.*)

JOHNSON: We're all going to want lunch when they get here.

(*BIRD exits. Pause.*)

JOHNSON: Fuck, women are sensitive. She's just like my mother was, all full of sensitivity. Jesus, you fart and they're running out of the room and slamming the door.

TURNBOW: I'm gonna register and be a first class citizen. (*indicating WAYNE*) When this boy firs come to me I didn't know what he meant about register to vote. He tol me every day, he helped me pick my crop and he tol me register and be a firs class citizen. I didn't want none to do with it, but then he tol me not one black citizen is a register voter, he said. And Holmes County got 80% black people he tol me. Well, then I start meetin' with the others in Tchula—that's where I live, in Tchula with my wife and my girl. We meet in the church every night and finally we just decide to come on up here to Lexington to do it. And by god, this boy say which of you's firs and I say I am. I am gonna be the first black man to register in Holmes County.
GINNY: Mr. Turnbow, what's the gun for?

TURNBOW: We meetin' in the church and they start shootin' in my windows. They shoot up my livin' room real good and leave bullet holes all around there above my sofa. Then the sheriff come and say I do it. I say you think I shoot up my own livin' room and he say yeah and I say I never owned a 45 in my life. Well, he rested me anyway and then I got a trial and all this time I ain't even register. I just think about it. (*pause*) Yeah, I heard all about that non-violence. I heard Martin Lufer King say it himself, but I say every what the Mississippi white man pose with, he got to be met with. Meet him ever what he pose with. If he pose with a smile, meet him with a smile and if he pose with a gun, meet him with a gun. I got a 10-year-old girl and a cotton crop to protect and them shootin' up my house. Well, once they put me to trial for them bullet holes, I decide I'm gonna register. I don't know where all that there braveness come from. I just found myself with it. Other words, the shootin in my house. I have a wife and I have a daughter and I love my wife just like a white man loves his'n and I love my baby daughter just like a white man loves his'n and a white man will die for his'n and I say I'll die for mine.

(Pause.)

WAYNE: On the march, shit, so many wondrous things happened, but I think the most amazing of all was Stokely. He's been with us six years by now—he's been under the fear we've known here for six years. So they tear gassed us you know, several times, and we're getting pretty upset and wanting to fight back but Stokely, he just got hysterical. After all his talk about Black Power and be militant and fight back and kill whitey, he's hysterical. He's running around shouting, "Don't make your stand here," and he's sobbing and he's wandering around in circles saying, "I just can't stand to see any more people get shot."

(Pause. TURNBOW gets up, gets his briefcase.)

TURNBOW: Dinner hour's over. I'll be goin' to register now.
WAYNE: (*to GINNY*) The others are right outside town hall.
GINNY: We'll be there.

(WAYNE exits the freedom house.)

TURNBOW: I want to thank you for the sandwich.

GINNY: That's our pleasure.

(TURNBOW joins WAYNE, waiting for the REGISTRAR.)

GINNY: What am I doing here, David?
DAVID: What?
GINNY: (*as though looking out a window after WAYNE*) Look at him. It's like the Lord came down and whispered in his ear, "Wayne Pearson, your life's gonna be about helping your people get the vote." He's just straight ahead doing it, no fear, just doing it.
DAVID: You're doing it too.
GINNY: I'm scared to go out there and be with those people at Town Hall.
DAVID: We're all scared. We'd be crazy not to be.
GINNY: Wayne really got his head busted on that march.
DAVID: Look, I have no problem with Wayne. He's the one who has a problem. (*beat*) I love you.
GINNY: If it wasn't for Wayne pulling me down under this table a dozen times, I wouldn't be here for you to love. (*beat*) I've been in Lexington over two years, and if we get this guy registered, he'll be the first.
DAVID: Then let's go do it.

(GINNY and DAVID exit.)

*(A couple beats, then **SEVERAL GUNSHOTS**. The following actions happen simultaneously.)*

(WAYNE looks around him, startled; GINNY enters at a run.

AIDE, alone now in the study, goes to the window and looks out.

LEROY and BUTCH stand, looking around for where the shots came from.)

LEROY: Man, there's a million cops out there.

GINNY: Somebody shot at us.
WAYNE: Anybody hurt?
GINNY: They shot at us through their car window as they drove by. Sheriff's car.

WAYNE: (*to the world*) We are registering these people, goons.

LEROY: We been crawlin' with cops ever since Malcolm. Those Black power cats causin' it.
BUTCH: Black power cats ain't doin' it, man. Cops the ones doin' it. Tony got caught up in one of those riots after Malcolm was killed.
LEROY: He got Black Power on his mind now.
BUTCH: No, he just like what Malcom got to say. He told me he feels we got rights. Right to gather in a public place, right to demonstrate.
LEROY: Fuck demonstrate. How about hot water in winter, man? I'm concerned about my right to hot water.

WAYNE: You better get back to those folks. They're probably scared out of their minds.
GINNY: Who isn't? (*She starts to go, turns back to WAYNE.*) You're gonna get this guy registered, Wayne. I know you are.

(*She exits. WAYNE turns to TURNBOW.*)

WAYNE: Everything's all right now, Mr. Turnbow.
TURNBOW: I'm sittin', waitin'.

(*More* **GUNSHOTS**, *in Harlem only.*)

LEROY: We got to get off this street, man.
BUTCH: What about Tony? Where Tony at?
LEROY: We got to get off this street. (*pulling BUTCH along*) Duck in this hallway, we can see Tony comin' from there. (*LEROY and BUTCH exit.*)

(*WAYNE turns to TURNBOW.*)

WAYNE: It's time. You ready?
TURNBOW: I been ready

(*WAYNE and TURNBOW exit.*)

(*BIRD enters the study.*)

BIRD: (*to AIDE*) We'd love to have you for dinner.

AIDE: I'd love to stay. (*beat*) I don't know how you do it.
BIRD: I've had the same thought about you.
AIDE: I thought I heard gunshots earlier.
BIRD: There's hunting here sometimes, close enough so we can hear it. Deer. (*pause*) The first time I heard that gunfire, I was so frightened I turned on every light in the house. I sat very still in the living room until Lyndon came home two or three hours later. He was amused. He told me about a time nearly the exact thing happened to his mother. He was very sweet, he loves Rebekkah terribly. I imagine he's told you this story.
AIDE: He's told me hundreds of stories.
BIRD: This is the one in which Rebekkah is pumping water in the dead of night and there are shots—
AIDE: Mr. Johnson's father is away at Austin?
BIRD: Yes. Rebekkah is pumping water, very frightened. She's sobbing, and Lyndon comforts her. He toddles out to the porch, all of three years old, puts his arm around her and says, "Don't worry, Mama. I'll protect you." You've heard it?
AIDE: I've heard it.
BIRD: I'll wager it's true. Perhaps it was not quite the dead of night and almost certainly Lyndon was—say, five or six—but it's very like Lyndon. Don't you think so?
AIDE: Yes, now that you mention it.
BIRD: The man has a heart unlike any other I've come across. He lives alone with his heart. I'm allowed a tiny piece of it. No one else is allowed any of it. It's up to the rest of us to fill that heart up with love, and especially with admiration, and of course, no one wants to because he won't give any of it back. (*pause*) He's a very frightened man.
AIDE: I think that fear is going to cost a great deal.
BIRD: Please stay.
AIDE: I will.

(*Bird exits.*)

(*The lights come up on the freedom house. GINNY and DAVID are sitting at the table, WAYNE near them. A Temptations album is playing.*)

WAYNE: Turnbow did not blink an eye. The guy said please read and interpret this section of the Mississippi constitution and the guy just did it. Shit, I'm not sure he knows what interpret means, but he did it.

GINNY: (*excited*) 12 registered voters!
WAYNE: That's just the beginning. I know it's just the beginning.
DAVID: You've done an incredible job, Wayne.
WAYNE: Yeah, thanks for your help.
DAVID: You've really stuck it out, stuck with it, had a lot of courage.
WAYNE: Look, you don't have to do that. All right?
DAVID: Maybe I'd be better off back in Berkeley.
WAYNE: Maybe you would.
DAVID: I'd have gone back months ago except for Ginny.
WAYNE: You know what? This is a movement here, not some white boy romance. This guy's scared shitless he's going to get run off his land, his family's going to be murdered, and you're over here playing kissy face. Maybe you're too stupid to realize that our lives are on the line and nothing pisses these crackers off more than white men lovin' black women. (*beat*) Except maybe black men lovin' white women.
DAVID: I was trying to help.
WAYNE: Kissy face does not help.
DAVID: (*beat*) Doesn't hurt.

(*GINNY laughs.*)

WAYNE: Real funny. Just understand this movement is about black folks and black folks are gonna run it.
DAVID: Who's trying to run anything? I'm not trying to run anything. You tell me what you want, Wayne. Say it, I'll do it. Go home, work the streets, register the farmers, transfer to another office. I want to help.
WAYNE: I don't want your fucking white boy help.
DAVID: Mine, or any white—(boy's?)
WAYNE: Yours. I don't want to work with you.
DAVID: Why not, Wayne?
GINNY: You two don't knock this shit off, I'm clearing out. Jesus, it's like being home listening to mama and daddy again.
DAVID: (*to WAYNE*) Why not?
WAYNE: Because I don't want to have to look at you loving this woman day in and day out.
DAVID: Because I'm white.
WAYNE: No. Not because you're white. (*pause*) Let me turn this record over.
(*WAYNE moves to the stereo.*)

(JOHNSON enters the study and goes to the window, looks out.)

JOHNSON: Will you look at that?

WAYNE: *(to GINNY)* I've got something for you. *(He exits.)*

GINNY: Like he doesn't have enough to deal with.
DAVID: I know. I'm going back to Berkeley. I want you to come with me.
GINNY: You want a lot, huh?

(WAYNE enters with a cake and puts it on the table.)

WAYNE: Happy birthday, Ginny.
DAVID: Oh, crap, did I miss your birthday?
WAYNE: It was the same day as the march. Happy birthday and happy Selma to Montgomery.
GINNY: Is that coconut cake? Oh, my God.
WAYNE: Made it myself.
GINNY: You made me a coconut cake with your own hands? Wayne Pearson, I love you.
WAYNE: Made it last night after you all went to bed.
GINNY: I want to eat it ALL right now.
WAYNE: *(looking hard at DAVID)* You may be good at kissy face, but I bet you all 12 of those newly registered voters you can't make a coconut cake.
DAVID: No. No I can't. *(beat)* Wayne, if I'm causing . . .
WAYNE: Forget it. Get some plates and forks.

(As DAVID moves to do this, a knock and yelling.)

JASPER: *(off)* DAVID DOUBIAGO, ARE YOU IN THERE?
DAVID: Jasper?
JASPER: David Doubiago, open this door.
DAVID: *(letting him in)* Jesus Christ. Jasper!

(They hug. They jump around the room in each other's arms.)

GINNY: This must be Jasper.
DAVID: Yeah. Yeah. Jasper, this is Ginny.
JASPER: Ah. Sweet Virginia. I have heard about you in letter after letter. You

have swept this man off his feet.
DAVID: Wayne. Jasper.
WAYNE: How you doing?
JASPER: And Wayne Pearson, the crown prince of the southern Mississippi civil rights movement. It's an honor. (*He extends his hand.*) Jasper Peders. With a "d".
WAYNE: (*shaking Jasper's hand, then a pointed look toward David*) Crown prince?
DAVID: Fuck, Jasper, what are you doing here?
JASPER: Simply, I had to see you, Dave. (*to WAYNE and GINNY*) As you both probably know, I am the vice-resident of the Berkeley chapter of SDS. Purely a social experiment. I would not dabble in real politics, but I'm excellent on such issues as students' rights to petition for an extra class and the creation of co-ed dorms.
DAVID: Jasper, what the hell are you doing here?
JASPER: (*proffering a letter*) Our man in the white house may be securing for all of you Mississippi residents the right to vote . . .
WAYNE: Oh yeah.
JASPER: What he's securing for vice-presidents of radical student organizations is an all-expense paid trip to southeast Asia.
DAVID: (*looks at the letter*) You got drafted?
JASPER: Pay attention, Dave. Yes. I got drafted.
WAYNE: Oh, man.
JASPER: I believed you'd take it better hearing it straight from me and I knew I'd take it better after discussing it with you. I brought Bob Dylan along, as well as a couple candles and a great deal of good wine, so we can have a long talk if I can stay the night.
WAYNE: Yeah. Have some cake.
GINNY: It's my birthday cake.
JASPER: (*kissing her hand*) Many happy returns.

(*TONY enters and calls quietly to BUTCH and LEROY.*)

TONY: Come on out. It's quiet now. Cops are gone.

(*LEROY and BUTCH enter.*)

BUTCH: I been looking for you. Where you been?
TONY: I found a place, Butch. (*turning to LEROY*) Listen, Leroy. Me and

Butch been talking about moving downtown.
LEROY: You full of shit.
TONY: No, man. Butch don't want to tell you this but—
BUTCH: I can't get behind the life up here no more. I'm working now and I want to go back to school. Maybe go to college later.
LEROY: Yeah, great, baby, you get on out.
TONY: He only stayin' this long because he knows you in trouble with shit. But I told him you got to find your own way. I wish I never got involved with those junkmen.
LEROY: Everybody got somethin" someone else wish he had. Butch wish he could paint like you.
TONY: That so?
BUTCH: Yeah. You lucky with that.
TONY: You don't got to worry cause I found us a place and my taxi job is steady and I got the cash for my painting. I'm seein' different items I'm needin' now, paints and all what I'm needin'.
BUTCH: When you get yourself straight, you come on downtown with us, Leroy.
LEROY: I'm gonna get clean. I swear.

(In the freedom house, GINNY, DAVID, WAYNE and JASPER sit on the floor gathered around a couple candles, drinking wine. DAVID's arm is around GINNY. Bob Dylan music plays.)

WAYNE: We'd just lay out in a field in the evening and rest for the next day's walk. Pretty beautiful first night, stars out and all. Crackers everywhere hassling us. But there's so many of us, you know how that is, and we're just feeling good. Second night, we get to real, live partying, man. It's pouring out, but we're singing and dancing and knowing we're gonna make it to Montgomery. We just know it. (*He takes a gulp of wine.*) Yeah, my daddy was good for something. He went ahead and died without ever speaking to me again, but he kept me out of Vietnam. I told 'em I was mama's sole support and she backed me up, so I'm 1-Y. (*pause*) They don't need to send me over there to die. I'm gonna die right here.
GINNY: No you're not. Now I never want to hear you talk like that.
DAVID: I got out on my asthma. I had a massive asthma attack right in the middle of my physical. Funny thing. (*long pause.*) You gonna go, Jasper?
JASPER: I believe I am.
DAVID: (*he can barely get it out*) Social experiment?

JASPER: Refusing to go takes courage. I don't have it.

(DAVID *starts to cry.*)

JASPER: Don't be foolish, Dave. Nobody's going to kill me.
DAVID: Okay.
JASPER: And I'm not going to kill anybody.
DAVID: Shit, you're not on the planet long enough at one time for anybody to get a good shot at you.

(LEROY *enters, paces a bit, waiting. After a couple beats,* TONY *enters.*)

TONY: Leroy, am I late? What time is it?
LEROY: You not late, man.
TONY: I swear, if this meetin' about smack, I'm getting back in my cab and—
LEROY: I told you it's not that, man. Butch asked me to take his mama to a doctor appointment, you know, cause he couldn't get off work. She can walk it, but it take about a half hour, Butch says, and he don't want his mama walkin' it alone. I get to her place and she's cryin', man. Then she calms down a minute and tells me Butch got a letter from the draft board. Those fat cats in Washington tryin' to draft Butch.
TONY: Shit.
LEROY: Can you pick him up from work and carry him to his mama's? She in a bad way, Tony.
TONY: You comin' with me?
LEROY: That's why I asked you to come on uptown and pick me up. Better if we both tell him.
TONY: (*several beats*) You think he's gonna go?
LEROY: Don't have much of a choice.
TONY: Black man'd be crazy to go. Man, everybody got some choice. It's not our war and I don't think Butch should be goin' to no Vietnam.
LEROY: You know Butch. He gonna go over there, think he's got to protect everybody, and get his ass blown off.
TONY: Not me. I got a mama usin' and whorin' and two little sisters need me to support them. I'm not goin' to no Viet Nam.
LEROY: I been to mama's church. I tol' God if he keep me outta the draft, I'll start goin' to church regular.
TONY: (*a smile—maybe the first we've seen. He puts his arm around* LEROY.)

Get in the cab. Let's go get Butch.

(TONY and LEROY exit.)

WAYNE: Shhh. Listen. (*WAYNE gets up and turns off the music. Silence on the stage. For a beat or two.*) You hear that?
GINNY: Pick-up truck?
WAYNE: Yeah, Jesus, that's a pick-up.
GINNY: Quietly now. Back door.

(Each of them moves slowly toward the door.)

JASPER: What's the significance of a pick-up truck?
GINNY: Quietly.

(She waits and lets JASPER go ahead of her out the door and off. She follows, then DAVID and finally, WAYNE. A few seconds later, a bomb comes through the window of the Freedom House and explodes.)

(Silence for several beats.)

JOHNSON: I like these big trees here. It's a good place to walk and rest. When I come here and stay two or three days it's a breath of fresh air; it's new strength. I go away ready to challenge the world. Sometimes when I come back here I think that I just might stay because there's no other place—no Virgin Islands, no Miami coastline, no boat trips across the Atlantic—that can do for me what this soil, this land, this water, this people and these hills, these surroundings, can do. (*pause*) When my daddy was dying, I carried him back here from the hospital in Austin. His doctors didn't want him to leave, but he needed to be here. He said to me, "Take me home, Lyndon. I want to be where people know when you're sick and care when you die." And that's that I want. I'm gonna die here too.

SCENE 3

(The scene takes place between January 1968 and May 4, 1970.

In the dark, we hear the Buffalo Springfield singing "For What It's Worth." The song continues as the lights come up.

JOHNSON *is sitting in his study with* BIRD *and the* AIDE. *He and* BIRD *are holding hands, as he watches a football game and drinks orange soda.*

TONY *is sitting on a stoop, drawing.*

JASPER *is standing near some candles, going through various yoga poses. He is wearing short shorts and a tee-shirt. He has a muslin bandanna tied around his head with an owl's claw sticking up out of one side of it, and a rose sticking up out of the other. He is barefoot. He has a gold hoop in one of his pierced ears. In this space should now be an open trunk.* DAVID *and* GINNY *are lying on the floor. "For What It's Worth" is playing on the stereo.)*

JOHNSON: Will you look at that? That man looks like a fuckin' gazelle. Shit, when are the Cowboys going to wise up and get ourselves a running back like that? (*to* BIRD *and* AIDE) That's the way to look at my job, like that game. I have to find the hidden legislative path between the south and the north, the public power men and the private power men, the farmers' men and the union men, the bomber boys and the peace lovers, the eggheads and the fatheads. I imagine a football team and I'm the coach and I'm also the quarterback. I have to call the plays and I have to center the ball, run the ball (*he does this*), and pass the ball (*he does this*). I'm the kicker. I'm the tackle. I'm the passer. AND I have to catch the pass.

(*He runs across the room as though to catch the pass. He does, and acts like the impact was so great it knocks him down. He falls down, laughing.* AIDE *and* BIRD *laugh with him.*)

BIRD: (*extending her hand to him*) Can I help you up, Lyndon?
JOHNSON: (*to* AIDE) Look at this little gal, thinks she can help me up.
BIRD: (*extending her other hand as well*) Come on, darling. Ready? (*She pulls, laughs. He stumbles to his feet.*) How about I fix something to eat?
JOHNSON: Yes, I'm ready.
BIRD: All right then.

(*She kisses his cheek, then exits.*)

JOHNSON: That woman's grown on me, I'll tell you. At the beginning, I wanted her, that's for sure, married her less than a year after I met her. Would have married her the same week I met her if she'd let me. And she just grew on me. There's only been two women I've loved in my life, besides my mother. (*indicating BIRD*) That woman (*quietly*) and Alice. (*pause*) She couldn't have been more different than Bird, tall and independent, all full of herself and her opinions. Wanted to change the world. Wanted me to change it. When I sent troops over there, she wrote me a letter, first time I'd heard from her in more than 20 years. "I realize now I never knew you. The Lyndon Johnson I knew could not have perpetuated this immoral war." That woman made me forget that principles will kill you in politics. I look at all these fucking doves now and think they're soft, the ones who mean it, and the ones who don't, which is most of them, are just full of shit. But Alice convinced me that principles made you strong, not weak. (*pause*) She never minded that I was married, she was nuts about Bird. Bird liked her too. (*beat*) Now I know better about Alice. She's a fucking communist sympathizer.

(*TONY sits on a stoop, drawing. LEROY enters. The music changes to Aretha Franklin's version of "I Can't Get No Satisfaction."*)

LEROY: Hey, man.
TONY: (*not looking up*) Hey, Leroy, what's happening?
LEROY: What you got there that's so interesting?
TONY: I'm drawing it from a letter I got from Butch when he was in the war. I find myself re-reading those couple letters he sent—don't know why, just find myself doing it.
LEROY: Let me see that work.

(*TONY hands him the drawing.*)

LEROY: (*looking at the drawing*) I'm gonna pray for those boys.
TONY: You spendin' a lot of time at that church.
LEROY: What you doin' up here so much, Tony?
TONY: I'm waitin' on you. I can't keep a place downtown by myself so I'm stayin' with mama waitin' till you're ready.
LEROY: You know I got myself a girl now.
TONY: You mean you got yourself a Holy Roller.
LEROY: I got myself the most gorgeous, God-fearin' woman in Harlem, brother.

(Pause. Then TONY speaks as he draws.)

TONY: That's good, man. When am I gonna meet this gorgeous girl?
LEROY: Tony.
TONY: What you want?
LEROY: You not waitin' for me.
TONY: I'm serious, Leroy. I can't afford—
LEROY: I know you not drivin' the cab no more, Tony.
TONY: Yeah. I got this paintin'. That's takin' all my time.
LEROY: What you doin' for cash, man? You back runnin' the middle for those junkmen?
TONY: *(after a sigh)* I'm fine, Leroy. When Butch get back, we just get ourselves a new place.
LEROY: Butch not comin' back, Tony. He got himself a new life in California.
TONY: Then I'm gonna have to wait till I can make it on my own. (*TONY draws for a few beats. LEROY stands watching. TONY puts down his pad and pencil and looks LEROY straight in the eye.*) We ain't got no kids in Harlem.
LEROY: What's that?
TONY: I ain't seen any. I've seen some real small people actin' like kids. They're too small to be grown and they might look like kids, but there ain't no kids in Harlem. You ever been a kid, Leroy?
LEROY: Yeah, I seem to remember it.
TONY: Damn, you lucky. I ain't never been a kid, man. I don't recall ever bein' happy and not scared. What I recall is some man around beating on my mama. One cat after another. I look at her sometime and she just say, he got a lot of the dog in him today, Tony. He just feel doggish.
LEROY: My mama in church, yours in the saddle. Shit. (*A long pause.*) I realize somethin' now, though, now I'm clean and have the Lord's grace.
TONY: What's that?
LEROY: They did what they had to. One day I'm gonna have kids comin' up here and there's some fear in it. How you gonna take care of 'em? Your mama got a few bucks from this cat, that cat. Mine found a place where she don't have to think about me doin' shit, found a way to believe I ain't gonna turn up dead in the hallway one night. I dig bein' with my mama now. Makes me wonder how cats who come up in Harlem could be anything but strong men, because they come from such strong women. (*pause*) I'm keepin' you in my prayers, Tony.
TONY: I appreciate it.

(In Berkeley. There is a poster of Alan Ginsberg up and a blackboard visible on which is written the word "SOLIPSISM." There's a desk with several open books on it. HARMONY enters. She is a 17-year old girl with hair that looks like it might never have been cut, wearing a wrap-around skirt and a faux-jeweled blouse. She looks at JASPER doing yoga, then at the candles. She kneels on the floor, mesmerized by the candles' flame.)

HARMONY: Wow.
GINNY: Listen, David. Honey, I want to go, but I've got to study. My final's tomorrow, baby.
DAVID: You are forever in the library. I don't see you anymore. Ginny, come to this demonstration with me.
GINNY: Baby, I'm finally going to get this degree. I finally have enough money to eat every day. I finally get to relax sometimes. If there's a demonstration or something at a time I don't have to study, I'll go. Otherwise—it's someone else's turn. I'm putting myself first for a change.
DAVID: Fine. *(to everyone in the room)* You think we could turn on some lights here already? *(a beat, then he blows out the candles and flicks a light switch).*
HARMONY: What's the matter, David? Jasper got us some wonderful hash, David, you want some? *(She goes to DAVID and puts her arms around him.)*
DAVID: *(pushing her away)* Will you get away from me? You may be used to balling everyone you bump into, but we don't do that here.
HARMONY: No, David. I thought you might want some of this dope. That's all. *(She giggles.)* I have screwed a lot of guys though.
DAVID: Yeah, I bet you have.
HARMONY: But there's no harm in that, was there? I wasn't hurting anyone, was I?
DAVID: How do I know?
HARMONY: But, David, Ginny and I are friends, I would never—
DAVID: I'm sure you'd never do anything to hurt anyone, Harmony. Peace and love, right?
HARMONY: Right.
DAVID: More like sex and drugs.
GINNY: Lay off her.
HARMONY: That's all right, Ginny. *(She walks right up to DAVID)* Have I done something to make you want to be mean to me?
DAVID: Oh, for Christ's sake. *(He puts on a Doors album and turns it all the*

way up.)
HARMONY: I think that's too loud.

(*JASPER finishes his yoga.*)

JASPER: What's the problem, Dave?
DAVID: If she has to live here could you at least get her to keep her hands off me?
HARMONY: I offered him some hash, that's all. He's so uptight.

(*JASPER puts his arms around her.*)

JASPER: That was extremely generous, Harmony.
HARMONY: Should I start dinner?
JASPER: If you like.
HARMONY: (*to GINNY*) Will you be home for dinner?
GINNY: No. I'm going to the library.
DAVID: I'm going to campus.
HARMONY: I did not ask you.
JASPER: We'll save you some dinner.
DAVID: Jasper, come to this demonstration with me.
JASPER: No, I will not go with you. Demonstrations are beside the point.
HARMONY: I'll start dinner. Can I hold your claw, Jasper?
JASPER: Certainly, my darling.

(*JASPER gives HARMONY the owl's claw. She kisses him and exits.*)

GINNY: I'm going.

(*As GINNY starts to exit, BUTCH enters. He is wearing old army pants and a tee-shirt, and he limps. GINNY kisses his cheek as she goes.*)

GINNY: Hi, Butch.
BUTCH: Hi, baby. You gonna study tonight?
GINNY: Yeah.
BUTCH: Catch you later.
(*GINNY looks at DAVID, who doesn't speak to her. She exits.*)

JASPER: Good evening, Butch.

BUTCH: (*laugh, imitating him*) Good evening, Jasper. What's happening?
JASPER: Our Dave is off to a demonstration.
BUTCH: Yeah? You mind if I join you, man?
DAVID: Are you joking?
BUTCH: No, man. I figure the time has come to do one of these DEM-ON-STRA-TIONS. I got a buddy in Harlem did that thing long time ago and you too, right, Jasper?
JASPER: That is in the past, Butch.
BUTCH: And I figure I got to redeem my name. My name's Johnson too, isn't it?
DAVID: Yeah, come if you want to.
BUTCH: Sure thing, let me just get cleaned up. I had a hard day making pizza, you know what I mean?

(*BUTCH laughs and exits.*)

DAVID: Is he serious?
JASPER: He appears to be.
DAVID: I've been feeling pretty lonely out there with you not coming anymore, and now Ginny. (*He walks to the blackboard. Reading.*) "Solipsism."
JASPER: The word for the day.
DAVID: Yeah, but what's it mean?
JASPER: The dictionary on my desk is open to the correct page.
DAVID: Okey dokey. (*He looks it up. Reading.*) "The theory that nothing exists or is real but the self." (*pause*) You left something over there, Jasper.
JASPER: Someone.
DAVID: Not just Ky. (*pronounced "Q"*) Something else.
JASPER: Don't be alarmed. We'll have a new word tomorrow.
DAVID: Jasper, listen. I know I've been a prick lately. I've been irritable and hard to get—
JASPER: You're not smoking enough un-stimulants.
DAVID: All the worry about me and Ginny and, you know, will this war ever end?
JASPER: I know.
DAVID: But, well. I love you, Jasper.
JASPER: Thank you.

(*BUTCH enters.*)
BUTCH: Here we go.

(BUTCH and DAVID exit. Low murmurs. A demonstration quelling.)

JOHNSON: I don't understand who these young people are that are opposed to the war. I never meet any of these young people. The young people my daughters bring around are not like that.

AIDE: Do you think it's still just the young people, sir?

JOHNSON: You come down here all the way from Washington to ask me, the leader of the Western world, a chickenshit question like that? You sit there and talk to me like that, you sound like a jackass. You got a suggestion? You got an idea to offer about that Hanoi and that motherfucking Ho Chi Minh?

AIDE: No, sir.

JOHNSON: No, I didn't think so. Course, Bobby Kennedy's got an idea. Oh, yeah, Mr. Charmed Life Kennedy's got an idea Ho's some kind of fountain of integrity. I ask Kennedy last year, "What's his price?" and he tells me Ho has no price. He tells me Ho believes in what he's doing, Ho can't be bought. You and I both know what a pile of horseshit that is, and Kennedy's been in politics long enough to know it too. Every human being has his price, or if not his price, then his soft spot. If I can't buy off that yellow bastard, then I'm gonna find his soft spot and I'm gonna shove my fist through it. We cannot afford to lose this war and we're not going to lose it. You know why? Because it doesn't matter how hard you explain it or how well, defeat is not the same as victory—and don't let anybody tell you different. Now that fuckin' Kennedy's running all across this country screaming about those Asians and their courage and integrity and me and my—

(JOHNSON stops abruptly, moves very close to AIDE, speaks very softly.)

JOHNSON: We're not gonna let him beat me though, are we? He runs against me, we're gonna beat his Boston ass, am I right?

AIDE: Yes, sir. No one's going to beat you. You're the president.

JOHNSON: I'm the president, that's right. *(He tousles AIDE's hair.)* Ah, I love you. You know I love you, don't you? Christ, I couldn't have come this far without you. You've been here with me the whole time, haven't you, right here with me. I know I don't tell you enough, but I appreciate all you've done. I'd be lost without you. You know that.

(JOHNSON picks up a framed picture of himself with his family.)

JOHNSON: Here, I want you to keep this as a momento of your visit to the ranch, but for God's sake, don't embarrass me by leaving it in a whorehouse someplace.

(AIDE laughs. JOHNSON goes to the window and stares out of it.)

(JASPER meditates. HARMONY sits on the floor near him. GINNY enters with a letter in her hand.)

GINNY: *(referring to JASPER)* He gone again?
HARMONY: He's in a peaceful place.
GINNY: He's probably the only person in the country.
HARMONY: Do you read?
GINNY: I read my behind off.
HARMONY: Does reading make you feel peaceful?
GINNY: Comin' in first in my class is going to make me feel real peaceful.
HARMONY: That would be a wonderful accomplishment. We're going to do acid tomorrow.
GINNY: Have fun, you hear?
HARMONY: You're welcome to join us.
GINNY: I'll pass. Harmony—hey, what's your real name?
HARMONY: My name is Harmony.
GINNY: What was it before Harmony?
HARMONY: You'll laugh.
GINNY: I might.
HARMONY: Harriet. *(pause, sees GINNY isn't laughing)* I thought I'd keep the H. I like the H. *(beat)* You have any nail polish remover?
GINNY: No.
HARMONY: Shoot.
GINNY: Sorry. I'll get you some if you want.
HARMONY: Would you? Because I want my toenails orange now. Don't you think it's about time?
GINNY: Definitely. *(beat)* You ever think you might like to get out of the house sometimes, find something to do?
HARMONY: Like a job, you mean?
GINNY: Yeah, like a job.
HARMONY: No. See, Jasper takes care of me. I prepare his food and give

him sex when he wants it and he takes care of me by paying for the food and getting me some acid and giving me sex when I want it. It's a groove.
GINNY: Uh huh.
HARMONY: Jasper and I have real togetherness, real peacefulness.
GINNY: Real love?
HARMONY: Jasper says love is not to be talked about. The very next morning after our first time together he said (*She giggles*) he said, pay attention because I don't want to ever have to repeat this to you. Love is beside the point.
GINNY: What's the point?
HARMONY: He didn't tell me that.
GINNY: When you were a child, what did you want to be?
HARMONY: You mean, when I was Harriet?
GINNY: When you were a little girl. What did you think it would be like when you grew up? Can you remember?
HARMONY: Well. Well. I thought I'd be a veterinarian. I thought I'd heal sick animals. (*pause*) Jasper says it wonderful to heal. He says I'm healing him.
GINNY: (*looking at Jasper*) You think he doesn't hear us?
HARMONY: Oh, no. He's away.
GINNY: You're healing him?
HARMONY: Yes.
GINNY: What are you doing for you?
HARMONY: That's the same thing. (*a long pause; HARMONY is thinking hard*) Ginny, I think you and I are each other's opposite.
GINNY: I'll buy that.
HARMONY: My energy goes to Jasper and Harmony. Jasper and Harmony are together, we are one. Ginny and David—
GINNY: We are not one, that's for sure.
HARMONY: You're not even together. (*pause*) Did you get a letter?
GINNY: It's from a friend of mine who's in prison.
HARMONY: What's his name?
GINNY: Wayne.
HARMONY: Why's he in prison?
GINNY: For helping people avoid the draft.
HARMONY: I didn't know they could put you in prison for that.
GINNY: It came as a surprise to him too.
HARMONY: Is he a black man?
GINNY: He's the original black man. First mint.

HARMONY: Is he like Butch?
GINNY: No, honey. He's not like Butch.
HARMONY: Don't be sad. Jasper says the time will come for us to stop being together too. Jasper says that's natural. Good-night.
GINNY: Good-night. See you tomorrow.
HARMONY: Okay.

(GINNY and HARMONY exit. A beat, then JASPER gets up, puts something soft on the stereo. He moves around the space, picking up a few objects that are placed about—odd things, perhaps an enormous feather, a paperweight, a tea kettle, the Alan Ginsberg poster—and puts them in the trunk. Then he selects other items from the trunk and places them about the space. At one point, he pulls out dog tags and holds them up high.)

JASPER: Good evening, Jerry. Come join me.

(He displays the dog tags somewhere prominent. Then he erases the blackboard and writes "INSOUCIANCE" on it.)

(LEROY enters dressed for church and TONY passes by quickly, hardly noticing him.)

LEROY: Tony? (*beat*) What's up?
TONY: I got to get home. I'm drawing a new—
LEROY: You drawing? Then why you out on the street? (*beat*) You lookin' for some shit, Tony? All this time clean and now you lookin'—
TONY: You don't know nothin' about it.
LEROY: I don't know nothin' about it? Brother, I know everything about it. (*beat*) You all full up with somethin', Tony, like always. You all full up with somethin' and I don't know what it is. But I know shit ain't gonna help. Shit ain't gonna help, man.

(Smokey Robinson music fills the air.)

LEROY: There's that Smokey. He is fine. (*beat*) I got services. (*beat*) Walk with me a ways?
TONY: I got to finish my drawing. (*pause*) I'll walk with you.
LEROY: (*as they start to walk*) You write Butch?
TONY: A few times. Yeah, I write him.

LEROY: You got to give me that address. Meantime, next time you write him, tell him I'm clean.

(LEROY and TONY exit.)

(JASPER takes a letter out of the trunk and opens it. Sits near the candle for light. He reads to himself and then starts to read out loud.)

JASPER: *(reading)* I was at one with the earth, the air, the upland fields, the paddy, and the seedbeds of my village. During the harvesting and planting season, I and my friends in the village would sweat and labor together, under the sun and rain, contending with the poverty and miserable conditions, continuing the farmers' life of the centuries. But then you came and I could feel the trembling of the earth and the shock from the sounds of arms exploding around my village, the noise of airplanes circling about in the heavens, the bombs roaring and at night, your voice in my ear, your pleasure in my body.

(DAVID and BUTCH enter. BUTCH moves toward JASPER. DAVID stops him.)

JASPER: *(reading)* Each day I would share news with the neighboring villagers of the damaged houses, the injured, the dead. And you in my bed at night.

DAVID: Jasper?

(JASPER looks at him.)

DAVID: Put that away.
JASPER: Perhaps you're right.

(BUTCH disappears for a moment, then returns to a corner of the room. JASPER puts the letter away.)

JOHNSON: I am not well liked. I mean, personally. *(A long pause. Then he turns to the AIDE.)* Why don't people like me better?
AIDE: *(a beat, then in a quiet voice)* Well, you're not a very likable man, Mr. Johnson.

(JOHNSON nods, waits a minute.)

JOHNSON: You think I don't know what's happening over there? I get nothing but bullshit from over there. Morale is high. Shit morale's not high. Our boys are dying over there, how could morale be high? I know that. *(He looks sharply over at one of the three TV sets.)* YOU HEAR THAT? What in a cow's ass is he talkin' about I won't negotiate? I'll negotiate anytime anywhere with anyone. LISTEN TO THAT. *(imitating newscaster)* President Johnson seems not to be aware of the loss of life being suffered in Southeast Asia. Stupid prick. *(He walks right up to the TV, gets face to face with the TV screen.)* OF COURSE I'M AWARE. TELL ME WHAT I SHOULD DO INSTEAD.

(A long pause. Finally, AIDE gets up and goes to JOHNSON, touches him lightly.)

AIDE: Mr. President?

(Johnson looks up at him, then stands up slowly and moves a bit away from him.)

JOHNSON: Those kids screaming, that newscaster, Bobby Kennedy, how many others? They believe I enjoy this war. They think death gives me a thrill. Or that I'm indifferent to it. *(to AIDE, delivered directly to him)* Think about that. Thousands of people callin' me a killer, thinkin' I'm indifferent to it. *(pause)* And you? What do you think?
AIDE: *(very uncomfortable)* I don't know what you mean, Mr. Johnson.
JOHNSON: You agree? You think I'm a killer?
AIDE: Of course not, sir.
JOHNSON: But then I pay your salary don't I? *(beat)* Tell me the truth now. *(pause)* Should I run again?
AIDE: Mr. Johnson. I just can't advise you on that.
JOHNSON: Why the fuck can't you? You're supposed to be a goddamned advisor.
AIDE: Sir, there is no one in your employ who would advise you against running for president. I think you know that.
JOHNSON: Yes. *(He bangs his hand on something.)* I cannot believe the people of this country don't want me to lead them anymore. I can't believe it.

DAVID: Write her, Jasper.
JASPER: No. *(JASPER goes to his trunk, pulls out a picture, hands it to DAVID.)*

DAVID: (*drawing in breath*) Jesus Christ.
JASPER: A man in my outfit snapped that. A friend of mine snapped that. After he did that to her, he took a picture of it. (*pause*) I believe that might have happened to Ky. If not, the war's not over. Me inside her, somebody's bayonet inside her.
DAVID: No, Jasper, she's all right.
JASPER: HOW DO YOU KNOW THAT? (*long pause*) Whether or not she's all right is beside the point.
BUTCH: (*far away voice*) Yeah, man, you don't even know what you're protestin'.

(*DAVID looks over at BUTCH, who has just finished shooting up. The strap is still around his arm. DAVID goes to him quickly and pulls the strap off.*)

DAVID: What the fuck are you doing? For Jesus fucking Christ's sake, are you doing smack in my living room? (*to JASPER*) Great, pal, you brought a junkie home from the war. A 17-year-old runaway crawlin' up my ass every minute's not enough for you, you brought home a junkie too. (*to BUTCH*) What the fuck are you doing to pay for it? You buying junk off pizza money?
JASPER: Dave.
DAVID: Dave what? You expect me to live with a junkie?
JASPER: I'm paying for it.
DAVID: You're—. You have fucking lost your mind. YOU'RE FUCKING CRAZY.

(*BUTCH moves toward DAVID threateningly. JASPER puts a hand on BUTCH's shoulder.*)

JASPER: Stop.
BUTCH: He talkin' shit about you, Jasper.
JASPER: He doesn't know any better.
DAVID: I don't know any better? You're supplying this man with fucking heroin and I don't know any better?
JASPER: PAY ATTENTION, DAVE.

(*HARMONY enters.*)

HARMONY: What's going on in here? You woke me up.

JASPER: (*to HARMONY*) Shhh. (*then*) Dave. Occasionally, we'd get the better of the Viet Cong.
BUTCH: Yeah, if we caught 'em sleepin'.
JASPER: Correct. Our C.O. adopted the practice of sending pairs of us back into the field after such a battle to shoot the wounded. That's how Butch and I became friends. We shot wounded Vietnamese soldiers together.
DAVID: Sounds delightful.
JASPER: Our Dave didn't realize until now that I killed people, Butch.
DAVE: Shut up, okay, Jasper? (*beat*) Okay, I'll bite. Why are you buying him junk?
BUTCH: Man, over there it's easier to get on a habit than in Harlem. Shit comin' out of everyone's ears. I could get it and I could nod.
JASPER: Butch looked so comfortable at night. I wanted him to share. (*He touches BUTCH's arm with affection.*) Butch explained that it was far wiser to "stay off shit." I was suffering the greatest anxiety of my life. I had left Ky. We had finished with her village. I had left the calm I knew with her, and I felt I would never experience that calm again. I told Butch this and asked him again for heroin. He said, exactly, "You want the calm you felt with that chick, baby? I'll give you that." Which he then proceeded to do. He made me calm that night and many nights thereafter. He made it possible for me to get through my tour without dabbling in heroin.
DAVID: What are you saying?
JASPER: Love is where you find it, Dave. Don't fret. I never killed a baby.

(*GINNY enters in a bathrobe.*)

DAVID: You had sex with this guy?
JASPER: Butch. Say Butch.
DAVID: I can't believe it.
BUTCH: You can't believe Jasper and me took care of each other over there? That what you can't believe? You can't believe I use shit and you can't believe Jasper and me took care of each other over there and that says somethin' to me. That says to me nothin' ever really hurt you, man, so now I want you to come clean. You want me to come clean, I want you to come clean.
DAVID: What are you talking about?
BUTCH: I'm talking about suffering, man. Tell me about how you suffered, go on, tell Butch all about it. Tell me about your friends dyin' from junk or cops or cold in the winter. Tell me about dreamin' about blood at night,

nothin' but red, and how you can't sleep till you get some shit in you so you don't see no more colors. Tell me how you shootin' some poor motherfuckers for doin' nothin' but surviving the goddamn battle. (*beat*) I'M TALKIN' TO YOU, DAVID.

(*BUTCH waits. A couple beats. BUTCH sits. After a beat, HARMONY goes to BUTCH and sits beside him, puts her arms around him.*)

HARMONY: Butch, you saved Jasper's life.

(*Now GINNY also sits beside him.*)

JASPER: (*to DAVID*) Know whereof you speak.

(*JASPER goes to BUTCH and extends his hand. Butch takes it and stands up.*)

JASPER: I regret that I couldn't save your life in return, Butch.
BUTCH: (*small laugh*) You doin' your best, Jasper.
JASPER: (*to HARMONY*) Will you come to bed?
HARMONY: Yes, I'm tired. You woke me up.

(*HARMONY and JASPER start to exit, pass the blackboard.*)

HARMONY: (*reading, mispronouncing*) "Insouciance."

JASPER: "Insouciance": gay heedlessness. Light-hearted unconcern.

(*JASPER kisses HARMONY.*)

DAVID: I love you, Jasper.
JASPER: Never fear. Love is rare. I'm going to keep it. I'm going to treasure it.
(*JASPER and HARMONY exit.*)

DAVID: (*to BUTCH*) I want you to forgive me.
BUTCH: You apologize to me, I'm gonna forgive you.
DAVID: I'm sorry, Butch. I—I'm jealous, you know?
BUTCH: No shit. (*beat*) Hey, David, man, I tell you what. I'm gonna be going to a lot of those demonstrations with you from now on. (*to GINNY*)

Good-night, baby. Sorry about the ruckus.
GINNY: See you in the morning, Butch.

(BUTCH exits. GINNY and DAVID put their arms around each other.)

DAVID: I want you to forgive me too.
GINNY: I've got nothing I need to forgive you for, honey. You're a crazy, passionate man. You go a little too far this way or that way, but most people don't go any way at all, so that's fine. *(beat)* I got a letter from Wayne.
DAVID: Do me a favor, Ginny. If you've got more bad news for me, tell me tomorrow.
GINNY: I just wanted you to know I invited him to stay here when he gets out. *(beat)* For a while. *(beat)* I figured we were gonna argue about it either way so I just went ahead and invited him.
DAVID: *(a sigh)* We're not going to argue. Wayne's my hero. Yes siree, I want to be just like Wayne when I grow up.
GINNY: You want to be a poor black sharecropper's son?
DAVID: Not exactly. But you love Wayne.
GINNY: I love you too.
DAVID: Not like you love Wayne. Never like you love Wayne. *(beat)* Never mind. I'm bushed. I've got to go to bed.
GINNY: David. You can't make a life out of going to demonstrations. It may not look like it now, but the war will end. Then what are you going to do?
DAVID: Then I'm going to start studying.

(The lights dim and then go out. A pause, then the sound of JOHNSON's recorded voice. Lights up on JOHNSON sitting in his study after the recording starts. He looks much older than the last time we saw him.)

(GINNY and WAYNE sit in the Berkeley living room. The blackboard says, "PERSEVERANCE.")

(LEROY sits on the stoop in Harlem. BUTCH stands somewhere on the stage, reading a letter.)

JOHNSON'S VOICE: Fifty-two months and ten days ago, in a moment of tragedy and trauma, the duties of this office fell upon me. I asked then for your help and God's, that we might continue America on its course, binding our wounds, healing our history, moving forward in unity, to clear the American agenda and to keep the American commitment for all our people. United we have kept that commitment. United we have enlarged that commitment. With America's sons in the fields far away, with America's future under challenge right here at home, with our hopes and the world's hopes for peace in the balance every day, I do not believe that I should devote an hour or day of my time to my personal partisan causes or to any duties other than those of this office—the presidency of your country. Accordingly, I shall not seek, and I will not accept, the nomination of my party for another term as your president.

(LEROY speaks, reading the letter that he wrote to BUTCH. Images of the painting LEROY describes should be projected.)

LEROY: Butch, I been wantin' to write you for a long while, but I been lucky—no time. What with church and mama and the girl I'm gonna marry. Bernadette. You ever hear a beautiful name like that? But now I got to write you, Butch. (*a big breath*) Tony's dead. He been workin' for those junkmen again. (*He stops.*) Nobody really know what happened, but he had a lot of bruises on his face and all over the rest of his body. I saw him dead, man. Looked like somebody been kickin' him. I went to his place, man, and I looked through all his stuff. I figure you gonna want these pictures he made, so I'm gonna send 'em to you. They the war. But they Harlem too. He made one of Luther Jones—that cat he run shit for. He paintin' Vietnam and he got Luther Jones in there too. I'm tellin' you, Butch. Tony got somethin' inside him we never did see.

(In the Berkeley living room, WAYNE and GINNY sit together on the couch.)

GINNY: I missed you.
WAYNE: I missed you, Virginia. (*beat*) You got that degree.
GINNY: It's official. I'm a social worker. Virginia Hawthorne, working within the system.
WAYNE: Wayne Pearson, ex-con.

(Riot noises get louder and louder as this sequence progresses.)

WAYNE: You ever think about moving back to Mississippi?
GINNY: I'd miss this house.

WAYNE: David?
GINNY: I don't know, Wayne.

(*WAYNE kisses her. JASPER enters.*)

JASPER: Good evening.
GINNY: Jasper, you scared me. (*beat*) Wayne and I—.
JASPER: I observed.
GINNY: Wayne and I are old friends.
JASPER: Ah. It's impossible to predict what's liable to happen between old friends.

(*JASPER sits on the floor.*)

GINNY: Meditation?
JASPER: Indeed. (*pointing to the blackboard*) I hope you appreciate the easy word.

(*Sounds of riot/demonstration continue to increase. The sound of VERY LOUD GUNFIRE FOR 13 SECONDS. A phone starts ringing. DAVID enters the Berkeley living room, where JASPER is meditating.*)

DAVID: (*pointing to radio*) Did you hear? (*He moves to JASPER, shakes him.*) Jasper, did you hear?
JASPER: What, Dave?
DAVID: The National Guard killed four students at Kent State.
JASPER: The war continues.
DAVID: Terry's there, Jasper. My sister's there. (*DAVID goes to a phone and dials.*)

(*The lights come up on JOHNSON's study. JOHNSON looks considerably aged. BIRD sits near him.*)

JOHNSON: I passed the baton to him and he sure did run with it. Now we've got kids dead on college campuses. That's his fucking law and order.

DAVID: Come on, Terry. Answer your phone. (*beat*) God, please answer your phone. (*Phone keeps ringing. Then—*) DAVID: (*into phone*) Terry?? Oh my God. Oh, thank God.

JOHNSON: I see that he's gone too far, but I understand it. We've got a national reputation to protect. Yes, I'm saying we've got to cover our asses. I believe his economic policy is the worst thing that's happened to this country since panty hose ruined finger fucking—

(BIRD stands.)

JOHNSON: Sit down there. I apologize. Now sit still.

(BIRD sits.)

JOHNSON: I know this shooting students in parking lots, in their own goddamn dorm rooms, it's horrible. It's barbaric. (*beat*) But I understand about Cambodia.

SCENE 4

December 1971 and January 1972.

(JOHNSON sits in his study, BIRD beside him. JOHNSON's hair is white now, and shoulder length. AIDE is somewhere in the room. JOHNSON is clearly ill.)

JOHNSON: What kind of staff we got here anyway? Where in goddamn hell is that cattle feed? We're going to lose half of 'em without it.
AIDE: I just called, Mr. Johnson. It's on a plane—
JOHNSON: I don't need it on any plane. I need it goin' down my cows' throats.
AIDE: It should be in this afternoon.
JOHNSON: That vitamin company going to pay for every head I lose between now and then?
BIRD: We're not going to lose any, darling. I promise. (*BIRD runs her hand through JOHNSON's hair.*)
JOHNSON: (*chuckling*) She promises. Woman power's the greatest untapped natural resource in the country, I'll tell you. I should have put this woman to some real work. Screw that planting trees and beautifying the highways and byways. If I'd turned it over to her, Bird would have probably won this war, which, need I remind you, is still going on, isn't it? So much for it all being my fault. Course Nixon's not Johnson, Nixon can get away with

all kinds of things Johnson couldn't.
BIRD: I believe you're confusing President Nixon with President Kennedy.
JOHNSON: I am at that. Could you believe that fucking Chappaquidick? Teddy Kennedy will get off scot free, but if I'd been with a girl and she'd been stung by a bumblebee, they would have put me in Sing Sing. Already my programs are forgotten. Lyndon Johnson means the war in Vietnam. I busted my ass and everybody else's ass to get my programs through. Not just civil rights, but—look at Medicare. I remember saying to Hubert at the time, I remember telling him this story. One man says to another, what would you do if you saw a train coming from the East at 60 miles an hour and you turned around and saw a train coming from the West at 60 miles an hour? Second guy says, I'd run and get my brother. He's never seen a train wreck. Well, Hubert, I says, if that expanded Medicare bill gets through committee, I'll run and get my brother. (*pause*) But I did it. I got it through. (*standing*) I've got to get ready to go. Long drive to Austin.
AIDE: The wind's terrible, sir. Are you sure it's wise to drive all that way?
JOHNSON: You know, for damn near twenty years you've been asking me if things are wise. Do I look like the goddamn oracle to you? It may be wise, it may not be wise, but they chose Austin for that Civil Rights Symposium and that means something to me, and I'm going. (*He exits.*)
AIDE: I'm not sure his heart can withstand the trip.
BIRD: For days, I begged him not to go. But he knows what he's spending and it's his to spend, so we should allow him to spend it the way he sees fit.
JOHNSON: (*off*) BIRD. My blue suit.
BIRD: *Excuse me. (She exits.)*

(*As she does, GINNY and WAYNE enter. GINNY is pregnant.*)

WAYNE: This is a good turnout, look at all these people. (*waving*) Some other folks from Tulane over there. Ginny. There's David.
GINNY: David? Where? (*She looks around for him and sees him as he enters.*)
GINNY: Oh my God. (*calling*) David!
WAYNE: Please tell me he already knows you're pregnant.
GINNY: I wrote him.

(*DAVID reaches them.*)

GINNY: David Doubiago as I live and breathe.
DAVID: As all three of you live and breathe. (*DAVID and GINNY hug. To*

WAYNE) Congratulations.
WAYNE: Appreciate it. I didn't expect to see you here.
DAVID: Well, that wasn't very bright, Wayne, given those excruciating months we spent registering voters together.
GINNY: He didn't mean—
DAVID: Relax. I'm joking. After I went on a rampage and destroyed all your pictures, I felt much better.
GINNY: Ha ha?
DAVID: No, I really did that. And I really felt much better.
WAYNE: I meant don't you have final exams?
DAVID: Not this term. Final papers. They're all done. It's a miracle—I'm a good student.
GINNY: I can't imagine you withstanding tax law.
DAVID: Stop trying. I wouldn't be caught dead taking tax law.
WAYNE: How the hell'd you get out of taking tax law? I didn't have that option.
DAVID: That's what you get for being smart enough to get into Tulane. Jasper tells me I'll be meeting the baby at our place come the New Year.
GINNY: We're planning on it. (*pointing*) He's starting.

(*JOHNSON enters and moves to a podium, his AIDE nearby. We can tell he's giving a speech, but we can't hear it. As JOHNSON speaks, MR. YOUNGBLOOD, an old, black porter, enters and stands near the others with a broom.*)

WAYNE: Yeah, I knew it. First he's gonna tell us about his accomplishments. You know, we ought to all get down on our knees and offer up a prayer of thanks. I never saw LBJ's ass in Mississippi registering anybody to vote.
YOUNGBLOOD: (*almost to himself*) I know somethin'. (*WAYNE looks at him.*) Why, this man bring his secretary to dinner at the country club in Austin and she a big black woman and that club white as chalk till that time. Except for us waitin' on tables. (*He laughs.*) One of those other colored waiters says to me—his eyes get so big, they 'bout to pop right out—and he says is that that Bird lady we been hearin' about?
JOHNSON: (*we can hear him now*) I knew that as president I couldn't make people want to integrate their schools or open their doors to blacks, but I could make them feel guilty for not doing it and I believe it was my moral responsibility to do just that—to use the moral suasion of my office to make people feel that segregation was a curse they'd carry with them to their graves.

WAYNE: Moral suasion?

DAVID: This guy is standing here talking to us about morality. I can't fucking believe it.

JOHNSON: When I appointed Thurgood Marshall to the Supreme Court—

WAYNE: (*loudly, to Johnson*) Tokenism. You got the black vote from that.

JOHNSON: I already had your vote.

WAYNE: Maybe you cared about us, maybe you didn't. Either way what you did is in the past and we've still got a long way to go and the man in the White House is terrible on civil rights.

JOHNSON: (*thunderous*) You think I don't know what hasn't changed? My secretary—riding in the presidential car—still has to get out and pee along the side of the road because your goddamn deep south bathrooms are still segregated.

GINNY: We know. We live there.

JOHNSON: Let me explain something about politics to you. There is everything right about a group demanding an hour of their president's time to talk, but you don't start off by saying he's terrible because he doesn't think he's terrible. Start by talking about how you believe he wants to do what's right, and how you believe THIS is right. Do it that way. All of you go back and counsel together and push off wrath. Indulge, tolerate and come up with a program with objectives, with organization.

WAYNE: You want a program? I'll give you a program. Stop starving us, stop keeping us out of work, stop killing us on our way to the polls. How's that for a program?

JOHNSON: What's your name?

WAYNE: Wayne Pearson.

JOHNSON: Wayne, that attitude's only going to hurt you.

WAYNE: (*moving closer*) Don't be telling me I have a bad attitude. You have all the money and power and privilege in the world, don't bad attitude me.

JOHNSON: Let me put it another way, Wayne. You don't know a fuckin' thing about politics. (*a beat—he collects himself and continues*) Let's watch what's been done and see that it's preserved, but let's say we have just begun and let's go on. Until every boy and girl born into this land, whatever color, can stand on the same level ground, our job will not be done.

(*His speech is over. Applause and the lights dim. As he moves toward the audience, YOUNGBLOOD lays down his broom and walks toward him.*)

YOUNGBLOOD: Mr. Johnson? (*JOHNSON looks at him.*) I know you don't remember me, but I used to wait on you when you came for lunch at the—
JOHNSON: At the country club here in Austin. Yes, I remember. You wore your name on your coat and it was—Youngblood. Am I right?
YOUNGBLOOD: Yes, Mr. Johnson.
JOHNSON: How are you, Mr. Youngblood?
YOUNGBLOOD: I'm just fine, Mr. Johnson.

(*Spotlight on JOHNSON and YOUNGBLOOD as they shake hands and grasp arms. Lights stay up on them during the first part of the following, then dim gradually.*)

(*The lights come up on the Berkeley living room, which now takes up most of the acting space. The table's set for dinner. JASPER meditates. DAVID enters and sees the word on the chalkboard, which is "LULL." DAVID erases it and writes "CELEBRATION." As he does, HARMONY enters breathlessly from outdoors, packages in her hands.*)

HARMONY: Jasper doesn't like it when you change his word.
DAVID: I've been handling Jasper a long time.
HARMONY: I know. But sometimes when he scolds you, you freak out and I don't want you to freak out. All right, David?
DAVID: Deal.
HARMONY: (*holding up packages*) Christmas shopping.
DAVID: Christmas was—like—a couple weeks ago.
HARMONY: David. You know it's the thought that counts.

(*GINNY enters.*)

HARMONY: Oh, how's the little baby? I love that little baby. (*as though DAVID were about to speak to her*) I know. Jasper doesn't want to have a baby of his own. But I love other babies. I love all babies.
GINNY: The baby's fine, but Wayne's not doin' too well. He needs some soap, you got any?
HARMONY: (*calling*) In the drawer to the right of the sink, Wayne.
GINNY: I'll get it. (*as she exits*) I keep telling him, you want hot water? Don't wait till five other people take a shower before you get yours.
HARMONY: You're doing much better with Ginny and Wayne than I

thought you would. I mean than I thought you could.
DAVID: It's been three years. Even I can get over something in three years.
HARMONY: I bet it's the baby. Don't you love him?
DAVID: Of course I do, Harmony. We all love him.
HARMONY: (*amused*) I bet even when I'm as old as my grandma, you'll still be patronizing me. But that did not deter me from getting you this Christmas gift.

(*DAVID takes the unwrapped gift suspiciously.*)

HARMONY: (*so excited*) It's a shirt!
DAVID: It is. It's a very nice shirt.
HARMONY: It's a shirt for you to wear to court.
DAVID: Alas. I'm still in Law School.
HARMONY: But you have to save it. You have to wear it your first time.
(*HARMONY hugs him.*) Jasper and I are so proud of you.

(*BUTCH bursts the room, struggling with a large package.*)

HARMONY: Look, Butch. (*holding up the shirt*) It's a shirt. For David to wear to court.
BUTCH: This from Leroy. (*to HARMONY*) We gotta wake Jasper up. (*He moves to JASPER.*) Hey, man. (*calling to him*) JASPER! (*asking for help*) Harmony?
HARMONY: (*touching him*) Jasper? Butch wants you.
JASPER: (*opening his eyes*) Go ahead, Butch. I'm listening.
BUTCH: Okay. I'm gonna open this. Where's Ginny and Wayne? (*calling*) GINNY! (*to everyone else*) I'm gonna open what Leroy sent me. GINNY!
GINNY: (*entering*) I'm here.
BUTCH: Leroy sent me a package. His card says it's that painting of Tony's he's been promising. He wrote he's sorry he can't come cause of his two girls and his laundry business got to be open all the time. But he says tell you thanks for the offer, Jasper.
GINNY: WAYNE, GET OUT HERE! (*to the others*) He's in the shower.
BUTCH: Then he gonna see it in a minute. (*to DAVID*) Help me get this paper off.

(*BUTCH and DAVID tear the brown paper off TONY's painting. Several beats.*)

HARMONY: Wow! (*looking at it closely, then to BUTCH, pointing*) Is that supposed to be you?
BUTCH: It's the war. Leroy says he got all kinda people in there.
HARMONY: That's sad. That's a sad painting.
JASPER: No, dearest. That's a beautiful painting about a sad circumstance.
HARMONY: I'm going to check on the roast before I start crying (*to BUTCH*) Do you mind?
BUTCH: Go on, it's all right.
HARMONY: (*calling*) Wayne! Come see Butch's beautiful painting about the Vietnam war. (*She exits.*)
JASPER: (*as WAYNE enters, wrapped in a towel*) Butch. Your friend Tony was an artist.
BUTCH: I know it.
WAYNE: (*seeing it*) Damn!
BUTCH: Wish he was here with us.
JASPER: (*toward the painting*) Tony. We salute you. (*JASPER and DAVID stand shoulder to shoulder and salute the painting. Then JASPER turns and sees the chalkboard*) What is this? Who did this? Dave? Is this your handiwork?
DAVID: Jasper, the war's over. We're all here together. Shit, Wayne hasn't called me a fuckin' white boy once in three and a half days. Pay attention, Jasper. The war's over. That stinking war is over.

(*Nevertheless, JASPER's got the eraser. Lights dim a bit on Berkeley and come up on JOHNSON, BIRD, AIDE.*)

BIRD: Lyndon, you shouldn't be out of bed.

JOHNSON: (*indicating TV*) They talking about the war being over?

(*BIRD turns off the TV.*)

JOHNSON: We lost it, didn't we? We lost that motherfucking war. (*beat*) It's finished. You suppose that's the most important thing? (*He shakes his head.*) I don't know what's right.

(*BIRD sits next to him, runs her hand through his hair.*)

JOHNSON: It was always just beyond my grasp. I remember when I first went to Washington. I worked 18 hours a day. I was a bulldozer, wasn't I, Bird?

BIRD: That was before I knew you, darling.

JOHNSON: I was. I ate once a day at a cafeteria, where egg sandwiches were a dime, ham and egg twenty cents. I'd always have the egg, but I'd always wish for the ham. What was I after?

AIDE: You wanted to be president.

(Lights back up in Berkeley. JOHNSON remains on stage. WAYNE is now dressed. TONY's painting resides in a place of honor.)

BUTCH: What kind of party you all call this? Ginny, what you doin' over there? Put on some music.

(JASPER moves toward the stereo.)

BUTCH: Not Bobby right now, Jasper, if you don't mind. We got ourselves a new time starting, maybe we don't need ol' Bobby no more.

JASPER: Bite your tongue.

BUTCH: *(turning on the radio)* We just gonna take our luck.

(Bluesy music plays.)

GINNY: Come on now, Jasper, anything can happen. David got into law school.

WAYNE: We got new children comin' up now.

BUTCH: Leroy says he's plannin' on one of his girls becomin' president.

GINNY: Oh, no. Anybody's black child gonna be president, my black child gonna be president. Maybe we got the first black president sleeping right there in the next room.

JASPER: One moment. *(He writes "LULL" on the board.)* I feel I must temper our celebration. It is true that all of us have played a part in an historic social experiment.

DAVID: *(laughing)* Jasper.

JASPER: But when the conversation turns to black presidents, I feel it is my duty to provide a rational voice. If we mean today to pause and honor our dead, I'm with you. Anything else is—

DAVID: Beside the point?

JASPER: Illusory.

GINNY: Lull. Like lullaby?
DAVID: Like calm down. Put to sleep.
JASPER: Induce. "To induce sleep."
BUTCH: I am not interested in sleepin'. I am interested in dancin'. (*calling to her*) Harmony, get your skinny ass in here and dance with me. (*He puts a record on the stereo.*)
HARMONY: (*off*) I'm basting.
BUTCH: Baste later.
DAVID: Hey, man, let her baste. I'm starving.
BUTCH: Then you gonna have to dance with me. (*He and David start to dance.*)

(*WAYNE and GINNY start to dance. Two beats. The baby starts to cry.*)

HARMONY: (*off*) I wanna get him!

(*Spotlight on JOHNSON, AIDE near him.*)

JOHNSON: I used to think, there ain't nothin' government can't fix. (*He shakes his head.*) I didn't know. I didn't know the president's biggest problem is not doing what is right but knowing what is right. (*He moves downstage and faces the audience, as though looking out a window.*) I'm going to show you the greatest thing you ever saw, the greatest treasure that no money can buy—sunset on the Pedernales.

(*JOHNSON freezes in warm light.*)

(*Folks, including JASPER are still dancing in Berkeley.*)

NEWSCASTER: Former President Lyndon Baines Johnson died today at the age of 65. Johnson's doctor said he suffered a heart attack at his ranch in Central Texas.

(*Silence. Then—*)

DAVID: (*quietly*) Pig.
JASPER: Dave. Generosity. Mr. Johnson is dead.
GINNY: No more war, no more Johnson. It's been quite a couple of days.
WAYNE: It means to provide a false feeling of safety. (*They all look at him.*)

Lull: to provide a false feeling of safety.
BUTCH: I don't know about false, but this just about the most safe I felt, all of us here together.
DAVID: We're going to keep being here together. That's how we got this far, right?
WAYNE: I suppose you're right. (*He grins.*) Although I hate to say it.
DAVID: Right, Jasper?
JASPER: Right, buddy.
BUTCH: Rest in peace, Mr. President. (*to WAYNE*) You think white folks ever rest in peace?

(*"What's Goin' On?" plays on the radio. Several beats.*)

BUTCH: (*singing along*) War is not the answer, for only love can conquer hate.

(*BUTCH continues to sing along as the radio plays. HARMONY enters.*)

HARMONY: DINNER'S READY!!

(*The people in Berkeley take seats or bring on food from offstage or both. The radio plays. Berkeley folks sing along at will.*)

RADIO:
   What's goin' on?
   Tell me, what's goin' on?
   Yeah, what's goin' on?
   What's goin' on?
   What's goin' on?

(*As the music continues to play and the action in Berkeley continues, the lights go out on JOHNSON.*)

(*Then the lights dim slowly and go out on the Berkeley living room.*)

END OF PLAY

TRUCKER RHAPSODY

CHARACTERS:

REGINALD DENNY, a long-haired, White truck driver, 36 at the time of the riot.
DAMIAN WILLIAMS, a young, Black man, trying to decide what direction his life should take, well-built—he's not nicknamed "Football" for nothing, 17 at the time of the riot.
RIOT 208, a young Black graffiti artist who paints in Queens, New York, 17 at the time of the riot.
TITUS MURPHY, a Back unemployed aeronautical engineer, who—despite his own formidable problems—saves the life of a truck driver he doesn't know, 28 at the time of the riot.
TERRI BARNETT, a Black interior designer, mother of a young daughter, TITUS' partner, rescuer of a truck driver, 28 at the time of the riot.
GEORGIANA WILLIAMS, DAMIAN's mother, a Black, Christian nurse from the deep South, trying to raise four children in South Central Los Angeles, mid-40s at the time of the riot.

ACT I: 17 scenes, some without text
ACT II: 25 scenes

Scenes take place in Los Angeles during the 1992 Los Angeles riot; in the jail cell in which DAMIAN WILLIAMS is incarcerated; in DAMIAN's childhood home; in the home of two of REGINALD DENNY's rescuers; during the trial of the four men arrested for attacking DENNY; and in a stage space where a New York City graffiti artist engages one of DENNY's attackers in confrontations of various kinds, and where DENNY teaches that graffiti artist how to country swing.

The following should be included in the program of any production of this play. "The inciting incident of this play is the beating of truck driver REGINALD DENNY during the 1992 Los Angeles riots. These riots were touched off by the acquittal of four police officers who beat Rodney King, a Black man whom they were trying to arrest for a traffic violation. Their trial was moved from Los Angeles to Simi Valley, a mostly White, middle class suburban community where the largest concentration of law enforcement officers in California resides. The beating of Rodney King was caught on video, as was the beating of REGINALD DENNY. Both videos were aired on television repeatedly."

Incorporation of these videos or other images relating to those incidents would be a welcome addition to a production of this play if a director so chooses.

I'm grateful to DAMIAN WILLIAMS and BEN VELAZQUEZ (RIOT 208) for their willingness to communicate with me. Without their stories and their generosity, there would be no play.

ACT I

SCENE 1

(*NWA music plays as a photo of the corner of Florence and Normandie Streets in Los Angeles on April 29, 1992 comes into focus slowly with its famous picture of REGINALD DENNY lying in the street near his truck, DAMIAN WILLIAMS standing over him with a concrete block raised above Denny's head. Sudden silence. DAMIAN steps through the photo, concrete block in hand.*)

DAMIAN: Can't take it back. Can't do it. (*He approaches the photo, speaks to it.*) Get up. Everybody knows you're not dead, man, so stand up.

(*DENNY stands up, walks through the photo. Country music starts to play. DENNY walks to a corner of the stage and takes a seat in a couple of chairs painted red that stand in for his truck. On the chairs is painted "208." He drives. He turns up the music. Lights out on both of them as—*)

SCENE 2

(*RIOT 208 enters—and the lights come up bright and we see his work brightly lit on a wall. RIOT is a graffiti artist; the work we see should contain his tag— "RIOT 208."*)

RIOT 208: I'm interested in learning things, I mean in learning all things, I am interested in learning every single thing under the sun. There is no subject that does not interest me, there is nothing I cannot learn, there is nothing I reject before I let it flow through me and see it for what it is and understand what good it does me to know this thing. So each day I paint with more knowledge and each time I throw my name up there I throw up a name that stands for a little more perception, a little more worldliness, more and more of the great and good human person that is me.

(*police siren*)

(*DAMIAN animates, looks around him for the police.*)

RIOT 208: (*turning to DAMIAN*) That's for me, not for you. I'm in New York City, you're in Los Angeles, this is a New York City police siren.

(DAMIAN *steps back several steps, still looking around.*)

RIOT 208: Believe me. (*a sigh*) They are going to chase me around a little while and try to confiscate my art supplies, then they are going to cover up my work. These particular police are not after you. Believe me. (*beat*) You got to trust somebody sometime.

DAMIAN: I trust my mama.

RIOT 208: That's a start. And by the way, put that down, did that weapon not get you in enough trouble?

(DAMIAN *looks at the concrete block, surprised that it is still in his hand.*)

RIOT 208: What now? You gonna tell me you have some special feeling for that brick? Put it down.

(DAMIAN *puts it down.*)

RIOT 208: Idiot.

SCENE 3

(DENNY *gets out of his truck. He walks to the center of the stage, then realizes the country music is very loud and returns to his truck to turn it down. Then he returns to the center of the stage.*)

DENNY: (*covering his eyes with his hand as though there's a light shining on them*) Reginald Oliver Denny. But you can just call me Hey You. Most people just call me Hey or call me Hey You. (*a small chuckle*) I'm kidding. That's a joke. So. (*he puts his hand down*) I was driving from—I was working. I picked up a load in Azusa and I was driving it to the plant in Inglewood. I saw, you know, a lot of commotion. I didn't know about the verdict at all, I hardly knew who Rodney King was. I knew, but only a little bit. There was a medical truck of some kind stopped in the road in front of me, so I had to stop too. (*He turns around and points to* DAMIAN.) He was there, I guess. I don't remember him being there because I had 92 skull fractures. I had more cracks in my head than Humpty Dumpty.

Someone ripped open the door to my truck, see—and that's the last thing I remember about that day. So I have to take everybody's word for what happened. The doctors, the police, my friends, and the angels. God sent them to me, and they saved my life. Here's how He did it. He showed me dying to them—on television. The Lord works in mysterious ways. That's the truth. (*DENNY walks back to his truck. Just before he gets there, he falls to the stage floor as though struck. He holds himself up, dazed, and crawls toward the truck. He lifts himself up into the truck slowly.*)

(*TERRI BARNETT enters quickly, sees DENNY.*)

TERRI: God almighty. He's going to die. (*She gets in the truck and sits beside DENNY, as TITUS enters. She looks around helplessly.*) I can't drive this thing. Jesus, Titus, can you drive this truck? (*She looks down at DENNY.*) Jesus. (*She gets out of the truck and TITUS gets in. TERRI walks center stage and looks back at DAMIAN. She shakes her head.*) What in the name of God is the matter with you? Look at this man.

(*TITUS has figured out that he can't drive the truck either. He gets out and looks around for help—maybe even exits and re-enters quickly, as TERRI turns away from DAMIAN abruptly. She returns to DENNY.*)

TITUS: (*referring to someone we can't see*) Baby, this guy—what's your name? (*a beat as he gets the name*) This guy Bobby says he's a truck driver, he has a license to drive the truck, so he wants us to—
TERRI: Oh God, Titus, he's gonna die. I think he's gonna die.
TITUS: (*pointing to the offstage "Bobby"*) This man will drive the truck. He wants us to lead him to the hospital in our car.
TERRI: (*a big breath*) Then let's just get in the damn car and drive.

SCENE 4

(*TERRI walks away from the truck and into her apartment, followed by TITUS.*)

TITUS: Who's talking about getting credit? Nobody's talking about getting credit.
TERRI: All I'm saying is I'd lay money on those gangbangers get all the press coverage. That's all I'm saying.
TITUS: You're probably right, okay? (*looking at the television*) Man, that

trucker's gonna be in surgery for a week.

TERRI: Look at me. (*She holds out her arms.*) I can't stop shaking. How am I gonna finish any project today? I can't finish any project today, honey, I can't hold a pencil in my hand. (*looking behind her*) You think she's okay? She's just sitting there, staring out the window.

TITUS: She'll be all right, Terri, just give her a minute.

TERRI: A man half dead in his truck, that is not exactly the thing I want my daughter to be witness to.

TITUS: (*distracted by the television*) You hear this? This kid spray painted some poor guy's balls black.

TERRI: Very artistic. The kid—what's his name?

TITUS: I don't know. They keep calling him Football something or other.

DAMIAN: Hold up.

TERRI: Mr. Football probably thinks of himself as some misunderstood graffiti artist.

DAMIAN/RIOT 208: Hey!

DAMIAN: My name is Damian Monroe Williams. And that wasn't me.

(*DAMIAN and RIOT 208 cross to TERRI. TITUS watches the television.*)

RIOT 208: (*introducing himself to TERRI*) Riot 208.

DAMIAN: What kind of name you call that?

RIOT 208: Spray painting a person's genitals is not art, and graffiti is not vandalism. Let's keep these things separate, it's bad enough the police are confused on this particular subject, we got do-gooders all over New York covering up our work, let's not add fuel to the fire. Please. Please. Do me that favor.

DAMIAN: You deaf or something? It was not me did that, but who did it did it so the dude gets the chance to feel what it is to be Black. That's symbolism.

RIOT 208: Oh, that's symbolism.

TERRI: (*overlap*) You're joking.

RIOT 208: You want to do symbolism, how 'bout you write a short story?

DAMIAN: You telling me you never got to deal with color at all? You tell me those sirens are for you, but you don't understand what I'm talking about? You got sirens, but you're buying this Rodney King verdict? You not just deaf, you blind too? You got no problem watching six white housewives with nothin' better to do let those police off? Well, maybe you think a little different when you're the person getting the shit beat out of you by the cops.

RIOT 208: And you're what? Some avenging angel? You fixed those nasty white cops, huh? You showed their asses, huh? Kill some trucker, go to prison. That'll show 'em.

DAMIAN: Fuck you, all right?

RIOT 208: I am asking you for only one small thing—leave spray paint out of it. Can you do that for a brother?

TERRI: (*amused, to RIOT 208*) Where'd you come from?

DAMIAN: I told you two times already, I did not spray paint a goddamn thing.

DENNY: (*suddenly, from out of nowhere*) And I—

(*DAMIAN glares at him.*)

DENNY: Excuse me, this is kind of important. I am the wrong guy too where this is concerned. I—. Um, I mean, not my balls. Somebody else's balls.

DAMIAN: (*overlap, in on "somebody"*) And I didn't kill anybody. And I didn't run into the street and riot all by myself. And I didn't spit at somebody for no reason. I have a life inside me. I have a reason.

(*DAMIAN exits.*)

SCENE 5

(*TERRI's apartment.*)

RIOT 208: So what's this can't keep a pencil in your hand? You an artist?
TERRI: Yeah, I think so.
RIOT 208: You got to know so.
TERRI: Yeah. I know so.
RIOT 208: What's your work?
TERRI: Interior design. I do store windows, so far. But I've done a couple homes.
RIOT 208: Can you make a living off that?
TERRI: Sometimes. You can't possibly make a living off graffiti.
RIOT 208: Right. Although you can get arrested doing it.
TERRI: I see.
RIOT 208: This gentleman?
TERRI: (*sigh, looks at TITUS*) He's not working right now. He's an engineer,

laid off over a year ago and can't find anything. He's looked, I swear, but all he's been doing is temp work—a week here, a week there, he got one lasted five months but nothing permanent yet. See him watching that television? So absorbed in the tube, he doesn't hear us over here.

RIOT 208: That's not because of the tube, that's due to we are artists, he is not. (*TERRI is amused—this guy cracks her up*) That's our reward, right? When we don't get money, sure don't get recognition most of the time. We do get some little piece of that one universal creative con-scious-ness. So I'm over here in South Central from New York City communicating with another artist such as myself.

TERRI: You flatter me.

SCENE 6

(*Big swell of country music, and here comes DENNY, trying to dance along to it. During this scene, on the other side of the stage, TITUS continues to watch television. TERRI, meanwhile, gets up on a stool with a measuring tape and measures a window in their apartment.*)

DENNY: These country singers are artists too, aren't they? In their own way, aren't they?
RIOT 208: I prefer Tupac.
DENNY: Tupac. The rap guy? I like the way they talk quick in those songs. That makes me laugh.

(*A Tupac song comes up. RIOT 208 dances to it. DENNY watches, haltingly tries a step or two. Gives up. Several seconds of dancing, then DENNY speaks, looking at Riot 208 with affection.*)

DENNY: Riot 208. (*laughs softly*) A young man in Queens, New York named himself after my truck. I am trying to accept that as a compliment, but it's hard because I know I'm nothing special. (*all of a sudden, to RIOT 208*) But wait. Tupac's dead, isn't he? (*Music off abruptly.*) Didn't I read how he got shot?
RIOT 208: He wasn't shot yet when the riot happened.
DENNY: (*thoughtful*) He was alive at that time. (*beat*) Now he's dead, shot down in the street like in a western movie. Too bad.
DAMIAN: (*from another part of the stage*) I am telling you there's a life in me.

SCENE 7

TERRI: Titus, hand me that notebook, would you, baby?

TITUS: Look, honey, they're interviewing Lei. (*pronounced LEE*)

TERRI: I figure I can take these measurements anyway. Then maybe tomorrow I'll get back to the design. I'm warning you though, our apartment's going to be a guinea pig and I'm thinking about some bold colors and patterns for these curtains.

TITUS: Lei held that man's bloody head in her hands.

TERRI: Titus? Will you hand me—

TITUS: (*still focused on the television*) Where the hell did she come from? Suddenly she's sitting next to Denny, praying and singing over him while Bobby's driving the truck to the hospital. (*a chuckle*) I swear, she is the original Jesus freak.

(*TERRI gives up—she's not going to get his attention. She gets down off the stool.*)

TERRI: All right, well, I don't go for that born again nonsense, but that woman is surely a Christian. She is the genuine article.

TITUS: (*pointing to the TV*) Terri, they got Bobby on TV right now.

TERRI: (*hugging him from behind*) I was sure Denny was going to die. But Lei knew different.

RIOT: 208 I've discovered that actual real faith in God is rare.

DAMIAN: My mama's a Christian.

DENNY: She sure is. (*beat*) Praise the Lord.

DAMIAN: Don't work though. Faith in God. Don't seem to work.

RIOT 208: (*to DAMIAN*) Try to guess why I took "Riot 208" as my tag.

(*No answer.*)

RIOT 208: I'm watching the television in Long Island City, New York, and you know what? I was crazy pissed about the King verdict. I was blowing off steam like crazy. (*He pauses, remembering that crazy pissed off feeling, then shakes it off.*) But how it is with me, I am interested in learning everything, I want to know everything there is to know. So, I watched the TV. I read stories in the newspaper about him, about you, I followed your trial with your big defense lawyer and your splendid mama trying to keep you out of harm's way.

TITUS: Baby, look at these guys—they got the guys who beat him here on

TV.

RIOT 208: So, after all that I wound up taking Riot 208 as my tag. Try to guess why.

(Still silence from DAMIAN. DENNY walks all the way to the edge of the stage and leans forward.)

DENNY: See here? Look. Feel that? Big piece out of my face that's never coming back. Feel it? Those doctors? (*as though he was talking about the most miraculous thing that ever happened*) They built a muscle out of PLASTIC! PLASTIC! PLASTIC! And my eye sits on that plastic muscle! Can you imagine? Otherwise, it would still be pushed down into my sinus cavity. How great to be a doctor, isn't it? How great to save life. But this girl (*pointing to TERRI*) saved life too, and this man (*pointing to TITUS*) saved life too. He's not a doctor, he's not even employed. And the other lady—a nutritionist named Lei with her unstoppable Christian faith—they just jumped up from their chairs in front of their TVs and ran into the street. (*more and more excited, like he was explaining the plot of an action adventure movie*) Then a big rig driver named Bobby stopped his truck and hopped in mine (*a small laugh*) and that's how those four became the angels who made it possible for me to be standing here today. Can you imagine that?

SCENE 8

(All characters present.)

RIOT 208: I haven't been doing all this listening and learning and understanding and painting for nothing. I learned something.
DAMIAN: You want to listen to that trucker. Because why? Because he's too stupid to be mad at the people who stomped him?
RIOT 208: You question why I don't want to listen to you. Maybe you should listen to yourself a while, then I think you'll get my point.
DAMIAN: Oh, I have to get your point, but you don't give a fuck about my point, that right?
TERRI: (*to DAMIAN as in "okay, if you're going to talk that way"*) I've got to pick up my daughter.
DAMIAN: Listen to me now.

(TERRI stops and looks at him, as do the other characters.)

DAMIAN: I'm in trouble again.

TITUS: Shit.

RIOT 208: What kind of trouble?

DAMIAN: I got arrested again.

TITUS: (*after a big sigh*) I'll listen. But please don't tell us anything that will push me over the edge, okay? Coping with unemployment is delicate. You're an aeronautical engineer, a few years have to go by before you can face the possibility of taking a job as an office manager. Lots of job openings at McDonald's, right? Hold your head up and be unemployed simultaneously.

TERRI: I keep telling you I'll stick by you, baby.

TITUS: And I keep telling you it's not about will you stick by me. It's about I am good at what I do, I have a degree from USC, I graduated in the top 10% of my class, and I can't find a job and I have to keep living in South Central which is not exactly what I had in mind when I was coming in first in my physics class.

TERRY: Second.

TITUS: Woman, do not piss me off right now.

TERRI: Did you just call me "woman?"

RIOT 208: Okay, now we have this same problem in what the newspapers love to call the graffiti culture. The graffiti culture is a male culture, sort of like the football culture, or like the drag the truck driver out of the car and beat the living shit out of him culture, or like the police culture. I know, I know, I know, I know—lots of female police officers but how often do I see them wailing on somebody with a baton and somebody who's lying on the ground at that? Not too often. How often do I see females picking up big blocks of concrete and smashing some trucker's brains in? Not too often. How often do I see females tagging or throwing up? Alas. Not too often. I am a revolutionary as far as that goes. My crew's called TEAM for The. Eternal. Artistic. Mind. I'm a spiritual motherfucker. My crew is me, another male artist and one female artist. Yup. I'm also a progressive motherfucker.

TERRI: Have you forgotten my name?

TITUS: No, I have not forgotten your name. I'm only saying I am worried about this kid–all right, several years have gone by, he's not actually a kid anymore—-but I'm worried about him. You heard what he said, right? He's in trouble again.

DAMIAN: Listen to me!

(DENNY goes to DAMIAN, puts a hand on his shoulder.)

DENNY: Didn't I listen during the trial? Heck, I listened from a hospital bed. I'm a good listener.

DAMIAN: Do not be touching me. Listen with your ears only, keep your hands to yourself.

SCENE 9

DAMIAN: One of my best memories is my mother's accent. She's from Mississippi so she speaks in an accent that I love. Very much.

GEORGIANA: *(nurse's hat on her head)* Are you out of those pajamas, Dame? You want to be dropped off at school, you got to be in your clothes in a couple more minutes.

DAMIAN: *(7 years old)* I'm dressed, mama. See me dressed?

GEORGIANA: Eat your breakfast quick then, we got to fly this morning.

DAMIAN: *(7 years old)* Can I have some milk, mama? *(an adult—to the other characters)* My mama watched me eat, can I tell you that? She was gonna make sure everything she provided for me from that job in the hospital was making it down my throat to my stomach. I was gonna grow. I was gonna thrive.

DENNY: That's nurses. Those nurses took special care of me. They would not let me see pictures of myself in the paper all beat up and they would not let me look in the mirror. They wanted to protect me. That's why they're called that—nurses. They nurture you, put their hands on your forehead, take your temperature.

DAMIAN: My mama didn't need a thermometer. She could just touch my head with the tip of her finger, and she knew what it was.

GEORGIANA: That's 101 degrees, my baby, you got the flu, you get back in that bed.

DAMIAN: She's the best cook all the time but when I'm sick, she's even better.

RIOT 208: That's not nurses, that's mamas. You're just lucky you got both in one.

TITUS: That's not all mamas. Mine could not cook a lick. Dinnertime was something I had to gather my strength for.

RIOT 208: Now that's wrong. My mama cooked her brains out. That too was part of my education and I paint that part too. I paint those fruits and vegetables sometimes. I learned hundreds of things about vegetables from my mama, do you know that?

TITUS: I learned that vegetables are limp and taste like dishwater.

DENNY: (*like a kid trying to fit in*) My mom couldn't pay me to eat a vegetable. I don't know if she cooked them good because I would not eat a vegetable no matter what she did, no matter how much she threatened me. No way. No vegetables.

DAMIAN: I'm the youngest so sometimes the greens all gone by the time they get to me. Mama say, "Save some for Dame. Save some for the baby." When she's at home, which sometimes she is not because she has to work at night sometimes. I tell you, my mama can cook vegetables like nobody else.

GEORGIANA: (*suddenly shouting*) JUSTICE FOR THE L.A. FOUR! JUSTICE! JUSTICE! JUSTICE! JUSTICE!

DENNY: His mom has invited me. It's true. She invited me for Christmas dinner, after her boy was convicted, after he went to prison. She has true generosity.

GEORGIANA: That District Attorney replace the judge because he's Black? How those boys supposed to get a fair trial?

DENNY: I thought it was awfully sweet of her to invite me but of course I couldn't attend. I have my daughter. I have my friends. I have a new and very deep understanding of how much it means to spend every second you can with your loved ones so I appreciated it very much, but I could not go there for a holiday meal.

GEORGIANA: (*to passers-by in front of the courthouse*) Go ahead, look. Look all you want to look. But don't think you gonna be starin' me down. Georgiana Williams don't get stared down. I am going to get justice for my boy. JUSTICE! JUSTICE! JUSTICE FOR the L.A. FOUR!

DAMIAN: I missed mama most. And my baby.

TERRI: You have a child?

DAMIAN: You should see how he grew up when I was away.

DENNY: My daughter's eight.

TERRI: Ashley was 12 when it happened. She's a young woman now.

TERRI: (*to DENNY*) Wish you could have seen my little girl, looking out the back window at your truck following us to the hospital.

DENNY: I wish I could have too. That would have been nice.

TERRI: She said to me "I hope you save him, mama," kept looking back out the window when she said it, didn't turn to me, spoke to me without taking her eyes off that truck. She sat looking out her own bedroom window a long time after we got home.

DAMIAN: You know a lot better what your mama means when you see how fast they grow.

RIOT 208: You gonna tell us something about being a daddy now? You hauling rocks at people's heads and you got the nerve now to try to tell us something about being a daddy? You running with a gang—

DAMIAN: Maybe I was. What's it to you?

RIOT 208: Nothing. (*beat*) It's nothing to me.

DAMIAN: I'm saying since I had my son, I know some things my mama was talking about.

RIOT 208: I'm not gonna believe you know one thing about being a daddy.

DAMIAN: I am saying I know what my mama meant now, about the future. You got to put everything off in your understanding till later. Why we got to move back to Mississippi, I miss my friends, I miss the city, I don't know anybody here. Mama tells me she has to take care of her own mama, and I'm too young to understand now, but I will understand. That will come later. Little things and big things, do what I say, understand later. Football too. Practice. But I don't get playing time. You'll get playing time later. Practice now, get playing time later? It's all like that, always that way. That day of the verdict on those cops too. They beat some brother half to death, we got it down on videotape, those police get off. Be patient now, you get justice someday, you get justice later.

SCENE 10

(Lights change. Country music plays.)

RIOT 208: I made as many pictures of riot as I could imagine. I threw up dozens of riotous combinations of colors to commemorate the police brutality, then the in-com-pre-hen-si-ble verdict, then the in-ev-i-ta-ble riot, then the gla-mour-ous trial. The more I observed and learned and understood, the more work I did. Paint begets more and more paint. Every piece inspires twenty more pieces. It's glorious, it's thrilling.

DENNY: Painting sounds nice. How about New York? Is New York nice?

RIOT 208: It's life, you know. It's pizza on every corner, it's the noisy elevated train, it's more people than you could ever have time to say excuse me to when you bump into them. Tell me what you mean, is it nice.

DENNY: Something you know won't harm you.

RIOT 208: (*laugh*) Definitely not nice.

DENNY: That's all right. I guess L.A.'s not nice either.

SCENE 11

GEORGIANA: Los Angeles. I'll say this. It's not Mississippi. This city smells bad.

DAMIAN: Yeah. This city stinks.

GEORGIANA: Yes it does. You remember what Mississippi smells like? Mississippi smells like flowers. It fools you with its sweet smell.

DAMIAN: No it does not. That place smells like clothes got left overnight in the washing machine.

GEORGIANA: Uh uh uh. Like flowers. Sweet and juicy.

DENNY: My grandfather used to tell me the same thing about California. (*quoting his grandfather*) There was a day hereabouts had character. (*big laugh*) He didn't call Los Angeles "Los Angeles." He'd call Los Angeles "hereabouts." There was a day hereabouts smelled clean like lemons, he told me. Smelled like opportunity.

GEORGIANA: Oh, my Lord, lemons. Do you know I love that smell of lemons? I have a product to polish my furniture with that features that fragrance. (*big smile*) Don't I wish I could use it to wipe this city clean? Eliminate that smell of burning disintegration you have to contend with each time you step out of your home or your church, just hangin' in that brown air every minute. (*chuckle*) If I could do that, Georgiana Williams would be some kind of hero. Wouldn't I though?

SCENE 12

TERRI: Baby, you're making yourself sick about this.

TITUS: I just think the four of us have to stick together. One of us does a television talk show, gives a magazine interview, makes a movie deal, we all do. All of us or none of us. That's the only way we're going to manage this without resentment.

TERRI: I say we tell everybody no.

TITUS: You know I can't afford to do that.

TERRI: What does that mean? "Come on, baby, they're gonna kill this guy, we've got to help him" was an alternative to a finding a job?

TITUS: That is not true, and it is not fair.

TERRI: Shit, I didn't mean that.

(A pause. Then from another part of the stage.)

GEORGIANA: Justice! Justice! Justice!

TERRI: Titus, I'm sorry.
TITUS: It's Monique's bedtime.
TERRI: Honey, I did not mean that. *(glances at GEORGIANA, then)* I'm freaked out about all this attention we keep getting, about the trial coming up, about that kid's mother screaming in front of the courtroom.

GEORGIANA: Justice! Justice!

(TERRI turns to GEORGIANA then, and after a beat, back to TITUS.)

TITUS: Go put Monique to bed, will you, Terri.
TERRI: Say you forgive me.

SCENE 13

(Spotlight on DAMIAN.)

DAMIAN: My mama freaked everybody out, all right? And that is one thing I do not and will never understand, all right? The police chief arresting me in some big ego public way I might not like, but I understand. Folks in the United States of America want to throw me away because all they can think about is the truck driver got spit on. I might not like, but I understand. Things the cops do and say, things the prosecutor do and say, things the Los Angeles Times write, I might not like, but usually I can follow. Television newscasters call me a Big Black Thug I might not—I do not like. *(beat)* They don't want to know my name and that does not surprise me. But here my mama finds me a lawyer, here she gives me a hug and a kiss, here she stands outside the court and tells everybody on the street she will see to it this trial is fair or she will die trying—people write she is blind to what a gang-bangin' animal I am, people write she does not care about the victims of this riot. She is my mother. I came from her body. She gave me life, and she knows that life, and she loves that life. How do folks expect her to turn her back? Those police beat Rodney King got off. That is crazy. Folks don't believe in our anger about those police got off. That is crazy. *(He really is dumbfounded by this.)* But nothing as crazy as people truly expect my mama to abandon me. That is crazy. That is wrong. Give my mama some respect.

SCENE 14

GEORGIANA: I want nothing from you except an explanation. How many times do I have to receive this phone call? I do not need a math teacher to tell me you are a bright child.

DAMIAN: That's it right there, see that? I'm not a child. Why'd he call me a child?

GEORGIANA: You are my child, Dame.

DAMIAN: Look at me. I'm a man.

GEORGIANA: You are 14 years old and you do not attend your math class. Don't make me move you back to Mississippi permanently.

RIOT 208: Now she's going to tell you how disappointed she is in you.

DAMIAN: My mama's not disappointed in me.

GEORGIANA: Don't disappoint me, Damian.

DENNY: That's how mine always nailed me. No way I would have passed algebra except she was always telling me how disappointed she'd be if I flunked.

RIOT 208: It's a trick. They're not really disappointed. They just know how you hate to let 'em down, so they bring it on, try to get you to do what they want.

DAMIAN: I made the football team, Mama.

GEORGIANA: I'm proud of that too. But football is football. Math is math.

TITUS: My mother was like a cheerleader, I swear. "You go, boy. You show 'em, boy." And anybody gave me a hard time, she was down at that school, "Don't you tell me about my own son, he's first in his class, he's gonna get a college scholarship, you don't know nothing and if I hear you're bothering him"—she says this to the Vice-Principal, right? 'Cause I'm necking with some girl under the stairwell he called her in, you know? "If I hear you're bothering him, I will take him out of this school and I can promise you that will harm this school's reputation because there IS no brighter boy than my boy. You want this school to be known as a place bright boys transfer OUT OF?" (*beat*) Guess you could say I represented hope in my mama's mind.

TERRI: Mine didn't speak of disappointment. She grabbed her slipper and smacked me on the arm with it.

DAMIAN: Shut up. With a slipper?

DENNY: I hope it was one of those soft ones.
TERRI: It was but it hurt.
RIOT 208: What? No belt?
TERRI: Nope. A slipper. Your mama hit you with a belt?
RIOT 208: My mama never hit anybody her whole life. Some people hit, some people get hit. My mama got hit.
TERRI: Nobody was gonna dare touch my mama.
TITUS: Oh, you can say that again. This woman's mother is fierce. I'm telling you, she has got herself a temper.
TERRI: I have had to lay down the law about my daughter. No hitting. My mother just can't understand that.
DAMIAN: Mama didn't have that rule. I got a smack from time to time.
DENNY: My mother and father are both Christians so they didn't hit me.
RIOT 208: What are you saying now, did I hear you say Christians don't hit people?
TERRI: Dream on.
DENNY: (*shrugs*) My folks didn't hit me.

SCENE 15

(*GEORGIANA turns to DAMIAN as the others step out of the scene for a few moments.*)

GEORGIANA: Where you been?
DAMIAN: Nowhere. Hanging out.
GEORGIANA: I provided you with a Christian education.
DAMIAN: You're the only one of them Christians ain't full of shit.
GEORGIANA: Say that to me again, you will feel it on your face.
DAMIAN: Thank you for the Christian education.
GEORGIANA: Are you ridiculing me, Dame? (*Silence.*) Did I just hear you make fun of me?
DAMIAN: I'm sorry.
GEORGIANA: At some point in your life, you will learn to value what is valuable.
RIOT 208: See? That's what I'm saying.
DAMIAN: Shut up. You're not my mama;
RIOT 208: You bet your ass I'm not your mama. What are you thinking?
GEORGIANA: I should never have allowed you to go to that public high school.

DAMIAN: I do not like school, it has nothing to do with you should have done this or that. You take me from the Christian school, you put me in the public school, then another, then another, and I keep telling you the school does not matter, I do not like school. Let it be that simple, Mama. Please.

RIOT 208: I say there it is right there.

DAMIAN: And I say I hope every brother in New York City does not run off at the mouth like you or that's gonna be the noisiest goddamn city on earth.

RIOT 208: Where is your curiosity? What do you want to know? What hunger do you have for knowledge?

DAMIAN: I don't have hunger for knowledge. I have hunger for justice, man, everybody's not the same as everybody else, you know that?

RIOT 208: I'm not the one who beat up on the truck driver.

SCENE 16

(Lights up bright. DAMIAN sits on a stoop with a boom box blaring rap music. The music is interrupted to make an announcement. The police who beat Rodney King have been acquitted. The responses come rapidly one right after the other.)

DAMIAN: *(astounded)* Acquitted?
TITUS: *(also astounded)* Not guilty?
TERRI: *(to TITUS)* Not guilty? How those police not guilty?
RIOT 208: You're kidding me. *(to his radio)* Tell me you're kidding.
GEORGIANA: Oh, Lord. Lord, Lord, here we go one more time.
RIOT 208: That is fucked up.

(Beat. GEORGIANA prays. TITUS watches television.)

DAMIAN: Wouldn't you just know that? Man, wouldn't you just know it? *(changing the station)* I don't want to listen to that bullshit, give me something else.

(RIOT 208 spray paints in response to the verdict. Denny enters, gets in his truck, talks on a CB radio.)

DENNY: I'm thinking I'm going to take a short cut. I figure I can get there in probably less than an hour that way.

(We hear country music alternating with Tupac. RIOT 208 spray paints wildly. He paints "I am here. I am here. I am here.")

VOICE THROUGH MEGAPHONE: *(off)* Step forward, Sir. Step forward.
DAMIAN: *(talking to someone we can't see)* What'd you do, man? You got to go. You got to run.
VOICE THROUGH MEGAPHONE: *(off)* You are under arrest. Do not try to resist. You are outnumbered.
DAMIAN: Bro, what'd you do?

(DENNY sings along with the country song. Riot 208 paints feverishly.)

DENNY: *(into CB radio)* I'm exiting the freeway. I'm taking side streets. I bet you I can beat you back. *(beat)* I bet you I can too. Yeah, just keep your eye on the clock and we'll see what's what. Yeah, 10-4.

(SOUND OF rap music coming up louder and louder, competing with country music. SOUND OF many many many police batons smacking against hands. SOUND OF police with batons.)

(RIOT 208 paints. DENNY gets up, walks to DAMIAN who freezes.)

DENNY: It was months before I could leave the hospital, and it was two years before I knew the police arrested his brother. *(points)* Him. Damian Williams. The police arrested his brother for stealing a car. 30 minutes before I reached that corner. His brother didn't steal the car. He didn't go to jail for stealing the car. He got justice. Before he got justice, he got surrounded by 30 cops. *(beat)* 40 cops? I can't remember these details.
DAMIAN: How many of you does it take to arrest one PERSON for God's sake?
DENNY: Dozens of police officers. Handcuffs. No police officers left over for the corner of Florence and Normandie. No police left over for me *(beat, to DAMIAN)* Of course, that's not an excuse for what you did. I have a dented temple. I swear, my right temple is dented. *(DENNY gets back in his truck, drives along, sings along.)*

DAMIAN: You want to see what I think of y'all hundred fucking cops coming to arrest one man for stealing one car?

(DAMIAN turns his back to the audience, drops his pants, moons the police we don't see who are arresting his older brother. A beat. Then DAMIAN quickly stands up, pulls his pants back on. Pictures of the riot starting to happen projected.)

TITUS: *(watching the television)* Shit, this is gonna be bad. Baby, look at this.

SCENE 17

(Pictures of the riot continue, accentuated by rap music. The pictures fight for stage space with RIOT 208's painting. The rap music fights with DENNY's country music. Sounds and visuals battle for prominence.)

SCENE 18

Riot 208: I heard that verdict, I threw up, I kept throwing up. I kept thinking while I'm throwing up, learn something. Come on, I'm yellin' at myself. I'm yellin'. Come on, learn learn learn learn learn learn learn. Come on. Come on. Learn learn learn learn. *(beat, then worn out)* Those cops got off. *(He suddenly throws the spray can down.)* WHAT THE FUCK? *(beat)* Learn something. *(then with some anger and despair)* I knew that already.

(Now DENNY and DAMIAN move toward one another. Each arrives at the corner of Florence and Normandie. There is sudden silence, then the sound of glass shattering—a brick has been thrown through DENNY's truck window. DENNY reacts, then falls onto the stage floor as though having been pulled from his truck.)

TITUS: *(watching this on TV)* Terri, oh my God.

(DAMIAN picks ups the concrete block and holds it high over DENNY'S head.)

TITUS/TERRI/RIOT208/GEORGIA: DON'T!

(DAMIAN throws the block at DENNY. Silence.)

DAMIAN: Too late.

ACT II

SCENE 1

(Spotlight up on DAMIAN, on trial in the present. RIOT 208 somewhere else on the stage.)

DAMIAN: (*pleading*) Not guilty. (*to RIOT 208*) What happened to you, you believe the police before you believe me?
RIOT 208: I have given up on you, Mr. Damian Williams. I have given you up for a deranged crime-monger who is too immature to respond to a situation in any fashion besides with whining childishness.
DAMIAN: You know what? FUCK YOU AND THE L.A.P.D. I DID NOT DO IT. I went to prison after that riot—and that is why the cops think they got it easy, they can lay this new crime on me.
RIOT 208: So, what? You telling me now the cops arrested you for a crime you did not commit because of what you did to Denny all that time ago?
DAMIAN: You tellin' me New York City cops followin' you around relieving you of your paint brushes or spray cans or whatever it is? Yes, I am telling you the police have not let up on me since I got out of prison. But forget that, I did my time. I DID NOT DO—

(Spotlight suddenly out on him, and DAMIAN disappears into black.)

SCENE 2

(RIOT 208 walks across the stage, looking back at the darkness where DAMIAN stands. RIOT 208 stands still a moment, lost in thought, then sits down. DENNY sits beside him. A pause.)

RIOT 208: You want to know something? My wife is pregnant.
DENNY: I didn't know you were married. You're so young to be married, except who am I to talk, you know, because I was married before I turned 21 and then the divorce came fast.
RIOT 208: I wasn't married then. When the riot happened. I'm married now.
DENNY: Ah. See? I have these—sort of—black outs. (*grin*) I have a hole in my head. (*pause*) You read in the newspapers about this—this crazy bloody violence—being the "defining moment" of my life. I know I'm

not the smartest person who ever walked on this earth, but I've figured out life is better without a defining moment. (*beat*) Because with a defining moment, you forget things, you forget people get older and get married and people who used to not have children have children now. Because in your mind, everything goes back to that goddamn defining moment. (*This is the most upset he has been through the play. He stops talking; he doesn't like to be upset.*)

SCENE 3

(*We see TITUS hang up a telephone as DENNY moves forward into a spotlight and raises his right hand as though he is testifying at a trial.*)

TERRI: (*off*) Titus, come on and get in this shower.
TITUS: I got another one.
TERRI: (*can't hear you*) What?
TITUS: (*moving to the door so she can hear him*) That's the third call I got asking why I want to testify against a brother. Want to? Who said anything about want to?

(*TERRI sticks her head out, a towel around it, nearly bumping into TITUS.*)

TERRI: Those people calling were not there, so they don't know what they're talking about. Now we have got to get to that courtroom on time, so come on. I'll wash your back.
TITUS: (*a grin*) I'm gonna take you up on that.

(*TERRI and TITUS exit.*)

SCENE 4

DENNY: So help me God. (*hand down, pause*) Um (*a laugh*) no, too many skull fractures to remember anything. (*looking over at the defendants*) I don't recognize any of them. (*pause*) All I want to say is—um—just that it was something that happened in a moment because they—people—were pushed to their limit. I'm not saying it was right, what they did to me, it was wrong. But I don't think it—um—reflects that they are criminals. Not really.

(DENNY moves off the witness stand, he passes GEORGIANA.)

DENNY: Hello, Mrs. Williams.
GEORGIANA: Call me Georgiana. I insist.

RIOT 208: Man, when I watched it on television, I watched you approach that intersection man, and those punks were out on the street, I wanted you to run them down. Pleeeeeeaaase, I kept praying to you, please run them over.

(Lights up suddenly on DAMIAN.)

DAMIAN: You heard him, I am not a criminal, now how come he can say this with his head bashed in and you do not see it?
RIOT 208: Because you are a punk, you are a gangbanger, you take no responsibility, you are not man enough to stand up and admit that you did wrong.
DAMIAN: And you are not man enough to admit I had a reason. *(shaking his head)* And you call me an idiot.
RIOT 208: You know something, my daddy was a gangbanger. He took responsibility for nothing. My mama got most of the punches, but I got a few and I am telling you your little boy is not safe if you can't face up to your wrongdoing.
DAMIAN: *(furious)* I would never hurt my son.
RIOT 208: You would though.
DAMIAN: Mama takes care of him.
RIOT 208: That's what I mean. No responsibility. But what the hell, you gonna be going back to jail anyway, right?

SCENE 5

(TITUS enters, reading a newspaper, dressed for work—nice shirt, tie.)

TITUS: Look at this, baby. That kid who served time for trying to kill Reginald Denny got arrested again. You remember him? Baby?
TERRI: Titus, honey, I can't find those earrings with the jade insets. Do you have any idea—
TITUS: In your bathrobe.
TERRI: My bathrobe?

TITUS: You put them in your bathrobe pocket, right before you said these jade earrings are in my bathrobe pocket, baby, so when I can't find them and ask you where they are, they're in my bathrobe pocket.

TERRI: When'd I do that?

TITUS: Whenever your sister's engagement party was. You were loaded, baby, you were as drunk as I've ever seen you.

TERRI: No wonder about that, I am not right with her marrying that man, suppose he never gets a job?

TITUS: Guess I should be grateful you didn't feel that way about me.

TERRI: Titus—

TITUS: You remember how long it took me to get something?

TERRI: Titus, that's not what I'm talking about. Come on, now. Mama says he's not even looking. The century has turned now, Titus. Enough is enough, my sister should not marry a person who has no job.

TITUS: The century has turned. What does that mean, the century has turned? Now if a man can't find a job, he has no one to blame but himself? I see. So I couldn't find work last year because that was before the century turned.

TERRI: I'm just saying I'm worried, okay, that's all I'm saying. She's my little sister, okay?

TITUS: You think people were worried about you? All the time I was unemployed, you think people were worried about you?

TERRI: All the time you were unemployed, you were working temp, you were killing yourself trying to find something.

TITUS: How do you know he's not killing himself? Inside, where nobody can see it?

SCENE 6

(RIOT 208 crosses to her and taps TERRI on the shoulder.)

RIOT 208: This future brother in law got a name?

TERRI: Leonard.

RIOT 208: What kind of work does—

TERRI: No. Sorry. Leroy.

RIOT 208: What kind of work does Leroy do?

TERRI: No kind. That's the problem. (*beat*) I am generally not so judgmental. This is my baby sister.

RIOT 208: And you've got a teenage daughter. I understand. My wife's pregnant.

TERRI: (*big smile*): Congratulations. Good for you.

RIOT 208: I'm moving furniture. For cash. Weird to move furniture in New York City, giant trucks driving down narrow streets with grand pianos inside. I've moved some rich ones, you know that? I get a knot in my stomach sometimes handling those items, but more than that I get a good feeling, looking at beautiful rugs and carrying precious rare sculptures and other works of art. (*pause, realizing*) Because I'm an artist. (*excited by this new insight*) See that? There is something to learn every day, isn't there, don't you think so? Being near those magnificently beautiful paintings or vases or statues—I'll tell you, rich people in New York own any and all things you can think of. Being near those things makes me gasp out loud sometimes and then I get embarrassed in front of the other guys on the job. (*beat*) I used to think that knot in my stomach was from knowing where my mom has to live compared to these places, but now, I think it's not. I think it's touching that beauty created by someone like me.

TERRI: Don't you feel resentful?

DENNY: (*holding out his hand to TITUS*) Reginald Denny.

TITUS: (*shaking*) Titus Murphy. (*beat*) We've met.

SCENE 7

TERRI: (*shaking*): Do you? Feel resentful?

RIOT 208: I feel inspired.

TERRI: Because I know I sure do feel resentful when I bid on a job and someone else gets the job and when I see the finished project, I think well well well. My my, this girl has not got a lick of talent, how do you suppose she landed that job?

DENNY: I feel resentful sometimes. When you're in the hospital with your head all wrapped up in bandages, you have a lot of time to think and the thoughts just take on a life of their own. You can't control 'em. (*beat—then on to happier things*) I remember when you wrote me in the hospital, remember?

RIOT 208: Yeah, it made me feel so humble when you wrote me back, man.

DENNY: When I read your letter, it took me a long time to figure out what a tag was. But I did figure it out and I was thinking that it would be hard to paint pictures on the wall and then have someone paint over them. I was thinking if you kept painting, that took some kind of courage.

(*self-conscious*) Or something like that.
TERRI: Titus, listen, this young artist has a job moving furniture.
RIOT 208: I'm so excited about the baby coming. I would do anything.
TERRI: See, that's what I'm talking about. Men work.
DENNY: Excuse me.
TITUS: You know what your problem is?
DENNY: Could I—just—say something about this?
TERRI: (*overlap*) No, what's my problem?
TITUS: You want to generalize.
DENNY: Excuse me.
TITUS: (*overlap*) You make an exception for me, but then you still want to generalize.
DENNY: Listen. (*beat*) I don't work.

(*Pretty long, pretty awkward pause.*)

TITUS: See?
TERRI: That is completely different.
TITUS: I KNOW THAT. THAT'S MY POINT.

SCENE 8

RIOT 208: (*to DAMIAN*) You have something you'd like to add here?
DAMIAN: (*after thinking*) I'm a hell of an athlete.
DENNY: That's why you have that nickname.
DAMIAN: Do you have to talk to me?
DENNY: Well. Yeah.
DAMIAN: (*to the others*) My mama shows me pictures of me when I'm two. I'm bigger than most kids when they're five. I'm big, I've already got big arms and shoulders. If you looked at that picture, you'd say I had a destiny. As I'm growing up, I get picked first. Every time. Damian's on my team. Damian's the quarterback. But I'll tell you something. You read everyplace that all little Black boys want to play sports when they grow up, all little Black boys want that fame and fortune, poor little Black boys don't realize it's not going to happen, it's a stupid dream. Well, that what you read is not true. We do realize even when we're small, even when we're nine or ten, we do realize it's a stupid dream. Only in some little far away corner of our mind.
TITUS: But you were good at it. Football.

DENNY: You see? That's why you got the nickname. Damian Monroe Football Williams.

DAMIAN: (*overlap*) You realize even more when you're good at it. You get older and all of a sudden there's other big boys. You get a little older and they're everywhere, other guys who play football as good as you and what you have to do is, you have to work even harder. You have the dream and you know it's a stupid dream and the more you know it's a stupid, useless dream, the harder you have to work if you have any chance whatsoever of making it come true, which you know you don't.

RIOT 208: I hope you don't expect us to believe you tried to make your dreams come true, Mr. Football Williams.

TITUS: That's beside the point.

TERRI: Now you've really gone off the deep end, Titus. How is that beside the goddamn point?

TITUS: Because whether or not you "did your best"—whatever that means—when you have talent or skill or a dream or all of those and you can't live that, your heart is broken. If you come in second in your class at USC and you can't get a full-time job for eight years, your heart is broken. When you realize at age 14 that the dream is impossible, your heart is broken. When you're willing to do any work you can find—and do not contradict me, Leroy is willing to do any work he can find—and you can't find any, no matter when you give up the search, your heart is broken.

DENNY: When someone throws a brick at you and makes it impossible for you to drive your truck anymore, your heart is broken.

(*DAMIAN looks at DENNY.*)

DENNY: What?

SCENE 9

GEORGIANA: Dame, I am telling you I do not want that man here. Damian, you get back in this living room and listen to what I'm saying to you.

DAMIAN: (*returning to the stage*) I'm almost 30 years old, Mama, I got a child in high school, don't be telling me to get back in this room. For Christ's sake.

GEORGIANA: What did you say?

DAMIAN: Nothin'.

GEORGIANA: You are never NEVER going to be too old for me to wash that smart mouth out with soap, am I making myself as clear as the Lord will allow?

DAMIAN: (*a smile*) Yes, Ma'am.

GEORGIANA: Are you smiling at me?

DAMIAN: Smiling at you? Why'd I be smiling at you, Mama? That would mean I like you, wouldn't it?

GEORGIANA: I am telling you that man is trouble and I will not have that trouble in my home.

DAMIAN: He's a friend of mine, all right?

GEORGIANA: Do you think your mama is stupid, Dame? Now that you're grown, have you decided that you have a stupid mama?

DAMIAN: Come on, Mama, be nice.

GEORGIANA: Don't "come on be nice" me. That man is a drug dealer. That man walks up and down the streets of this neighborhood and sells drugs to children.

DAMIAN: He does not—

GEORGIANA: ARE YOU GOING TO DEFEND A DRUG DEALER IN MY CHRISTIAN HOME?

SCENE 10

TERRI: (*straightening TITUS' tie*) This tie is perfect with this shirt. Two months on the job, you already got a promotion. Honey, one day you're going to own that company.

TITUS: (*holding out the newspaper to her*) I was telling you that kid who threw the brick at Denny?

TERRI: Which one?

TITUS: The one who threw the brick. The one who danced all around him, remember?

TERRI: Yeah?

TITUS: He's in jail again. For killing some guy. Some drug deal gone bad.

TERRI (*taking the newspaper, then throwing it down*): Loser. (*She picks up a pad and begins to sketch.*)

SCENE 11

DAMIAN: I did not do it.

RIOT 208: Explain why you're hanging with the man. Didn't I hear your mama tell you not to?

DAMIAN: I don't have to explain a damn thing to you.
RIOT 208: Explain it to yourself. I'll just stand over here and listen.
DAMIAN: Listen to me, I got the best mama who ever lived on this earth and if she understand about the life inside of me then that's the only understanding I am going to care about. (*He turns to GEORGIANA*) He does not sell drugs to children, all right? (*pause*) I have not seen him sell drugs to children. (*pause*) I maybe seen him making one sale to a person who looked kinda young. (*pause*) I probably seen him sell to a teenager of some kind. (*pause*) I was not there when he whacked that dude. That's the truth.
RIOT: 208: What now? You think your mama don't know you're using?
DAMIAN: Riot whatever your name is, I think you a little confused.
RIOT 208: Oh. I'm confused.
DAMIAN: See, 'cause smoking marijuana—that's not the same thing as shooting somebody.

SCENE 12

(TERRI is still sketching.)

TITUS: He's in jail.
TERRI: Well, Titus, that's what generally happens to people who kill other people.
TITUS: He says he's innocent.
TERRI: No surprise there.
TITUS: Terri?

(She waits.)

TITUS: Come down to the jail with me.
TERRI: No way. What for? (*beat*) You are not seriously going to take time off work to visit some gangbanger in the county jail.
TITUS: After work. I wish you would come with me.
TERRI: I'm not going to. Titus. I think it's the wrong thing to do.
TITUS: I disagree.

SCENE 13

(RIOT 208 is painting, DENNY watching, playing country music. DENNY

then practices country swing dance steps as RIOT 208 paints. DENNY sings along with the music a little bit, then interrupts himself to say aloud the steps he is trying to follow. Correcting himself, then singing again. DAMIAN sits alone somewhere else on the stage—in jail.)

DENNY: (*pretending to hold a partner*) One two three four. One two three four. No, faster. One two three four. One two—faster, faster. (*pretends to be twirling his partner around*) Under. Oops. Wrong way. (*He stops. Sings, tapping his foot, starts again, pretends to twirl his partner. RIOT 208 turns to him.*)
RIOT 208: That music bites, brother.
DENNY: Give me a hand here, I'm trying to figure this out.
RIOT 208: You want me to dance with you?
DENNY: Pretend. This is country swing so it goes by awfully fast and the thing is if you don't twirl your partner in the right direction, you get all mucked up, your feet get all on top of her feet and then she might fall.
RIOT 208: We wouldn't want that to happen.
DENNY: That would be embarrassing. So here—(*he extends his hand to RIOT 208, who takes it hesitantly*)—if we're dancing one-two-three-four see and if you turn under like this—(*DENNY twirls RIOT 208 around. RIOT 208 loses his balance.*)
RIOT 208: I see what you mean.
DENNY: Yes, see? So if you go the other way, let's see.

(*TERRI enters, sees RIOT 208's graffiti.*)

TERRI: Oooh, look at these colors. That's vibrant work.
RIOT 208: You got here just in time. You gotta save me.
TERRI: That's vibrant.
RIOT 208: I like that word. Vibrant. (*to DENNY*) I am far too vibrant to swing with this country shit now, hear?
DENNY: Maybe you'll help me then.

(*DENNY falls to the ground, as though hit by the concrete block, starts crawling to his truck. TERRI watches him a moment.*)

TERRI: Of course I'll help you.

(*DENNY stands up, jubilant.*)

DENNY: Great. You know, I've been trying to learn to do this for a long time. I just have two left feet as the saying goes. I think maybe that's why my wife divorced me, because she still liked me and all, but I couldn't country swing with her and she liked to go out of a night. You should have seen her dancing even when she was real pregnant. Friend of mine tried to tell me don't let her dance like that in her condition, she's gonna hurt that baby. But I knew she wouldn't. I knew she'd make the baby—just—real lively, like she is. And I was right, Ashley is real lively, just like her mom. She's like what you said about his painting. Vibrant, that's larger than life, right?

TERRI: Something like that.

DENNY: That guy, that friend of mine, he was just all wrong. (*to TERRI*) Did you change friends after the riot? When I had my brains back, that same guy talked to me about what happened. And he calls the people in the riot a whole bunch of bad names, because he always did hate Black people. "Those Blacks" he would say, or sometimes "those Black monkeys."

TERRI: Oh did he really?

DENNY: All of a sudden, he thought I was going to agree with him but I didn't agree with him before I got hurt, why's he think I'm going to agree with him now?

TERRI: Sounds like he doesn't know you very well.

DENNY: Nope. No. He doesn't.

TERRI: I received some unpleasant letters—calling me a traitor, that kind of foolishness. I paid them no mind.

DENNY: Oh, you should have seen some of the nasty letters I got in the hospital. (*to RIOT 208*) Not yours, yours was nice. Takes some big crisis to find out who your friends really are, that's just a fact of life. Even to find out who you really are—maybe not for everybody, but for me anyway.

RIOT 208: (*to DAMIAN*) You hear that? You think maybe you'd be wise to consider who your friends really are? Why you even hanging with that guy? The man is a drug dealer.

DAMIAN: Everything plain and simple for you, huh? You are one lucky brother.

DENNY: (*holding out his hand to TERRI*) Would you?

TERRI: I would be pleased. And I'm a good dancer so you're in luck.

(*DENNY shows TERRI how to do the country swing and practices twirling her around. Lights fade on them dancing.*)

SCENE 14

(Spotlight on RIOT 208 as he speaks to DAMIAN. Rap music comes up. Rap music and country music fade in and out.)

RIOT 208: I watched you on TV, you know that? Oh, yeah, you some big television star, Football. I was screamin' furious about those cops getting away with all they got away with. But nothing beat the look of the people in South Central, and boy did that look scare me. Furious and frustrated faces—I watched that whole entire uprising unfold, and I just couldn't believe it. Out of all my years living in bad New York neighborhoods I never saw anything like it. (*beat*) I started feeling very sad and gloomy. Then here comes a humungous red truck making its merry way towards the intersection of Florence and Normandie. That's where you came in, right Football, you the avenging angel? (*pause*) You made me cry. (*pause*) The moment that forever will be etched in my brain was when he finally was able to get up off the ground and try to drive his truck. (*pause*) The day after the riots I called Los Angeles and asked for the address to the hospital in which Mr. Denny was staying and proceeded to write him a letter. After a few weeks I received a small card and a handwritten note signed by him and his family. I was so happy. I felt like I made a difference for once in my life. I felt strong and full of energy, I felt like celebrating, and I did so by changing my tag to Riot 208. I did it because my name now stands for strength, along with guts and glory. I learned something very touching and special from Reginald Denny that day. Whenever I do my paintings with the Riot 208 tag, my backgrounds consist of clouds and birds and a lot of pretty light colors. People are fooled into thinking that my tag stands for murder and destruction when in fact it's the other way around. (*a grin*) Bet I fooled you too.

DAMIAN: For the life of me, I do not understand you.

RIOT 208: You understand pride, I believe.

DAMIAN: Yeah.

RIOT 208: You understand the total dazed joyful shock of having a child.

DAMIAN: I do that.

RIOT 208: You understand guts and glory, right, Football?

DAMIAN: Yeah. I remember glory.

RIOT 208: You think you're riding back to glory hanging out with that drug dude? If I'm following this, he killed a guy.

DAMIAN: (*a beat*) I think yeah. I think he did. (*to GEORGIANA*) How I know he's gonna kill some motherfucker, Mama?

(*GEORGIANA crosses to him and slaps his face.*)

GEORGIANA: Language.
DAMIAN: How I know he's gonna kill someone?
RIOT 208: Explain to me why you hangin' with him.
DAMIAN: That's the thing though. (*beat*) I can't explain it.

SCENE 15

GEORGIANA: There is nobody on God's earth going to make me believe you're not a decent, God-fearing young man, Dame. I don't care how many video cameras take your picture, I don't care how many times the police frame you up, you are decent and I know you have the Lord's grace. Dame. Why you call that murdering criminal your friend, my baby?
DAMIAN: Okay. Mama, you're right. He's not my friend, but—. Sometimes I need to chill so—. I buy drugs from him sometimes.
GEORGIANA: Damian Monroe Williams!

SCENE 16

(*TERRI and DENNY resume dancing as country music overtakes the hip hop music.*)

TERRI: Did you know Damian Williams got arrested again?
DENNY: No.
TERRI: Murder.
DENNY: Oh.
TERRI: There were drugs involved.

(*Pause. DENNY stops dancing.*)

DENNY: If he did it, I hope they put him away for it.
DAMIAN: (*to GEORGIANA*) I know the guy, all right? I buy drugs from the guy, all right? I'm a customer, just like the guy he shot's a customer. I had nothing to do with that shooting.

(DENNY walks to his "truck," looks it over like it was an old friend's grave. He sits in it. The music plays more loudly. Riot 208 crosses to Denny and gets in the truck beside him.)

RIOT 28: Where you want to go?

SCENE 17

GEORGINA: Bad judgment is not murder.
TERRI: Now that I have a teenager on my hands, I'll tell you I look at that girl and I say right out loud, "Who are you? You are somebody I do not know."
GEORGIANA: Yes indeed.
TERRI: My friends tell me be patient, she'll be back. Be patient? I say to them you have yourself a teenage daughter, then you tell me to be patient. Please.
GEORGIANA: It's a trial and it's joy. I never had a daughter. Four sons. Dame's my youngest. 16 years old and crying to me late one night he's got some little girl pregnant. First thing you want to do is bring down the whole wrath of God on him with your scolding. But then you think I raised up four by myself, with the help of God, I can raise up another one. That's where the joy comes in and you'd do well to let yourself have it.
TERRI: Least I don't have to raise her alone. Her father's right there with me, just as mystified as I am.
GEORGIANA: How things do change. When I realized Dame's father was gone, I was inconsolable. I cried day and night, I believe my friends were ready to send me to the hospital in an ambulance. Now I don't remember how tall he was.
TERRI: Things do. They change.
GEORGIANA: Sometimes in a second. Sometimes not fast enough.

SCENE 18

(TITUS enters and takes a seat across from DAMIAN, who also sits.)

TITUS: Hey, man.
DAMIAN: Do I know you?
TITUS: No, I don't think you know me.
DAMIAN: You a lawyer?

TITUS: No. You have a lawyer, don't you? Same one you had for the Denny trial?
DAMIAN: What you want?
TITUS: I watched that trial.
DAMIAN: You gonna tell me who you are and what you want?
TITUS: In person. I was in the courtroom. I testified.
DAMIAN: That was a long time ago.
TITUS: You remember there was a car leading Denny's truck to the hospital?
DAMIAN: No.
TITUS: You're lying.
DAMIAN: What do you WANT, man?
TITUS: I was unemployed at that time. I was part of the rescue, one of the angels.
DAMIAN: One of the angels.

(Lights up on DENNY and RIOT 208 in DENNY's truck, RIOT 208 driving. They come to a stop and get out of the car. DENNY leads RIOT 208 to a spot on the stage.)

DENNY: *(pointing)* Florence. Normandie. I was lying right here. I'm sure. Right here.

(DENNY leads RIOT 208 to a door, where he knocks or rings a bell. GEORGIANA answers. Silence for a few beats.)

DENNY: I wonder if you remember me.

(GEORGIANA reaches for DENNY and takes him in her arms.)

GEORGIANA: I have asked the Lord to help Dame.
DENNY: Well, then He will. I think we both know that.

TITUS: Did you do it?
DAMIAN: I pled not guilty.

GEORGIANA: Each week I gather my boy's supporters at our church. We're collecting money and prayers.
DENNY: *(after nodding in response to her)* We visited the spot where I fell from my truck. Um—oh. This is—*(DENNY looks at RIOT 208, realizing*

he doesn't know his real name.)
RIOT 208: (*holding out his hand to her*) Ben.
DENNY: Ben's an artist. He paints graffiti.
GEORGIANA: How do you do? (*to both of them*) Will you join us at the church later today?
DENNY: I was wondering if you know. Did he do it?
GEORGIANA: No! The Los Angeles Police Department has not let up on him since—
DENNY: Since those riots?
GEORGIANA: Since the uprising. He is an easy target.
DENNY: I'd like to go see him.

TITUS: (*to DAMIAN*) No more bullshit. Did you do it?

SCENE 19

DAMIAN: That Denny trial? I was scared at first, but it turned out good. My mama stood beside me, that's the thing that makes me proud. At the time, I'm thinking how it turned out so much easier than I feared and how I got off with just a little jail time. But then I did the time and that was the first I realized there is no such thing as "just a little" where jail time is concerned. And that's when whatever it is happened happened. I'm lying there one day right and I'm missing my neighborhood and my house and all that's outside. I'm thinking about being ten years old. Gangs are not on my radar yet. I believe with all my little boy heart I am going to play football my whole life. Mama has not dragged me down to Mississippi yet. No Rodney King got stopped by no police. Reginald Denny still driving his truck around the city, man. I'm lying on that cot and I'm thinking about my imagination of my future at ten years of age, and then I kind of come to or something, and I look around and (*in astonishment, as though realizing it for the first time*) I am in a jail cell. I think, those police who pounded Rodney King ain't in no jail cell. But I'm not angry. I'm not— nothin'. I just feel numb, I'm like a piece of paper nobody's ever wrote on yet. I am in prison: I cannot figure out what this means. My head hurts when I try to figure out what this means. Every time I try, my head hurts. So I stop trying. Then I get out—it's like I've been in jail my whole damn life till then—that's how it feels. I get out and thinking is doing me no good, and feeling is doing me less good than that. I meet the guy, all right, and he's doing business, he's got his drugs. Do I know he's a lowlife? If I think about it, yes, I know he's a lowlife. But do I think about it? No, I don't think about it. I smoke and I tell myself, I say, you doing nothing but smoking dope every day, Football. This is not making your mama proud. Then I shrug.

SCENE 20

(DAMIAN turns back to TITUS.)

TITUS: Did you do it?
DAMIAN: I already told you.
TITUS: Tell me again. Make me believe you.
DAMIAN: Brother, I do not know what concern it is to you in the first place.
TITUS: It is of monumental concern to me.
DAMIAN: Why's that?
TITUS: What did you feel when Denny didn't die? Were you relieved? Were you thankful you didn't take a life?
DAMIAN: Thankful to who?
TITUS: To me. The four of us, we got him to the hospital in time and he didn't die. I stood in the way of your taking a life.

(Long pause.)

DAMIAN: Thank you.
TITUS: You're welcome.
DAMIAN: I—. Feel—. It's good he didn't die.
TITUS: You know that now.
DAMIAN: That's right.
TITUS: You didn't know that then.
DAMIAN: I didn't care about him then. It was justice then.
TITUS: But now you know better.
DAMIAN: Not I know better now. Now I'm glad the man is not dead. But it was still justice.

(DAMIAN gets up and moves quickly to RIOT 208.)

DAMIAN: That's my point. You been doing nothing but running off at the mouth about your point—well, that's my point. It was justice. Okay? We clear? Now don't you have something more important to do than be over here getting' on my ass?

TITUS: Damian?

(DAMIAN turns to TITUS.)

TITUS: Swear to me you didn't kill this man.
DAMIAN: I do. I swear.

SCENE 21

(RIOT 208 crosses to center stage.)

RIOT 208: Looks like you have got something to teach me after all, which is how brick-throwing, gangbanging and drug smoking move us closer to justice. Enlighten me.
DAMIAN: You think you so funny? You think you so smart? All right, you enlighten me. What you gonna be teaching that baby when he comes? Watch daddy draw cartoons on the wall?
RIOT 208: Yeah, I'm gonna teach my baby to draw. Yeah, that's his legacy. I was painting since I was 12. I was running around the subways, I was throwing up on as many trains as I could, I was thinking of it as ruining government property and I know you know what I mean. I thought destroy the property and at the same time make pictures of the beast in my daddy, expose his true self.
DAMIAN: Oh, you destroyed government property. So no matter about all that jabberin' you hidin' behind, you runnin' around Queens New York taking the law into your own hands.
RIOT 208: I create art. You created chaos.
DAMIAN: (*really angry now*) HOLD UP. I did not create that chaos. While you teaching that baby something, how about you explain to him what goes on out there?
RIOT 208: How about I teach him not to throw things at people?
DAMIAN: How about you teach him people gonna want to throw things at him, people gonna want to accuse him of shit he didn't do?
RIOT 208: How about I teach him violence begets nothing but more violence?
DAMIAN: Then you'd be teaching him a lie.

(RIOT looks at DAMIAN in amazement. This is certainly not the thing he expected to hear. They both freeze.)

SCENE 22

TERRI: Honey? What do you want for dinner? You want to go out?

TITUS: No, let's—. Could we stay here? You want to order something from the Shack?

TERRI: Sure. (*beat*) How'd it go?

TITUS: I believe him.

TERRI: You listen to me, Titus. No matter what that kid did or did not do, all those years ago you did a good thing. We saved a life.

TITUS: A thing happens, you know. You feel rotten about your life. Can't get work, live in a shitty neighborhood, everything that's come before feels like nothing but a waste of time, you feel like you've been tricked, you know what I'm saying? And a thing happens to you, and you don't give it much thought, it occurs to you fast that you have to do the right thing, and you're lucky enough to know what that is. That man's face was bleeding, little bones were sticking out all over the place, we could see into his head for God's sake.

TERRI: I remember.

TITUS: I saved his life. He is alive because of us. Because of me.

TERRI: Fuck football quarterbacks, Titus, you are a hero.

TITUS: It's like right that second, the second I got up off the couch and ran to the door, I learned everything about myself that's important, and I believed—I don't know, I believed my life had meaning. I believed *life* had meaning.

TERRI: You are not going to let this worthless piece of trash throw you into despair.

TITUS: He is not a worthless piece of trash.

TERRI: I don't care if he's the Sultan of some filthy rich foreign nation, Titus. Goddammit, you're a better man than he is.

(TITUS looks at her for a beat. He goes to her and kisses her.)

TITUS: Thank you, baby. (*beat*) You're wrong. (*a grin*) But as long as you're gonna be wrong, I'm glad you're in my corner. (*another small kiss*) I love you.

TERRI: I love you. And I'm not wrong. Now what do you want to eat?

(We see TERRI and TITUS ordering food, puttering in their apartment as the play continues.)

SCENE 23

(RIOT 208 finally breaks from his astonished posture, but DAMIAN remains frozen. RIOT 208 paints for a moment. Then—)

RIOT 208: *(not to DAMIAN, to the universe)* A lie? *(RIOT 208 paints for a moment. Then—)* You know me by now, I am interested in learning all things including what does violence beget if not more violence? *(RIOT 208 paints for a moment. Then—)* Knowledge is always good, that is something I'm absolutely certain I'm right about, anything I can learn, that's a good thing. *(RIOT 208 looks at DAMION, pretty frustrated. RIOT 208 shakes his head, turns away to paint, turns back)* Suddenly I'm gettin' flashes of 1776 with men throwin' crates of tea into large bodies of water and other men with muskets and even with rocks and truth be told—because I always always attempt to tell the truth—those images are makin' me very uncomfortable.

SCENE 24

(RIOT 208 paints.)

DAMIAN: Suddenly you got all quiet and shit.
RIOT 208: Do not dare say the words American Revolution to me.
DAMIAN: *(did I hear you right?)* Don't say American Revolution?
RIOT 208: *(looks at him, a beat)* I'm not going to believe you had one thought about American Independence when you bashed Mr. Denny's head in.
DAMIAN: *(no idea what he's talking about)* All right.

(RIOT 208 paints.)

DAMIAN: Explain to me what you're doing. I'm serious. What good is that? The police just going to cover it up anyway.
RIOT 208: They can cover it up all they want but they can't stop me.
DAMIAN: Now I'm followin' you. *(indicating RIOT 208's graffiti)* Yeah, I think I finally got this figured out. You learned to protect yourself from

what's going on around you by turning away from trouble and painting on the wall. You want to say I did what I did because I'm a punk, but brother, gangs had nothing to do with it. Anger just came up over me. You tell me anger never come up over you I will not believe that.

RIOT 208: You're right. When it happens, I paint.

DAMIAN: You paint. Mama prays. Me? I hear that verdict, then I see the police coming after my brother with viciousness like he was some kind of mass murderer, and we both know they would not think twice about killing him. (*a beat, then looking hard at RIOT 208*) We both know that right?

RIOT 208: We both know that.

DAMIAN: You keep tellin' me people can learn things. Those cops arrested me and they know I did not kill anybody. They learning things? What about those ladies on that police jury? They supposed to learn things? How come we the only ones have to learn something?

RIOT 208: Brother, we can't control—. (*He stops himself from talking. Thinks for a beat.*) That's a good point.

(*Pause, as RIOT 208 paints.*)

DAMIAN: What's that you're painting?

RIOT 208: That's my baby. Any day now I'm gonna get lucky like you and become a daddy.

DAMIAN: There's a baby in there? (*looking at the painting*) How you know what he looks like already?

RIOT 208: Football. You got to use your imagination.

(*A couple beats, then DAMIAN returns to his "cell."*)

SCENE 25

(*RIOT 208 paints. TERRI and TITUS sit together having dinner. DENNY crosses to DAMIAN.*)

DENNY: I was talking to your mom. (*beat*) She said I could come—you wouldn't mind. (*beat*) Do you? (*beat*) You're Damian Williams. Aren't you Damian Williams?

DAMIAN: Yeah.

DENNY: I'm—

DAMIAN: I know who you are.
DENNY: Who am I? (*a beat, then*) Say my name. Please.
DAMIAN: (*beat*) Reginald Denny.
DENNY: You're Damian Williams. Damian Football Williams.
DAMIAN: I swear to God.
DENNY: What?
DAMIAN: My lawyer says I'm gonna get acquitted. I'm thinking all the time about getting out. I got a guy in here been talking to me about the Nation of Islam. Got me thinking about—. Got me thinking about taking control of my own life. I swear. I didn't kill anybody.
DENNY: Did you want to?
DAMIAN: I never shot anybody, man.
DENNY: Not him. Me.
DAMIAN: Somebody. Not you. Somebody.

(*DENNY holds out his hand to DAMIAN who hesitates, then takes it. DENNY brings DAMIAN's hand up to the indentation in his head.*)

DENNY: Feel that dent? Like on a baby's head, that soft part?
DAMIAN: Yeah.
DENNY: You did that.

(*DAMIAN pulls his hand back.*)

DENNY: Did you feel your little boy's head when it was soft like that?
DAMIAN: No. I was afraid to touch him there, like maybe my finger would go right through his head.
DENNY: How old is he?
DAMIAN: 14
DENNY: How's he doing?

(*Silence. DAMIAN looks away from him. Several beats, then DENNY turns to go. Another beat. Then—*)

DAMIAN: He stays with mama.

(*DENNY stops.*)

DAMIAN: He's doin' good. (*beat*) How about you? How's your girl doin'?

(DENNY walks back toward DAMIAN as the lights go down.)

END OF PLAY

ARMOR

CHARACTERS

EUGENE KASTAKIS, about 50, a polymer scientist

ALICE KASTAKIS, mid-late 40s, his wife

CYNTHIA KASTAKIS, 17, their daughter

JEREMY GUNDERSON, 16, a piano student

MARY LOU GUNDERSON, 30's, early 40s, his mother

ANTON (TONY) BIXBY, 30s, a visitor

The play takes place about midway through the Iraq War (2003-11) in and around Washington D.C.

SCENE 1

(The light from a TV. An exercise tape is playing in a dark room. GENE exercises with great focus. He's right in the middle of it. In a few seconds, CYNTHIA switches the light on and enters.)

CYNTHIA: Dad? (*He exercises.*) Did you forget to call mom's students for today? Because one of them's here. (*He exercises. She crosses to him.*) Jeremy Gunderson's here for his lesson so I'm asking if you called to cancel mom's lessons for today.
GENE: (*still exercising, so speaking with difficulty*) He has a crush on you.
CYNTHIA: In your deluded mind, everyone has a crush on me.
GENE: (*still exercising*) He does. Dads know.
CYNTHIA: His sister's in my Family Living class.
GENE: (*still exercising*) That's the same thing as Home Economics, right?
CYNTHIA: It offers a bit of get-along-with-your-family-members psychology too. And apparently that will serve me well when I marry. Either way, it's an easy A, which I'm entitled to. Anyhow, Jeremy's sister says he's a homosexual and her mother's on the verge of having a nervous breakdown over it. (*how lame is that?*) Good grief. Although she—Jeremy's sister? Uses a different word than homosexual.
GENE: (*still exercising*) Sisters are not always the fairest.
CYNTHIA: I certainly know that firsthand.
GENE: (*still exercising*) The kid's madly in love with you.
CYNTHIA: Can't you stand still?

(GENE stops exercising.)

GENE: You don't want me to get flabby.
CYNTHIA: I have no interest whatsoever in whether you get flabby.
GENE: Look at your mother.
CYNTHIA: That's your job.
GENE: (*picking up his weights*) Good one.
CYNTHIA: Wait. (*He does.*) Should I call the rest of them, Dad? Because I doubt she's going to resume her lessons until Peter is—I don't know—miraculously able to walk again.
GENE: There's not going to be anything miraculous about it, Cynthia. Both his legs are broken. When he's released from the hospital, he'll do rehab, and when his legs heal, Peter will walk again.

CYNTHIA: Should I call the students or not?
GENE: Mom's list is tacked to the board next to the phone in the kitchen. My meeting's at 11:30 so I'm going to finish up.
CYNTHIA: It's Saturday.
GENE: Neither rain nor sleet nor gloom of night—nor weekends—shall keep the House Armed Services Committee from its appointed rounds.
CYNTHIA: Nor false testimony.
GENE: (*picking up the weights*) Get going.
CYNTHIA: I imagine people lie just as brilliantly on weekends as they do on weekdays.
GENE: Cynthia.
CYNTHIA: Well.
GENE: Focus your attention elsewhere. On the corkboard in the kitchen. Go.

(*CYNTHIA plants a kiss on her palm and touches it to his face. He resumes exercising as she exits the room and walks to wherever Jeremy is sitting. He moves his fingers around as though practicing piano in the air.*)

CYNTHIA: Air piano?
JEREMY: Why not?
CYNTHIA: If you're playing an air instrument, shouldn't you be making some sounds to accompany it?
JEREMY: Your mom says my fingering's not so hot so I'm trying to loosen them up. Your mom says my fingers aren't flexible enough, so . . .
CYNTHIA: Okay. Mom's not coming. She's at the hospital with Peter. You better call before you come next week too.
JEREMY: Nobody let us know.
CYNTHIA: She forgot I guess. So, I have to call the other students and you should get going.
JEREMY: No car. My mother drops me off and picks me up.
CYNTHIA: Your sister told me.
JEREMY: My sister told you?
CYNTHIA: That your mom makes sure she knows where you are at all times. Because of your—preference.

(*ALICE enters during the following.*)

JEREMY: (*as he whips out a cell phone and dials*) My mother drops me off and

picks me up because for the last couple months my father's had to work on weekends and there's no car for me to—(*into the phone*) Claudia? Is it not enough that my mother believes every idiotic rumor she hears about her son's sexuality? (*ALICE enters and watches, along with CYNTHIA.*) Why you would share that misinformation with Cynthia Kastakis of all people I have no clue, you bitch, because I told you: I'M-NOT-GAY. Don't talk to Cynthia Kastakis. Don't say anything about anything to Cynthia Kastakis. Don't even say good morning to Cynthia Kastakis. (*He flips the cell phone closed.*)
CYNTHIA: Goodness.
JEREMY: Apologies. I had to get that off my chest.
ALICE: Apologies all around. Sorry I'm late.
CYNTHIA: I thought your lessons were canceled today.
ALICE: Why'd you think that?
CYNTHIA: Jeremy came and you weren't here, so I assumed. I asked Dad and he—
ALICE: Your dad doesn't really know my schedule. Peter was sleeping, and he woke up right when I was about to leave, so I spent another ten minutes. I'm glad he's not old enough to call you a bitch yet, by the way. (*pointing to where GENE is exercising*) He in there?
CYNTHIA: Naturally.
ALICE: We'd better get going, Jeremy, only 45 minutes till your mom gets here.
JEREMY: (*to CYNTHIA*) Don't hold Claudia against me.

(*He exits. ALICE takes a step toward the room where Gene is exercising and calls to him.*)

ALICE: Careful about the time, Gene. Traffic's not so good.

(*ALICE follows JEREMY out. CYNTHIA looks around the room for something. The sound of JEREMY playing a piano exercise from one side of her. The sound of Dad's exercise video from the other. She searches a bit more, then the sound of the exercise video stops.*)

CYNTHIA: Dad? Did I leave my calculus notes in there?
GENE: (*off*) I don't see them.

(*CYNTHIA crosses toward the sound of the piano. It ceases.*)

CYNTHIA: Mom?

(But as she gets there, piano music starts again. It's her mother playing now. CYNTHIA listens as her mother plays several measures. Lights up on GENE. He is dressing now, putting on a suit and a tie—appropriate clothing for testifying in front of a Congressional committee. ALICE stops playing, then Jeremy is playing again. He starts, stops, starts, plays.)

Cynthia: Mom? (*no answer as piano playing continues*) Forget it. (*crossing back the other way*) Dad?

(GENE continues dressing.)

GENE: What?
CYNTHIA: I'm going upstairs to practice.
GENE: Did you find your notes?
CYNTHIA: I'm going to practice first.
GENE: See you later.
CYNTHIA: See you.

(CYNTHIA exits. GENE dresses. We hear JEREMY stop playing, then ALICE plays a couple measures, then Jeremy repeats them. Then silence for a couple beats. Then we hear a cello. CYNTHIA is practicing. GENE finishes dressing. A bit of just the cello. Then ALICE plays piano, and we hear piano and cello. GENE enters and walks across the stage while ALICE continues playing.)

GENE: I'm going, Alice.

(Piano stops. ALICE peeks out.)

ALICE: Knock 'em dead.
GENE: (*as he exits*) Let us hope.

(ALICE is back at the piano. Piano and cello play together.)

SCENE 2

(CYNTHIA is playing the last eight measures of a cello piece offstage. JEREMY

is playing poker on his phone. CYNTHIA plays those eight measures twice more. Then a couple beats. Then she enters and stands behind JEREMY and watches him play the game.)

JEREMY: What'd you play those eight measures—50 times?
CYNTHIA: I didn't count.
JEREMY: You know, my sister tells me things too. Such as Cynthia Kastakis threw her cake made from scratch in the garbage because the frosting was a little runny. You're a perfectionist.
CYNTHIA: I have very demanding parents.
JEREMY: Come on. You've got the sweetest mother in the world.
CYNTHIA: What are you doing?
JEREMY: Poker.
CYNTHIA: How old are you?
JEREMY: 17 as of 6 weeks ago. I signed up under false pretenses.
CYNTHIA: Are you winning?

(JEREMY holds up his hand as in "just a minute" as he shuts down his phone. Then—)

JEREMY: *And* your mom's a great cook. Occasionally she gives me a piece of rockin' homemade pound cake.
CYNTHIA: She's a fantastic cook. That's one of the reasons she wanted to live in this school district. She says I go to the only high school in the nation that still has an oven in one of the classrooms. If you had my mom, you would have thrown your cake in the trash too. Whenever we go out to dinner? Any little thing isn't exactly right—gravy's made with a little too much flour, not enough garlic in the scampi, glass of wine's from a bottle that's been open a little too long—that's it, we never go back, no second chance to see if the restaurant's maybe having an off night.
JEREMY: My father won't eat anything except peanut butter and jelly sandwiches, chocolate chip cookies, and beef.
CYNTHIA: That's the whole list?
JEREMY: Can you believe how incredibly lame that is? For God's sake, eat a pork chop.
CYNTHIA: We eat at home a lot more since we moved here. Now that my father works for Congress, he's literally on call 24-7.
JEREMY: Then how come I hear all these rumors about nobody in Congress showing up for work on a regular basis?

CYNTHIA: My father staffs the House Armed Services Committee. Our country's at war. His committee definitely shows up on a regular basis.
JEREMY: I thought your father was a scientist.
CYNTHIA: Yeah, he's a polymer scientist. He designs—
JEREMY: Polymers? Like—pantyhose?
CYNTHIA: Like truck armor. His committee's meeting right now. In fact, he's testifying today, which is highly unusual—for a staffer to actually testify.

(Spotlight on GENE.)

GENE: I'd like to start by saying that my support for the United States Army's current truck armor program does not preclude my support for the Mine Resistant Ambush Protected Program. I support MRAP 100%. I'm speaking to you today in the hope of convincing you that the army should continue to supply the troops with the truck armor kits known as "Hunter's Boxes" until such time as MRAP vehicles can be produced in sufficient quantities to offer a viable alternative. We started fielding the kits two years ago and we've continually improved them. They're fitted with a rapidly deployable ballistic shield that converts between a collapsed configuration for storage and transport and an extended upright configuration. The shield is fabricated from a composite fiber and matrix material capable of substantially inhibiting blast effects and preventing projectiles from penetrating it. Please allow me to point out that the truck armor situation is completely different from the debate this committee has undertaken about body armor. In that case, each side—Interceptor on the one hand, Dragon Skin on the other—contends that its body armor is more effective than the other side's. I'm not claiming Hunter's Boxes are more effective than MRAPs. I'm saying that MRAPs are simply not deliverable in the numbers we need. In the meantime, the kits have proven effective in the field. The soldiers love them. They have saved lives.

(GENE continues offering testimony in dim light. CYNTHIA talks; JEREMY listens as he tinkers with his phone.)

CYNTHIA: I'm thinking of doing something more along the lines of bio-terrorism defense. I haven't completely made up my mind, but polymer engineering? No. I'm much more attracted to biochemistry. It's important, what my Dad does but, honestly, I don't want to be doing science that's

about saving the lives of the guys on the front lines because—. I don't know. I just don't.
JEREMY: Because you don't want to take on such a big responsibility.
CYNTHIA: Way don't want to. (*beat*) He thinks you have a crush on me. My father. (*silence*) That's what he told me.
JEREMY: (*a pause, then a look at CYNTHIA*) I'm not saying he's wrong. Listen, here's how it happened. Some idiot saw me kissing another guy in a classroom.
CYNTHIA: That's a sure sign.
JEREMY: There's where you're wrong. You're going to become a scientist. You shouldn't make assumptions. Because we were rehearsing a scene for my advanced theater class which, by the way, my mom badgered me into taking. I'm pretty good at it and she loves coming to the play and applauding no matter how small my part is. Who pushes her son into taking theater classes three years in a row and then freaks out because she thinks he's gay?
CYNTHIA: That's almost exactly what I said to my father.
JEREMY: You told your father I'm gay?
CYNTHIA: After he told me you had a crush on me.
JEREMY: Oh my god. (*beat*) Anyway, the idiot who saw me kissing the guy told somebody, and that idiot told somebody else, and eventually somebody told my sister. Who told my mother, what kind of sister is that? I mean, would you rat out your brother like that? So my mother, who's not exactly a genius, put that together with I cried my little eyes out when I heard about somebody was murdered because he's gay on the news which, please, I was 8 or something, and drew her erroneous conclusions.
CYNTHIA: Please understand. Dad doesn't care whether or not you're a homosexual. He only commented because he thinks—. He's very open-minded.
JEREMY: For a guy who engineers truck armor.
CYNTHIA: Now who's making assumptions?
JEREMY: My sister says you speak Greek fluently.
CYNTHIA: French. I went to French camp last summer.
JEREMY: In France?
CYNTHIA: You bet.
JEREMY: She said Greek.
CYNTHIA: I only have a basic conversational grasp of Greek.
JEREMY: Then I definitely don't have a crush on you.

(CYNTHIA smiles, taking this remark in the spirit in which it was offered.)

CYNTHIA: At first, I was pretty excited about the whole truck armor thing. Because dad was so psyched about being called on to design this truck kit and about helping our guys in Iraq. And actually going to Iraq? He was thrilled. If you knew my dad you'd know that thrilled is just not a way he ever is. But then I realized we were going to have to move to Washington D.C.

(During CYNTHIA's speech, GENE, sans suit jacket, sits down at a kitchen table. ALICE joins him.)

JEREMY: Which. Good.
CYNTHIA: Right before my senior year in high school. So. Bad. And now Dad's—obsessed.

(CYNTHIA steps forward and looks toward GENE, remembering a dinner conversation.)

GENE: I configured the shield with a low-density, high-strength fiber and matrix material.
CYNTHIA: *(as she sits at the table)* A polymer. We know, Dad.
GENE: This material is incredible, Cynthia.
CYNTHIA: Dad, you—like—invented it, so of course—
GENE: The low-density material construction allows investigative radiography through the walls of the blast shield.
ALICE: Ah. That blasted blast shield again.
CYNTHIA: Mom please. *(calling)* Peter!
ALICE: Peter's eating in the living room.
GENE: So see—the bomb squad can assess the explosive device in safety. All they have to do is confine the device within the shield.
CYNTHIA: Pass the salad dressing.
GENE: I used a combination of fibers in the construction—spectra fiber, kevlar—
ALICE: Kevlar? That old thing? I wouldn't be caught dead in Kevlar.
CYNTHIA: Mom. Stop.
PETER: *(Off)* Mom, you were right. These guys are really funny.
CYNTHIA: Maybe we should just cancel Direct TV.
GENE: I'm thinking of adding a lining constructed of ceramic material that

would—
CYNTHIA: Seriously Dad? After you came to speak to my Physics class, Donny Templeton asked me, are you sure your Dad's a scientist because he sounded more like a salesman.
ALICE: Some nerve.
CYNTHIA: Does he pimp his own invention to the committee like he did to us?
ALICE: He called your father a pimp? I want that kid's phone number.
CYNTHIA: Dad's trying to figure out how to best meet the armed services' need for truck armor in order to save the lives of our soldiers who are fighting for Democracy, which includes free speech. So even if he's incredibly stupid, Donny's entitled to his opinion.

(Loud laughter from PETER offstage.)

PETER: *(Off)* Mom, you gotta see this.
CYNTHIA: So, Dad, I guess this means if Donny Templeton asks me to prom, I have to say no?
GENE: I've also incorporated a bladder—
ALICE: Gene, we're eating dinner.
GENE: *(overlap)* that can be filled with a blast-mitigating material like water or foam. The thing is, IED attacks are responsible for more than 70% of United States casualties in Iraq.
CYNTHIA: Dad, you've told us this. We know.
GENE: I honestly think this truck kit offers significantly more protection and survivability for our troops.
ALICE: Survivability? Like fewer guys get blown up?
GENE: That's it! The kits will save lives.
CYNTHIA: Dad!
GENE: What?
ALICE: I think she's wondering whether the four of us are ever going to sit at a table together again without discussing ballistics or MRAPs or—
CYNTHIA: Not that Peter's ever sitting at the table. So Dad, you're on the verge of forcing me to watch ancient "Honeymooner" reruns with my brother rather than sit at the dinner table with the adults.
GENE: I'm listening to you, Cynthia. Sure. Go to the prom with Donny Templeton.
CYNTHIA: *(raising her voice)* Donny Templeton didn't ask me to the prom!

(Silence.)

CYNTHIA: Sorry, Dad. (*beat*) Dad. I'm sorry.
ALICE: Gene, after dinner, I want you to listen to Cynthia play Dall 'Abaco's *Caprices*. She's going to blow you away.

(A beat. Then GENE speaks to CYNTHIA.)

GENE: Sure, honey. I'd love to hear that.

CYNTHIA: (*back to Jeremy*) That's the good part. I can play for my Dad and make everything all right again.
JEREMY: You play a beautiful, beautiful cello. (*an embarrassed pause, and then, the first thing he can think of to say*) I can't believe they let your brother eat dinner in front of the TV.
CYNTHIA: And that was before the car accident. I expect he'll be getting exponentially more spoiled once he comes home from the hospital.
JEREMY: That's intense about your father, man. That—you know—single-mindedness.
CYNTHIA: I know. I'm worried about him.
JEREMY: Yeah. Obsession can be dangerous. You wouldn't want him to die brokenhearted.
CYNTHIA: Jeremy!
JEREMY: No, I mean, wouldn't you rather not be brilliant if it's just going to lead to constant dissatisfaction? I mean, look at Einstein. He discovered all the important things in the universe—
CYNTHIA: Well, not exactly.
JEREMY: but he didn't figure out the Theory of Everything or whatever, so he was never satisfied with his work. Which sucks.
CYNTHIA: So, you're determined not to be brilliant?
JEREMY: I don't think I have much of a choice. I have no plans for my adult life if that's what you mean. I'm going to consider high school graduation a gigantic benchmark.
CYNTHIA: Well, it is.
JEREMY: Hey, but what about the cello? How can a girl who plays the cello like you do become a biochemist?
CYNTHIA: Right now, biology's my passion.
JEREMY: Can't argue with passion.

(Silence.)

CYNTHIA: But.
JEREMY: What?
CYNTHIA: Can you keep a secret?
JEREMY: Definitely.
CYNTHIA: I'm applying to Julliard. I felt I had to give it a try. My mom says I'm a great cellist, but she's my mother so I know she's biased. I haven't told either of them, which is going to be complicated if I get invited up there for an audition. My dad thinks I'm a great cellist too, but his heart's set on my going all the way through to a PhD in Biochemistry at Cornell. His Alma Mater. And Mom thinks I have a shot at Julliard, but I told her no. Because I just don't want to cause a conflagration in my home. But. For some reason, I want to audition anyway.
JEREMY: You want an objective assessment.
CYNTHIA: Yes. Exactly. How about you? And the piano, I mean?
JEREMY: Cynthia.
CYNTHIA: You're studying, so—
JEREMY: I don't come here to take piano lessons because I'm good at playing the piano.

(The doorbell rings.)

JEREMY: *(as though Darth Vadar or Freddy Kruger were at the door)* Oh my God, that's her.
CYNTHIA: It's a bit strange to spend a lot of money taking piano lessons if you don't like playing the piano.
JEREMY: I didn't say I didn't like it. I'm not that great at it, but when I do play something well, I love that. If I was better at it I could feel that feeling more often. Which would be cool. *(He shrugs.)* My parents can afford it.

(ALICE enters, MARY LOU following, talking to ALICE.)

MARY LOU: My heart just goes out to that boy. You give him my love.
ALICE: I'm going to go see him in a little while and I definitely will, Mary Lou.
MARY LOU: Your child in a hospital bed. My God, Alice. I'm so sorry. *(her arm around Jeremy)* If this boy got hit by a car, I swear, they'd have to cart me away and tranquilize me. *(to Jeremy)* You stay out of the street.

JEREMY: You have my solemn promise that I won't get hit by a car, Mom. I'll cross at the light. Or I'll follow the crossing guard's instructions.
MARY LOU: You hear him? He doesn't even believe in my love for him. He thinks my whole goal is to pester him.
ALICE: Kids. What are you gonna do? You feel like a cup of coffee, Mary Lou? I grind it fresh.
MARY LOU: I'm tempted.
ALICE: Come. It only takes a minute.
JEREMY: (*to Cynthia*) She grew up in Winston-Salem where I guess all the mothers tell their practically grown-up sons not to play in the street.
MARY LOU: She?
JEREMY: (*to Cynthia*): She hates when I refer to her as "she." (*to Mary Lou*): Which is irrational.
ALICE: Guys, come and have something with us. I made pita and tzatziki for Peter.
CYNTHIA: Mom? You're offering us Peter's homemade pita bread? I never thought I'd see the day.
ALICE: She teases me that Peter's my favorite.
CYNTHIA: He's your baby boy.
ALICE: He's in the goddamn hospital, Cynthia. What do you want from me? (*beat*) Yes, I'm offering you Peter's pita.
CYNTHIA: (*a groan*) Mom.
MARY LOU: Oh, I get the same thing from my kids—you like Claudia best because she's the oldest; you like Jeremy best because he's a boy. Makes you want to just wring their necks, doesn't it? But you don't because you know they don't mean it. It's a developmental stage, that's all it is. You think they're going to stop testing your limits at age four or six or nine or eleven or whenever, but sooner or later, you figure out it's never going to happen. Maybe once they're out on their own. The Good Lord willing.
ALICE: Jeremy, have something before you go.

(*As ALICE waves them toward her, lights dim a bit and GENE's spotlight shines. No one else on the stage.*)

GENE: Gun trucks offer several advantages. They can support a great deal of weight because they're heavy vehicles. Their elevation provides good vision and they're equipped with multiple guns, which protects if they're attacked from several directions. They're easy to armor with the kits, which consist of bolted 2 X 4 panels of triple steel and fiberglass. No welding. Two soldiers can put them together in 2-3 hours. The kit becomes a pillbox on the back of the truck and, with the ballistic shield mounted, the guys are doubly protected. Until such time as enough MRAPs become more widely available, I believe our best course is to continue to purchase and ship as many truck kits as the troops require. In making this recommendation, I'm not advocating for the members of this committee to "take sides." Everyone's on the same side. Everyone's on the soldiers' side. (*He takes a big, deep breath.*) Thank you, Mr. Chairman.

SCENE 3

(*ALICE, MARY LOU, CYNTHIA and JEREMY are eating and enjoying themselves.*)

MARY LOU: This is light on the garlic? Jeremy, can you fathom your father eating this?
JEREMY: Cucumbers—which are vegetables, yogurt—which is spoiled milk, garlic—which he associates with dark-skinned Mediterranean people. No, Mom.
MARY LOU: I know. Alice? You've got a beautiful daughter here. Are you aware?
ALICE: I am.
MARY LOU: Jeremy? Are you aware?
JEREMY: Mom? Are you aware that dozens of adolescent boys murder their mothers every year?
MARY LOU: Jeremy, I am on your side.
JEREMY: Mom. Quiet. Just—. Cynthia? You're a very beautiful girl.
CYNTHIA: Goodness.
ALICE: She means thank you.
JEREMY: And the way you play the cello?
CYNTHIA: Thank you.
ALICE: Mary Lou? Would you like a glass of wine?

(*pause*)

MARY LOU: Would you mind very much, Jeremy? I don't want to cause you to think you have to take sides between me and your father so I'm telling you right now, right out loud, I know dad doesn't approve of alcohol consumption.

JEREMY: Mom. Have a glass of wine.
MARY LOU: That's very . . .
JEREMY: Open-minded?
MARY LOU: That's very open-minded of you.
JEREMY: Remember that at Christmas.
MARY LOU: (*with real affection*) I will. (*to ALICE, with some excitement*) Yes. Thank you.
ALICE: What have we got, Cyn? (*looking*) I think we have a couple Pinots and a Zin. It's too early for a Cab. Oh, this. (*to ALICE*) Cotes de Rhone?
MARY LOU: It's the afternoon, isn't it? We're not drinking wine in the a.m., are we?
ALICE: It's one-thirty.
MARY LOU: All right then. Whatever you recommend.
ALICE: Or white?
CYNTHIA: Duh.
ALICE: You're right. (*to Mary Lou*) I'm just biased in favor of red.
MARY LOU: I like Chardonnay.
ALICE: All that garlic you ate? Chardonnay? Not so much.
MARY LOU: Really? (*to Jeremy*) This is very exciting, honey. I didn't realize there was so much to take into consideration. (*then to Alice*) I want the French one. That red French one. (*back to Jeremy*) Isn't this fun?
CYNTHIA: I'll have a glass of white. Something light, okay?

(*Jeremy and Mary Lou look at her.*)

ALICE: Mary Lou. Cynthia will be 18 soon, and Gene and I—. Well, we want her to be able to recognize decent wine. So if she drinks it at home—
MARY LOU: Since what age?
ALICE: Since 16.
MARY LOU: How do you know she won't drink it away from home?
ALICE: She promised.
MARY LOU: Oh. (*beat*) I see.

(*The doorbell rings.*)

CYNTHIA: I'll get it. (*Cynthia crosses the stage to very near the exit.*)

MARY LOU: (*to JEREMY*) Are you going to have a glass of wine?
JEREMY: Am I going to—? No thanks. I'll have some more of the cucumber

stuff.

ALICE: One little glass and then I have to get back to the hospital.

(*They chatter as ANTON enters, as though standing in the doorway.*)

CYNTHIA: Can I help you?
ANTON: I'm looking for Eugene Kastakis.
CYNTHIA: He's not home.
ANTON: Oh.

(*pause*)

CYNTHIA: Will there be anything else?
ANTON: Sorry, I'm trying to decide what to do. Leave a note, or—?
CYNTHIA: If you tell me who you are, I'll invite you in.
ANTON: Sorry. I'm Anton Bixby. I'm—
CYNTHIA: That's an interesting name.
ANTON: You think so?
CYNTHIA: The first name doesn't quite square with the surname. Which is interesting.
ANTON: Russian on my mother's side.
CYNTHIA: Languages interest me.
ANTON: More and more we're citizens of the world.
CYNTHIA: Increasingly. I'm Cynthia Kastakis.
ANTON: (*extending a hand*) You can call me Tony.
CYNTHIA: (*taking his hand*) Why would I call you Tony when you have a rare and exotic name like Anton?
ANTON: Call me Anton then.
CYNTHIA: Who are you, Anton?
ANTON: Has your father spoken to you about The Gathering?
CYNTHIA: Oh, yes.
ANTON: It's an annual reunion of Vietnam gun truck veterans.
CYNTHIA: He's spoken of it. Incessantly.
ANTON: I've just come from there. The guys all talked about your Dad.
CYNTHIA: He goes sometimes.
ANTON: I know. (*Cynthia waits.*) When I decided to go this year and I found out he wasn't going to be there, I wrote him a letter telling him—
CYNTHIA: Thank you for designing the truck kits?
ANTON: How disappointed I was that I wouldn't have the chance to meet

him. So, he invited me to come to Washington.
CYNTHIA: He did?
ANTON: We exchanged a couple of letters.

(pause)

CYNTHIA: You can't possibly be a Vietnam Vet.
ANTON: No. My dad—
CYNTHIA: You go to those reunions with your dad?
ANTON: No, my—
CYNTHIA: That's kind of sweet.
ANTON: My father was killed in Vietnam.
CYNTHIA: Oh no.
ANTON: He was a gunner on the Psychotic Reaction. The guys picked names for their trucks.
CYNTHIA: Psychotic Reaction?
ANTON: It's a song from the sixties.
CYNTHIA: Sung by whom?
ANTON: I don't know.
CYNTHIA: Are you sure? My mother has probably hundreds of CDs from that era and if she'd ever played that song I'd remember.
ANTON: It's a head banger song.
CYNTHIA: No kidding.
ANTON: The guys from dad's truck tried to find it on the internet to play it for me but by that time they were drunk, so—
CYNTHIA: Here he comes. *(pointing)* My dad *(calling, before we see him)* Dad! Guess who this is?

(Now the whole stage is the room where ALICE is finishing her wine.)

(CYNTHIA enters the room first, followed by GENE whose arm is around ANTON.)

GENE: Alice, guess who this is.
ANTON *(extending his hand)*: Anton Bixby.
GENE: My wife Alice. He's just come from The Gathering. How are you, Jeremy?
JEREMY: Pretty good.
GENE: And this is your mother, right?

MARY LOU: Mary Lou Gunderson. (*slightly buzzed*) Alice has fed us the most delightful food. With garlic. And wine. From France.
ALICE: You're welcome to stay, Mary Lou, but Peter's expecting me.
JEREMY: No, we're not staying.
MARY LOU: I know The Gathering. (*to JEREMY*) Your father's friend from high school, you know? The Mexican man? (*to ALICE*) He visits us from time to time. He and Martin are still just thick as thieves. Oh, honey, you know who I mean.
JEREMY: Jim Luna.
MARY LOU: Jim Luna! That's right. Jim Luna goes to those gatherings. (*beat*) Jim Luna's very handsome.
JEREMY: (*to CYNTHIA*) This is why my mom doesn't drink.
MARY LOU: What are you talking about? I do so drink. A little bit. (*to ANTON*) You should be very proud. Serving your country. And you know, Gene? So should you.
JEREMY: Come on, Mom.
MARY LOU: Definitely. We've got to go. Martin's going to be worried.
JEREMY: He won't be worried. But we should still go. You probably need a nap.
MARY LOU: Isn't he the living end? Thanks so much for the hospitality, Alice.
JEREMY: Bye, Cynthia. (*But CYNTHIA is distracted by her father and, especially, ANTON.*) Cynthia? (*CYNTHIA turns to him.*) Bye.
CYNTHIA: Bye, Jeremy.

(*MARY LOU and Jeremy are out.*)

GENE: I stopped to see Peter on the way home. Take off your coat, Tony. Have a seat. (*to ALICE*) You gonna take the pita bread? He asked about it.
ALICE: I'm on my way. How'd he seem?
GENE: Ah, he's Peter. You know how he is.
ALICE: How's his pain?
GENE: I authorized them to increase his medication.
ALICE: (*turning to go*) I don't mean to be rude, Tony, but our son's in the hospital and I'm on my way out the door.
GENE: He has a good doctor. She won't overmedicate.
ALICE: That medicine makes him act like a fruit loop. I can't stand him being out of it all the time.
GENE: You can't stand him being in pain either. Alice, be rational. Aside

from the obvious, being in pain inhibits his tissue healing and depresses his immune system, which makes him much more susceptible to infection.
ALICE: (*to ANTON*) Sit. Have a glass of wine, and there's cold cuts, Gene.
GENE: I wouldn't authorize more pain meds if I thought it would hurt him.
ALICE: What about your testimony, Gene? Did that go okay?
GENE: I think I made some progress, but they're politicians, so who knows?
ALICE: I'm sure you were brilliant.
CYNTHIA: Of course he was brilliant.

(a couple beats as ALICE gathers up her package for PETER)

ALICE: I'll see you in a couple of hours.

(ALICE exits. GENE fixes sandwiches and CYNTHIA gets beverages as Alice walks across the stage. She stops. She addresses her first line over her shoulder, as though to PETER.)

ALICE: I'm going to grab a cup of coffee, son. I'll be back. (*She lights a cigarette. She drags on the cigarette, then looks at it.*) In seven minutes, I'll be back. One more tiny step toward emphysema. (*beat, drag*) And that, Gene, is my choice to make (*referring to what GENE said to her*) Be rational. (*She drags, then looks toward where she left PETER*) I'd never leave that room if I had my way. That's what it's come to. Stroking his hair, stuffing him full of his favorite foods. When he comes home, he's going to be as fat as a little pig. (*She hums something she likes to play on the piano, stops abruptly, still thinking about the conversation she and GENE had.*) I stopped by the hospital on the way home and spoke to my son for a minute. Oh, what a good father am I. What a good provider am I. What a fantastic blast shield inventor am I. (*Cello music plays. ALICE drops the cigarette and steps on it to put it out. She sits on the ground, on a serious talking to herself jag.*) Those outdoor concerts at Stern Grove. (*She moves her head in time to the music.*) The best music, the best picnics, the best family. You put your life, your future, your happiness, your children's happiness in someone else's hands? Then no complaining allowed. No smoking allowed. No bursting into tears every time you see your son's broken femurs allowed. No buying pita bread in plastic bags at the grocery store allowed. And absolutely no offering an opinion about how much pain medication your son should be given allowed. Be rational. (*Pause. Cello music plays. ALICE listens in her mind.*) What would be wonderful would be for me and Cynthia to perform together. Nothing big, not Carnegie Hall. A recital for my piano students. Oh, wait. Members of the House Armed Services Committee sitting beside my piano students. Wait. (*She stands up. This next is her idea of an elaborate joke on her husband.*) We could host The Gathering next year: appetizers, good wine, Vietnam vets, my piano students, the House Armed Services Committee. Then Strauss' "Cello Sonata in F", me on piano and Cynthia on cello. Or Debussy's in D minor, or even Kurt Weill. (*Which now plays. ALICE closes her eyes and listens a bit. Then she opens her eyes. Solo cello plays again. She takes out a package of cigarettes, pauses, then puts it away.*) No. I've had my cigarette.

(*ALICE exits, returning to PETER. Cello lingers a bit.*)

SCENE 4

(*Cello music out. CYNTHIA has just finished playing. ANTON applauds.*)

ANTON: That was a treat. I've never heard live cello music before.
CYNTHIA: Why not?
ANTON: It's never occurred to me. But it will from now on. Really beautiful.
CYNTHIA: It's Prokofiev.
ANTON: I've heard that name. He's Russian, right?
CYNTHIA: That's why I chose him.
ANTON: You're a very thoughtful girl.
CYNTHIA: When I'm not in the chemistry lab.
ANTON: And smart.
CYNTHIA: Like my father. I know.
ANTON: I don't get a chance to meet girls like that.
CYNTHIA: Like that? You mean like me?
ANTON: Yes.
CYNTHIA: That's probably because you're not in high school.
ANTON: Most of the women I've dated graduated from high school years ago, but you seem smarter than any three of them put together. Is it boring for you to date boys in high school?
CYNTHIA: We don't have time for me to enumerate all the things in the world that are boring for me, Anton. Come on. My dad's going to wonder. (*quickly*) I don't mean—. He's not going to wonder anything wrong or anything.
ANTON: He's going to wonder what's keeping us.

CYNTHIA: Exactly. (*as she moves to where GENE sits, sipping wine*) Dad?
GENE: (*to ANTON*) What'd you think?
ANTON: Gorgeous.
GENE: You're telling me.
CYNTHIA: Okay. No more showering attention on your hero's child, Anton. Dad already knows I play a magnificent cello. What about you? What do you do?
ANTON: I own a moving company. We move people from one part of Philadelphia to another or from in the city to the suburbs or vice-versa.
CYNTHIA: You're in the same business as your dad was in the war. Moving supplies in. Moving people out.
ANTON: That never occurred to me.
GENE: I wanted to go to the Gathering this year, but my committee's embroiled in a dispute between two body armor manufacturers that's getting uglier by the minute. Somehow, we've managed to keep the *truck* armor negotiations civil, but . . . So, we've got hearings pretty much every day of the week. That should keep up for a while because—
CYNTHIA: Everybody's lying.
GENE: Cynthia.
ANTON: Who's lying?
GENE: There's some debate about whether the body armor the army is currently using is the best available. NBC did some testing which, unfortunately, disputes the army's contention that—
ANTON: Oh, man. The media.
CYNTHIA: Another bunch of liars.
GENE: Cynthia, what has gotten into you? In this house, we know better than anyone that these issues are complicated. Don't we?
CYNTHIA: We do.
ANTON: (*to CYNTHIA*) The Vets kept talking about what a debt of gratitude they owe your father. You know, because the truck kit—well, they're the ones who really invented the kit, those Vietnam vets—you know how necessity is the mother of invention. In Vietnam, there was nobody like your dad bringing any science to it. They scavenged whatever scrap metal they could find and armored their own trucks.
GENE: In Iraq too, at the beginning.
ANTON: These guys fought in Vietnam. They're not used to being appreciated. So when scientists and Congressman started seeking them out to help develop truck armor kits. You can imagine.
CYNTHIA: Did you travel here to tell my father thank you?

ANTON: Not really. (*to GENE*) I did want to meet you. But also, it was a little bit of an excuse. I'm going to go meet Gene Kastakis and tell him thank you on behalf of all the gun truck vets. Of course, I knew they'd already thanked you a hundred times over. But I'm here. So I'm thinking about going to the wall.
CYNTHIA: You've never been to the wall?
ANTON: No.
CYNTHIA: It's indescribable. A person has to see it for himself.
ANTON: I've heard. My mother. Other people who lost their fathers when they were real young. I've been afraid—of feeling overwhelmed, of not feeling anything. In the back of my mind, I think I decided well, if I come up with another reason to go to Washington, once I find myself there, I'll just go. Like jumping off the high diving board for the first time. Just go.
CYNTHIA: I'll go with you. If you want.
ANTON: Yeah. That'd be . . . I think going with someone else would help.
GENE: Cynthia.
CYNTHIA: What, Dad?
GENE: You've seen the wall half a dozen times.
CYNTHIA: I realize that. But now I want to go with Anton.
GENE: Let's think it over.
ANTON: I'd buy her some lunch first. Or . . .
CYNTHIA: I've never been to the wall with anyone who actually knew someone whose name is on it.
ANTON: (*to GENE*) To be honest, I think I had the idea in the back of my mind to ask you to go with me. There's a better chance I'll get myself there if I don't have to go it alone.
GENE: That'd be different.
CYNTHIA: You mean the three of us? Dad, I don't need you to babysit me. Anton's old enough to babysit me.

(*ALICE calls from offstage.*)

ALICE: Hello.

(*She enters, with more groceries than she can carry. Gene immediately gets up to help her.*)

GENE: (*to CYNTHIA*) Babysitting has nothing to do with it. (*He goes to help with the groceries.*)

ANTON: (*to CYNTHIA*) Listen, I'm sorry. I'm sure all this talk about the gun trucks and Vietnam vets are on that long list of things that bore you.
CYNTHIA: I have heard it all before. More than once.
ANTON: Don't worry about coming to the wall with me. Don't worry about that.
CYNTHIA: I think you're confused, Anton. The wall doesn't bore me.
ALICE: (*entering the scene with groceries, followed by GENE, also with groceries*) Let's hope not.
CYNTHIA: How's Peter?
ALICE: Peter's cheerful. Despite having two legs in traction. He'd like to see you.
CYNTHIA: I saw him two days ago and he wasn't that excited about it.
ALICE: You staying for dinner, Tony?

(*Beat. GENE and CYNTHIA look at him.*)

ANTON: Sure.
CYNTHIA: Great. You can tell us all about The Gathering.
ALICE: You haven't gotten that out of the way yet?
ANTON: We have.
ALICE: I was hoping.
CYNTHIA: (*overlap*) I was teasing you, Mom.
GENE: Quick shower before dinner.
ALICE: It doesn't have to be so quick. I'm not even sure what I'm cooking yet.
GENE: Whatever you decide will be fine. (*extending his hand for ANTON to shake*) See you in a bit, then.

(*GENE exits.*)

ANTON: I'm going to follow suit. I haven't even checked into my motel yet.
ALICE: Go ahead. You come back in an hour, we'll have dinner.
ANTON: Thank you. It's a pleasure to meet you and your family.

(*ANTON exits.*)

ALICE: What should I fix, Cynthia? What do you think?
CYNTHIA: I think too much.
ALICE: I'm not sure that's possible.

CYNTHIA: Even for Dad?
ALICE: Especially for Dad. I don't know what he'd do without that brain.
CYNTHIA: What does anybody do without a brain?
ALICE: Drugs. Knock over liquor stores.
CYNTHIA: Die in the war.
ALICE: That's a little harsh.
CYNTHIA: Send people to die in the war.
ALICE: Much better.
CYNTHIA: Jeremy says his mother has her car radio tuned to Rush Limbaugh all the time.
ALICE: There's a difference between not having a brain and not using your brain.
CYNTHIA: I get tired of using my brain.
ALICE: No problem. I'll make an executive decision. (*hand to head, as though channeling a cookbook*) Linguine, mushrooms, lemon juice, white wine, prosciutto. You dream up the salad.
CYNTHIA: Okay.
ALICE: I was wondering something. If you had to choose between Strauss' sonata for cello and piano in F and Debussy's in D minor, which would you play?
CYNTHIA: I can't believe you'd choose either of those. They're both so romantic.
ALICE: I have a romantic streak.
CYNTHIA: On the piano maybe.

(CYNTHIA *sways as though listening to first one of the pieces, and then the other.*)

CYNTHIA: I'd have to choose Debussy. If we're going for D minor, I really like the Shostakovich in D minor too. The piano part's especially wonderful.
ALICE: I was also thinking Kurt Weill's—
CYNTHIA: Uggh. No.
ALICE: Okay. Weill is vile.
CYNTHIA: Mom, that is so lame. I hate when you do that.
ALICE: Sometimes they just slip out.
CYNTHIA: So, Mom? How's Peter really?
ALICE: He's good.
CYNTHIA: Really really.

ALICE: Given the circumstances, he's doing fine.
CYNTHIA: (*overlap*) When did lying become *de rigueur* around here? He got hit by a car. He has two broken legs and a broken nose and bumps and bruises and scratches all over his body and you and dad are arguing about how much pain medication he should take. We have no idea when he's going to be able to walk again. He'll probably have to repeat the entire sixth grade. I ask how he's doing and you say he's good. He's not good. I know he's not good. Don't treat me like a baby.
ALICE: I didn't mean to—
CYNTHIA: Both of you seem to have decided that I'm a dumb child who couldn't possibly understand anything more complex than a game of Go Fish. (*beat*) David Brooks was indicted.
ALICE: I know.
CYNTHIA: Why hasn't Dad mentioned it?
ALICE: Dad's very focused on truck armor, Cynthia. Where body armor is concerned, he doesn't pay as much attention.
CYNTHIA: Why is he so protective of—whatever their names are—those army people when they're obviously lying? They're getting Interceptor from a company run by a guy who siphons off the profits to throw his daughter an eight-million-dollar bat mitzvah. He wore a pink suede pantsuit to that party. Pink. Suede. That's the guy who makes Interceptor.
ALICE: I don't think the color of the CEO's pantsuit has much to do with the viability of the body armor his company makes.
CYNTHIA: A 75-page indictment listing dozens of counts of insider trading, fraud, tax evasion, you name it, he did it.

(*GENE enters in fresh clothes.*)

GENE: You can't believe everything you read, Cynthia.
CYNTHIA: Are you contending that he wasn't indicted, Dad?
GENE: No. He was indicted. That's on the record.
CYNTHIA: And he's the CEO of the company that was awarded a no-bid contract to produce body armor.
GENE: The indictment doesn't necessarily reflect badly on the Interceptor line.
CYNTHIA: How about the army recalling 23,000 vests over the course of a year because they couldn't stop 9-millimeter bullets? Does that reflect badly on the Interceptor line?
GENE: Some of the vests were recalled and, so far as we know, the design

was improved.

CYNTHIA: So far as you know? If your committee doesn't know, who knows?

GENE: The thing is, Cynthia, I was contracted to design tank armor.

CYNTHIA: What does that mean, Dad? You did your job, the tank armor's cool, hooray, so if the company producing body armor's screwing up, oh well. Not my job?

ALICE: Cynthia, calm down.

GENE: You understand how it is with the truck kits, right? They're not perfect in terms of armoring the tanks, but they're the best we've got at this point. Something that might work better is in development, but meanwhile we're sending the best we've got out there. With the vests it's the same thing. Interceptor is the best vest available.

CYNTHIA: You know that's not true.

GENE: I don't like the turn this conversation is taking. Let's table it until after dinner when we can discuss it calmly.

CYNTHIA: (*calmly*) All your committee hearing transcripts are on the internet, Dad. Not that anybody but me or somebody writing a dissertation about the role of polymers in military history would want to read them. Even I had no interest in reading them until I saw in the paper that this Interceptor guy was indicted. I read the testimony from the guy who makes Dragon Skin. I read the testimony from the scientist who vetted the side-by-side tests that demonstrated Dragon Skin's superiority to Interceptor. You don't miss committee meetings, Dad, so I know you were there, I know you heard that testimony. So I've been waiting for you to talk about these things at the dinner table like you always do. I kept thinking any minute you'd start bombarding us with information about this.

GENE: You know my work takes place in a political arena. Some information is more sensitive than other information.

CYNTHIA: But you can't apply political strategies to scientific pursuits, right? Aren't I right?

GENE: Of course you are.

CYNTHIA: Thank goodness. Otherwise bio-terrorism defense probably wouldn't be a viable career choice for me. I'm asking you, as a budding scientist to a scientific genius, why won't the army conduct side-by-side tests like NBC did?

GENE: The army's response is that they don't test equipment against other equipment. They test against a performance standard.

CYNTHIA: But that doesn't mean anything.
ALICE: Cynthia, your father is answering your question.
CYNTHIA: He's not answering my question. He's telling me what the army's response is. But you're the scientist, Dad, so you know that side-by-side tests <u>are</u> conducted against a performance standard. They're just conducted on two different products at the same time. So for them to say they test products against a performance standard, not against each other, is just doublespeak, like in *Alice in Wonderland* where up is down.
ALICE: Cynthia, you know your father. Don't you know your father?
CYNTHIA: Yes. I know my father.
ALICE: That's what you have to think about. Television news, army spokespeople, political spins. You've known your dad for a long time and that's what you have to rely on. Listen. On the one hand, you've got two CEOs whose companies make body armor in a pissing match. You've got a gigantic bureaucracy; you've got our famously unreliable media. On the other hand, you've got your father whom you know through and through.
CYNTHIA: True. (*pause*) And I think he knows me through and through. I don't want you to come with me and Anton to the wall, Dad. We're going to visit his father who was killed in Vietnam and I don't think you should come.
GENE: What's that mean? His father got killed in Vietnam so I shouldn't—
CYNTHIA: That's not what I mean. I just mean—
ALICE: I don't know what that has to do with David Brooks and his pink pantsuit, but—
GENE: I asked you a question, Cynthia.
ALICE: (*as in "calm down"*) Gene. (*to Cynthia*) You're not going anywhere alone with a grown man we hardly know.
CYNTHIA: I can recognize a pervert when I see one. He's not a pervert.
ALICE: You are absolutely not going.
CYNTHIA: If it'll put your mind at rest, dad can drive me and I'll meet Anton there. (*pause, as ALICE looks to GENE*) And then I'll walk over to dad's office. And if I'm not there by—three hours—after dad drops me off, he can call out the National Guard. (*pause, as the parents look at one another again*) Dad. I just want to trust you. I want you to trust me. Anton's not a pervert and I'll be fine.
GENE: (*after a couple beats*) Make it two hours and you've got a deal.
ALICE: Gene!
GENE: I trust her.
ALICE: I trust her too. That's beside the point.

(The doorbell rings.)

CYNTHIA: That's Anton. Everyone smile politely.

ACT 2

SCENE 1

(Cello and piano sonata plays. ALICE and MARY LOU sit together at a café, with cigarettes and glasses of wine. They sit outside, wearing light coats.)

MARY LOU: I had no idea you smoked. A person like you.
ALICE: A housewife?
MARY LOU: I think of you as one of those healthy people. Takes her vitamins, eats her vegetables, that sort of thing. Not that there's anything wrong with being a housewife. But I already had my career going when I met Martin and I had no intention of giving it up.
ALICE: Mary Lou, I have no idea what kind of work you do.
MARY LOU: I'm a personal shopper.
ALICE: Really? Is that fun?
MARY LOU: It' probably be more fun if I lived in Hollywood, but I like it. I have good instincts—what blouse looks good with what color hair and eyes. I'm a whiz at picking out Christmas presents and anniversary gifts. But the people who employ me? All that money and no time to shop? Make time. Course I don't say that. That'd be cutting off my nose to spite my face if you see what I mean. *(takes a sip)* Alice, I swear, you've converted me. I'm enchanted by the world of wine.
ALICE: You must buy wine for your clients.
MARY LOU: Oh sure. I go into that Rumrunner over on Brighton? And I say give me a case of the best cabernet I can get for $35 a bottle. Anyway, I was saying how my job keeps me crazy busy and that means eating out a lot because Martin would rather starve to death than fix dinner. He has precisely none of the qualities it takes to cook a decent meal. Number one, there's only three things in the world he'll eat. Number two, I'm not entirely sure he could name the kids' favorite foods, and number three, he has no imagination, so there's no way he could come up with a dinner menu. How about you? Does Gene cook? I bet he doesn't have time with

that big government job he's got. I shop for those people, so I know the government of the United States is a very demanding employer.
ALICE: He likes to make breakfast some Sundays. He's an expert omelet maker. That's what we did on our first date—made omelets. I was in his Botany class in grad school, and—
MARY LOU: No disrespect intended, but you went to graduate school?
ALICE: Just a masters degree.
MARY LOU: In botany?
ALICE: Music theory.
MARY LOU: What in heaven's name does botany have to do with music theory?
ALICE: Not much less than it has to do with polymer engineering.
MARY LOU: Polymer Engineering? Polymers are what? Hard things made of proteins? Something like that? Because Claudia took physics last year. Well, she dropped it. But before she dropped it, she tried to explain it to me, which she couldn't do really. I guess that's why she dropped it.
ALICE: Suffice it to say, polymer engineering has very little to do with Botany. I took the class because I love to garden.
MARY LOU: Makes perfect sense to me.
ALICE: The course focused on the reciprocal relationship between people and plants, and Gene adores his houseplants, so I quickly began to suspect that was why he took the class. He loved those plants and he wanted to know more about them. Of course, he'd never own up to that.
MARY LOU: Well, you gotta love a man who waters the plants. And Gene's awfully cute. Were you smitten right away?
ALICE: I was pretty much instantly smitten, yeah. His big brain. I found that very sexy. After that omelet cooking date, engineered by me, we got into the habit of omelets every Sunday and when Cynthia came along, she joined right in.
MARY LOU: I hope you got married first—before Cynthia came along.
ALICE: Actually, we were married quite some time before Cynthia arrived.
MARY LOU: On purpose, or did you have a hard time getting pregnant?
ALICE: Hard time doesn't come close to describing it.
MARY LOU: Me too! You think it's just going to follow naturally, and you think you're prepared to take a baby whenever God decides to give you one, but it sure isn't that simple, is it?
ALICE: Simple it is not. (*pause*) I was so miserable, and Gene was such a wonderful comfort. Science can be surprisingly reassuring.
MARY LOU: Well, I suppose so.

ALICE: Conceiving Peter was a bit easier.

(Pause. MARY LOU puts her hand on ALICE's.)

MARY LOU: How's Peter doing?
ALICE: Peter's confused. No . . . more . . . disoriented. His world has collapsed into that one small room.
MARY LOU: But he's going to be all right.
ALICE: In time. (*beat*) Hey. Better nearby in a hospital than in the Middle East.
MARY LOU: That's a different thing of course. Seriously, I'd take Jeremy getting injured fighting for his country over a random car accident any day of the week.
ALICE: (*this is an honest question*) You would?
MARY LOU: Course I would. If Jeremy were to die—young, I mean. Before me, I mean. I'd want him to die for something that means something.
ALICE: I don't know, Mary Lou. Your son goes over there, he's out of your sight, communication's erratic. Maybe he survives, maybe he doesn't. Even if he does, imagine what life must be like over there, day after day. Dangerous. Frightening. Lonely. I can't believe that's a life you'd want for your son.

(MARY LOU takes a final drag, then puts her cigarette out.)

MARY LOU: You know what? How about we agree to disagree? (*taking one out*) You want another cigarette?
ALICE: I only smoke one cigarette a day.
MARY LOU: Don't you just have all the will power in the world?
ALICE: Possibly.
MARY LOU: I'm going have another. Unless you want to go on inside?
ALICE: I'm fine.

(CYNTHIA enters, leading ANTON behind her, one of his hands in both of hers. They have just seen the wall. CYNTHIA sits on the ground. ANTON sits beside her. She drops his hand. He stares straight ahead.)

MARY LOU: Alice, I'm going to confide something in you. I bet you're wondering, well, if you and Martin spend so much time going your separate ways, what's the point of being married?

ALICE: No. That's none of my business.
MARY LOU: The answer is Martin is great at one thing. Besides his job, and I don't really truly know if he's good at that, but he brings home a lot of money so he must be good enough. I'm talking about sex. He's always been very, you know, experimental, very rough and tumble. He enjoys it, so naturally I enjoy it. That and I love him, of course. The other day though? When we were talking about veterans and so on, that Jim Luna—that friend of Martin's I spoke about?
ALICE: Handsome Jim Luna?
MARY LOU: That's the one. The last time he came to visit, he kissed me. I walked him out to his car just, you know, just to be polite. Because he'd come a long way. He kissed me, and you know what he said? "I think you're beautiful, Mary Lou." Well, I'll just admit. I was thrilled. Oh my God, what would my kids say if they heard me talking like this?

(Not really listening, ALICE stands and takes a few steps away.)

MARY LOU: I'm sorry, did I embarrass you?
ALICE: No no. I'm just a bit worried about Cynthia.
MARY LOU: Tell me about it. Claudia is a pain in my ass. I'll tell you what I think. I think every school district ought to have a place where we can send our girls to live once they hit puberty. Good-bye, take out your bad humor on one another, see you in four or five years. What is it, Alice? Bad boyfriend?
ALICE: *(shaking her head)* I don't know. *(She turns back to MARY LOU.)* I'll take that cigarette.

ANTON: Those long lines are oppressive.
CYNTHIA: It's a good thing it's not Saturday or Sunday. They're even worse on weekends. Major tourist attraction.

(They lapse again into silence.)

ALICE: *(after one drag, dropping the cigarette and stepping on it to put it out)* I've got to get to the hospital.
MARY LOU: How about I come with?
ALICE: It's not fun, Mary Lou. I'm not sure you'd enjoy it.
MARY LOU: Silly. I want to poke my head in and wish Peter the best.
ALICE: All right. If you like.

(MARY LOU drinks her wine down.)

MARY LOU: (*as they exit*) If a person can't take a minute out of her day to say hello to a boy in the hospital, what's the world coming to?

(Silence continues for a couple beats till CYNTHIA breaks it.)

CYNTHIA: What'd you do yesterday?
ANTON: Watched football in my motel room.
CYNTHIA: We're still 49er fans.
ANTON: I watch all the games. I just like to watch 'em play. (*pause*) Kind of odd to see his name carved on there.
CYNTHIA: Virgil is a very unfortunate name.
ANTON: Eugene's a pretty dorky name too.
CYNTHIA: That's why dad likes to be called Gene.
ANTON: Virgil Bixby. (*beat*) You want to see a picture?
CYNTHIA: Of course.

(ANTON retrieves one from his wallet.)

ANTON: This one my mother gave me—that's him before he got drafted. The guys at the Gathering showed me pictures of him in his truck. I wish I could show you those. In pictures, it's so weird. He's a lot younger than I am now. And his hair got to be this brownish red color, real pretty color.
CYNTHIA: They didn't give you the pictures?
ANTON: They're going to send me copies. They won't give up the originals—they have hundreds of photos of gun truck vets who were killed, gun truck vets who were maimed, gun truck vets who survived and then died of cancer, gun truck vets at the Gathering year after year.
CYNTHIA: Did they sing "We Are Family?"
ANTON: Aren't you a smart aleck?
CYNTHIA: No. I just think that's kind of depressing.
ANTON: Yeah, for all the drinking and laughing and storytelling, the whole thing was . . . I don't know. It was raucous and somber all at the same time.

(Silence.)

CYNTHIA: Anyhow, they're going to send you photos of your father with his red hair.
ANTON: They promised. (*pause*) I know I could have stood there beside him longer, but you feel pressure with that long line, so you keep moving. (*ready to talk about something else*) So what? Your parents let you take off school?
CYNTHIA: One thing neither of my parents would dream of doing is allowing me to take off a day of school. It's "you're a big deal because you're a senior" day. One day a month, seniors get the afternoon off. My mom says it's what took the place of allowing senior girls to wear pants to school on Fridays. Why weren't girls allowed to wear pants to school?
ANTON: Don't know. That rule had passed by the time I went to high school.
CYNTHIA: Where you never met girls like me.
ANTON: Correct.
CYNTHIA: Did you date at all in high school?
ANTON: Not really. I was kind of a combination of inertia, sugar addiction, and trepidation about sex.
CYNTHIA: I promised my parents you weren't a pervert so don't let me down.
ANTON: You're a strange girl.
CYNTHIA: I thought I was the girl you've been waiting for all your life.
ANTON: You're a strange, fascinating girl.
CYNTHIA: I like you too, although I'm not sure why. Maybe because you were so swept away by my cello. (*getting up*) You want to walk me to my Dad's office?
ANTON: Sure.

(*They walk across the stage. GENE enters from the direction they're walking and then the three of them walk together.*)

GENE: Did you find your father?
ANTON: Yes.
CYNTHIA: Dad? You never leave work early.
GENE: This way I can spend a little more time with Tony. He came all this way—I can take a couple hours off.
CYNTHIA: Anything scintillating to report?
GENE: Nope. (*to ANTON*) Come home and have a beer with me?
ANTON: Absolutely.

CYNTHIA: I don't drink beer. It has a disgusting metallic taste.
ANTON: You're too young to appreciate beer.
CYNTHIA: I'm not too young, Anton. I just don't like it.

(They exit.)

SCENE 2

(We hear the cello, solo. Two nearly empty bottles of beer on the table. GENE enters, with weights. ANTON follows. GENE takes off his shirt and lifts in his undershirt for a few minutes. ANTON watches.)

GENE: *(lifting as he speaks)* I don't pretend to be an expert. When I first started, I watched a guy on television whose pitch was: in twenty minutes a day you can be stress free. Given the pressure of my job, I didn't expect stress free. But I can tell you *(pause, the lift he's doing is hard and he concentrates. He does it, finishes the set and puts down the weights)* I can tell you it calms me down. It does calm me down. So—try.

(ANTON struggles to lift the weights, which are too heavy for him. He drops them.)

ANTON: Man.
GENE: Right. Wait.

(GENE exits. ANTON looks around a bit, sits at the table, listens to the cello. GENE returns with two more sets of weights, puts one down and hands the other to ANTON.)

GENE: How's that?
ANTON: Better.
GENE: You sure? Don't start too heavy.
ANTON: I'm good.
GENE: All right. Try a set of six first. Like I showed you. Two counts up, two counts down. *(as ANTON does this)* Two up. Two down. Two up. Two down. Two up.
ANTON: Jesus.
GENE: Two down. Two up. Two down. One more time. Two up. Two down. How's that feel?

ANTON: Stressful. To tell you the truth.
GENE: Everybody's different. You want another beer?
ANTON: Yeah, thanks.

(GENE gets them both a beer and they sit at the table.)

GENE: But don't give up. You don't give up, right? You keep plugging away.
ANTON: Plugging away.

(GENE takes a big swig of beer.)

GENE: I want to ask you something, Tony.

(pause)

ANTON: So? (*He waits. Nothing.*) Ask.
GENE: Have you ever been terrified? No holds barred completely, irrationally terrified? You ever been there?
ANTON: I don't think so.
GENE: You ask the guys at the Gathering about terror. They'll tell you about terror.
ANTON: They won't in fact.
GENE: I guess maybe not.
ANTON: What I do know about terror, I learned from my grandmother. (*beat*) The whole seven months my father was over there she was terrified he was going to get killed. Then he did. (*beat*) She felt relief.
GENE: (*nodding his head in agreement*) There was maybe 45 minutes when we thought Peter was going to die. (*a swig of beer*) The only way to get through that in one piece is to force your mind to go completely blank. (*GENE finishes his beer in one more gulp, then points the empty bottle in ANTON's direction*) Another one?
ANTON: I'm okay.
GENE: (*as he gets another beer*) The timing was unbelievable. If I were a religious person or if I believed in karma or that kind of nonsense. He didn't want to move even more than his sister didn't want to move. But there can only be one father in a family.

(ANTON nods and swigs and waits.)

GENE: I never would have believed how much a person's life can change. I mean change *radically*.
ANTON: Your son gets hit by a car—that's pretty radical.
GENE: No, I mean before that. I was doing what I always expected to be doing. It was always going to be science; it was just a question of what kind of science. Tony, I worked at Livermore Labs for almost 20 years. I get a call out of the blue from Washington, DC, from the chairman of the House Armed Services committee. You know why? His brother and I took the same engineering class in college. He tells his brother the congressman I'm the right guy to solve the truck armor problem. (*shakes his head*) You never know what's right around the corner. So—long story short—we invited a couple of Vietnam vets to join the team, we developed the truck kits, and then I was offered the Armed Services Committee staff appointment. I wasn't a supporter of the war, so I wasn't sure. But then—see—I went to Iraq to teach the guys to use the kits. The soldiers were crazy with excitement. They wanted to practice over and over. It took three hours to put the kits together, but that was okay with them. Let's practice again. (*pause*) So I decided to take the appointment. (*shaking his head*) Alice worried I'd hate it. How can you not believe in the war and work for the Armed Services Committee? (*A swig of beer.*) I'll tell you how. Between my first and second trips over there, I got letters and e-mails. The truck kit saved my life, sir, an IED hit us and all seven of us got out alive. (*pause*) When the invitation to the Gathering came, I was excited. I went. Here they all were, with their memories of Vietnam, and photographs of their trucks. My father was a doctor. When I was growing up, I'd occasionally think, "Dad saves lives." Saving lives was an abstract concept to me, nothing to do with actual arms and legs and head wounds and bleeding. I didn't think of it like that. I thought, there are plenty of doctors. Let them save lives. I preferred to be immersed in the details of solving tiny parts of a much bigger puzzle, you know what I mean?
ANTON: I don't think so.
GENE: I'd figure out the mechanical properties of thus and such garden variety polymer, then pass that solution on to other people who'd try to determine different applications for it. (*pause—ANTON is listening intently trying to make sense of this completely foreign discourse*) It never occurred to me that my work could mean something beyond my having a skill set I could exchange for the income I needed to support my family. Meaning in my life? I was happy enough. My life was going as planned.
ANTON: And your family?

GENE: That's different. That's exactly as I expected it to be. Now what's happened is I have the desire to be more than a breadwinner.

(*Pause. Only cello music for several seconds. GENE takes a swig.*)

GENE Are you disappointed? (*ANTON stares at him blankly.*) In me? Am I different from what you expected?
ANTON: I don't know how to answer that.
GENE: You expected a genius, a hero, a defender of the enlisted man and—
ANTON: I didn't really expect—
GENE:—in the end, I'm just a guy who stumbled on—
ANTON: Seriously, my expectations were . . .
GENE: Were?
ANTON: Not that specific. I thought you'd be a smart guy, I guess. But mostly, I thought you'd be the guy who made the truck kit happen and honestly, I don't really care about the particulars.
GENE: (*a bit blustery, a bit intoxicated*) All right, change of subject. How was your visit to the wall?
ANTON: Strange. I'm running a fleet of moving trucks around the Philly area now, you know, and I'll catch myself thinking, Tony, you're making a lot of money. I wonder if your father would have been proud of you. But I don't know what kind of man he was. The kind who cared about how much money people make? And my mother only knew him from when he was 16 to when he was 22. My grandmother. (*He stops for a second—he's sad for her.*) She's told me stories about what he was like as a kid. So, I'm standing at the wall with some stories about 10-year old Virgil in my mind, and a photograph mom gave me of them on their first date—to the prom or something. Like at the Gathering, I met two guys who were on my father's truck for a time and what are they going to say? He was brave? Well, yeah, he was brave, he got killed while he was driving through an ambush to deliver supplies. He didn't get out of the truck and run away when the ambush happened? Well, of course not. How does that distinguish him from anybody else over there? (*pause*) His truck was probably armored with trashcan lids.
GENE: From what I hear, they did a little better than that.
ANTON: I mean, how's my visit to my father at the wall any different from watching George Bailey in "It's A Wonderful Life?"
CYNTHIA: (*entering*) The difference is George Bailey had a wonderful life.
GENE: Come on, Cynthia.

CYNTHIA: What?

GENE: Don't be rude. That's what. You don't make fun of something like that.

CYNTHIA: I wasn't. (*to ANTON*) I didn't mean to make fun of you.

ANTON: You're fine. My dad didn't have a wonderful life. (*to GENE*) I feel ripped off. That's one way I feel.

CYNTHIA: There's a lot of that going around. As a matter of fact, I'm on my way over to see my brother in the hospital now. I bought him the "Honeymooners Classics" DVD. 39 episodes. You staying for dinner, Anton?

ANTON: I've imposed on you people enough.

CYNTHIA: You haven't. Please stay. (*pause*) You probably want to be alone. (*shorter pause*) With thoughts of your father. Come by before you leave tomorrow, okay?

ANTON: You got it.

CYNTHIA: My dad must really like you. I haven't seen him leave his office at 4 o'clock ever.

(*CYNTHIA exits.*)

ANTON: I love her. (*GENE looks at him.*) Just a figure of speech.

GENE: (*pointing his beer in ANTON's direction*) You sure?

ANTON: Am I—? (*sees the beer bottle*) Oh. Yeah, I'm all set.

SCENE 3

(*Intense piano music plays. A couple beats, then JEREMY and CYNTHIA enter. They are in mid-conversation. CYNTHIA is uncharacteristically hyped up.*)

CYNTHIA: Bio-terrorism's not new. The Romans were throwing rotting animal carcases into wells to poison the water literally thousands of years ago. In the fourteenth century, bubonic plague was used—mostly just as a threat.

JEREMY: Yikes.

CYNTHIA: And plague is still on the table. As a biological weapon.

JEREMY: But you're on top of it. Which is reassuring.

CYNTHIA: As long as I get into a good college.

JEREMY: Oh, yeah. What college would want you?

CYNTHIA: But if they invite me to audition at Julliard. . . .

JEREMY: What's going on? Suddenly you're all "I wish I was good at stuff." I'll tell you what. When you find out when the Julliard audition is, let me know. I'll take the train down there with you.
CYNTHIA: (*almost a shout—like "I just have to get this off my chest."*) Jeremy.
JEREMY: Whoa! What?
CYNTHIA: (*collecting herself*) I appreciate your mother being late to pick you up. I've had a miserable couple of days.
JEREMY: How come? Does it have something to do with that Anton guy?
CYNTHIA: No. I like him.
JEREMY: That's what I thought.
CYNTHIA: Don't be ridiculous. He's, like, 30.
JEREMY: So are you. (*beat*) Why's your mother playing Rachmaninoff like the world is ending?
CYNTHIA: Because I went to visit Peter today.
JEREMY: And—he requested Rachmaninoff?
CYNTHIA: I gave him the "Honeymooners" DVDs I bought him. He told me he was feeling fine, but I think it was the drugs talking.
PETER: (*Off, clearly on drugs*) My legs feel fine.
JEREMY: Gotta love that pain medication.
CYNTHIA: I told him about this tug of war that's been going on between these two body armor manufacturers—Interceptor and Dragon Skin.
PETER: (*Off*) Cool name.
JEREMY: Wait, you told Peter—your little brother Peter?—about—
CYNTHIA: (*a bit of an explosion*) He's my Dad's only other kid so I thought he might have some insight.
JEREMY: I so have no idea what you're talking about.
CYNTHIA: I'm saying (*a breath, calming down*) NBC tested them both—
JEREMY: Dragon Skin and Interceptor?
CYNTHIA: At a ballistics laboratory. How these tests go. They shoot at this clay-like substance with the body armor on it. The clay stuff is supposed to simulate human tissue. They're interested in whether the bullet penetrates the armor and also in assessing the blunt force trauma. Because even when bullets don't penetrate the body armor, a blow with enough force can still kill a soldier.

(*CYNTHIA stands and takes a few steps toward PETER's hospital room.*)

CYNTHIA: Peter. Don't watch "The Honeymooners" now. I'm trying to tell you something. (*beat*) On the fourth round, the bullets completely

penetrated the Interceptor armor and even on the third round, the level of blunt force trauma was extremely high. But with Dragon Skin, the bullets didn't penetrate the armor after six rounds, and the blunt force trauma level was still very low. Four side-by-side tests, and the results were always the same. But, dad's committee . . . Well, the army . . .
PETER: (*Off*) Thanks for the cool DVDs, Cynthia.
CYNTHIA: Then the army did a whole press conference thing saying they conducted their own tests. They claim Dragon Skin, like, melted. But they wouldn't discuss the specifics because—some bullshit. National Security, blah blah blah. But the thing is, this scientist testified before Dad's committee and confirmed that Dragon Skin is far superior. Dad heard that testimony, but he didn't. . . (*She stops talking for several beats.*) I don't know. Something. He should have done something.
PETER: (*Off*) Cynthia? Dad's a really cool guy.
CYNTHIA: I know. But, see, first, the CEO of the company that makes Interceptor was indicted and now, this Colonel John Norwood, one of the army's procurement guys—(*she turns back to JEREMY*) That's when my mom showed up.
ALICE: (*entering*) Cynthia!
CYNTHIA: Hi, Mom.
ALICE: What are you doing in here?
CYNTHIA: I'm visiting my brother.
ALICE: Out. (*taking CYNTHIA's arm*) Let's go. (*to PETER*) I'll be right back.

(*ALICE and CYNTHIA "step outside" the hospital room.*)

ALICE: Explain what you're doing.
CYNTHIA: I wanted, I guess, his perspective.
ALICE: He's 11 years old.
CYNTHIA: But he's smart, Mom. He's not in freaking kindergarten.
ALICE: Watch your language.
CYNTHIA: I said "freaking." I was watching my language.
ALICE: He's in the hospital.
CYNTHIA: Which is why I came to the hospital to talk to him.
ALICE You really don't grasp how inappropriate this is? Your brother has enough to deal with, don't you think?
CYNTHIA: But mom. There's more now. In just three days, there's more. Colonel John Norwood is under investigation. Because he retired from his

job procuring equipment for the soldiers in the field, and went to work for Armor Holdings, which is owned by the company that makes Interceptor.

JEREMY: No way!
CYNTHIA: (*still with ALICE, outside PETER's room*) If that's not war profiteering, explain to me what is.
JEREMY: You said that?

ALICE: You're standing outside Peter's hospital room suggesting your father's a war profiteer? Did I get here just in the nick of time, before you had a chance to share this preposterous theory with your brother?
CYNTHIA: That is not my theory and even if it were, I would never tell Peter that. I would always protect Peter.
ALICE: (*her arms around CYNTHIA*) Let's just leave your brother out of it, all right?

(*CYNTHIA returns to JEREMY*)

JEREMY: So. Why is she playing Rachmaninoff like a crazy person?
CYNTHIA: I think because she's mad at me. I mean, she was yelling at me in the hospital corridor.
JEREMY: She probably just agrees with me that there's no way the perspective of an 11-year-old boy on drugs could be illuminating.
CYNTHIA: (*amused*) Probably.
JEREMY: Maybe I've just never heard her play something so passionate before. So maybe it's just really, really passionate piano playing. Which I'm not used to from your mom, so—
CYNTHIA: Jeremy? I'm a senior, and we get perks. One of the perks is the Sadie Hawkins dance in January. I never in my life thought I'd want to go, for several reasons. Especially because it seems stupid and juvenile, and also, you have to make a dress and make a shirt for your date that matches it. Seriously.
JEREMY: It's a great idea. Then if anybody's seen kissing a girl wearing a dress that doesn't match his shirt, he'll be exposed for the rotten cad he is.
CYNTHIA: The idea—Sadie Hawkins—is that the girls ask the guys. I can't sew at all, but do you want to go with me?
JEREMY: Even though I'm a junior? (*CYNTHIA shrugs.*) Definitely.
CYNTHIA: I'll figure out the sewing part. My mom can sew. Oh. If she were listening to this conversation, she'd say, "I can sew, SO?" and then laugh

her head off. So annoying.
JEREMY: She and my mother have taken to going out drinking. My mom's pretty late. I'm actually a little worried about her.
CYNTHIA: They went to a wine bar, Jeremy. Once. Anyhow, your mom wouldn't drink and drive, would she? (*beat*) She's only 15 minutes late.
JEREMY: Yeah. You're right. I'm not worried.

(*ALICE starts playing again, a calmer, quieter, beautiful piece.*)

CYNTHIA: The thing is.
JEREMY: What?
CYNTHIA: This is what's driving me crazy. The army's using Interceptor, but it's seems pretty clear that Dragon Skin is safer. If I know that, my Dad knows that.
JEREMY: But. Well, is there anything he could do? I mean, you've seen all those movies, right, about how the government is this behemoth that mows down everything in its path?

(*The doorbell rings.*)

JEREMY: I hope that's my mom.

(*The doorbell rings again.*)

GENE: (*off*) Hello?

(*CYNTHIA opens the door for GENE, who enters carrying a large bag and a briefcase.*)

CYNTHIA: Where's your key?
GENE: (*holding up the bag*) I couldn't get to it. Chinese food.
CYNTHIA: Yum.

(*GENE puts down the Chinese food, takes off his coat, hangs it up.*)

JEREMY: Anyway, would the army really keep using Interceptor if—
GENE: Are you still worried about that, Cynthia? Because I promise you—

(*The doorbell rings. CYNTHIA lets MARY LOU in. MARY LOU walks past her to JEREMY.)*

MARY LOU: I am so sorry, honey. Somebody rear-ended me at a stop sign on my way over here.
CYNTHIA: You promise me what, Dad?
JEREMY: *(to MARY LOU)* Are you all right?
MARY LOU: It was just a tap. His cell phone must have rung while he was coming to a stop or something. But then we had to exchange driver's licenses and insurance cards and all that. Because that's my Jaguar and those scratches are coming off. You ready to go?
JEREMY: Just a second, Mom. *(to CYNTHIA)* Listen, I bet they'll come around to Dragon Skin, you know, once they figure out how to save face and everything. *(no answer)* Don't you think?
MARY LOU: Dragon Skin's that body armor that doesn't work, right?
CYNTHIA: I believe it works. It works, right, Dad?
MARY LOU: Not according to the United States Army. I saw a big old press conference about that. In fact, they interrupted my regular programming to bring me that press conference.
CYNTHIA: That's only one side of the story.
GENE: *(to CYNTHIA)* Why don't you get ready for dinner?
CYNTHIA: I'm ready for dinner.
MARY LOU: The Army tested Dragon Skin. What kind of name is that? Sounds like a Sushi roll. They proved that what they use now works better. Shame on NBC. Honestly.
GENE: Where's Mom?
CYNTHIA: *(pointing)* Can't you hear her? *(to MARY LOU)* I've seen NBC's side-by-side tests of the two vests. You can watch them on You Tube.
JEREMY: Cool.
MARY LOU: I don't need to watch them. The army's word is good enough for me.
CYNTHIA: Appeal to Authority. Taking somebody's word for it rather than demanding evidence. Logical fallacy.
MARY LOU: Is that so? Well, tell me how logical it is to think the army would not provide our soldiers with the best possible equipment. Where's the profit?
GENE: What with my work on the committee, Cynthia's been giving these issues quite a bit of thought.
MARY LOU: I understand. You're involved in these things, and you're her father. Speaking of appealing to authority. Let's face facts. It's just a bad

idea to appoint someone who doesn't believe in the war to that kind of position.
GENE: I'm good at my job. I staff the committee without bias.
MARY LOU: I didn't mean to imply that you're biased.
GENE: Maybe you didn't intend to, but you did.
MARY LOU: But honestly, it follows that a person opposed to the war is going to pursue the goal of ending the war. That just makes sense.
GENE: Then I take it you're not opposed to the war. You're in favor of the war?
JEREMY: I'm ready to go, Mom.
MARY LOU: I'm not ashamed of being in favor of the war. Why should I be?
GENE: (*lifting a fist slightly, making fun of her*) Go war.
CYNTHIA: Dad, you're changing the subject. (*to MARY LOU*) There's a photograph on several internet sites of the Vice-President wearing a Dragon Skin vest as he gets off an air force plane in Iraq. Sub-standard body armor for our vice-president? Body armor that failed army testing for our Vice President?

(Piano music ends.)

CYNTHIA: (*to MARY LOU, as ALICE enters*) I'm sorry. (*to JEREMY*) I'm being ridiculous, arguing with your mother.
MARY LOU: Oh no, honey. Where would we be without independent thinkers? I have always encouraged my children to speak their minds. Haven't I, Jeremy? (*without waiting for an answer, to GENE*) I didn't mean to offend you.
GENE: No offense taken.
MARY LOU: Forgive my tardiness, Alice. Just a little car trouble.
ALICE: He did a nice job on Chopin today.
JEREMY: Thanks.
CYNTHIA: (*to JEREMY*) Watch that test on You Tube.
JEREMY: I'm going to, are you kidding?
MARY LOU: (*to ALICE*) Maybe wine sometime next week?
ALICE: Give me a call.
MARY LOU: Let's go home, Jeremy. We don't want your father to think we've left him to starve to death.
JEREMY: (*to CYNTHIA*) See you at your locker. In the meantime, get sewing.

(MARY and JEREMY exit.)

ALICE: What's going on?
GENE: Nothing's going on.
ALICE: Did you get the Chinese food?
GENE: Yep. I'll be ready to eat in a half hour. We'll have to re-heat it.

(GENE exits.)

ALICE: Get sewing?
CYNTHIA: I invited Jeremy to the Sadie Hawkins dance.
ALICE: *(thrilled)* Good for you. You want me to help you pick out a pattern?
CYNTHIA: You're going to have to help me do more than that.
ALICE: I'll help, but I'm not making the dress.

(We hear the exercise tape. ALICE looks in that direction.)

CYNTHIA: I'll need some guidance.
ALICE: Guidance I'm good for. You're making the dress. *(pointing)* Go. Wash.

(As CYNTHIA exits, we hear GENE's exercise tape.)

SCENE 5

(Open boxes of Chinese food on a table. Used paper plates and forks. CYNTHIA, ALICE, GENE each with a glass of white wine.)

GENE: The committee's looking at a new tracking system. Well, turns out it's not that new. Israel's been developing it for years. It detects and tracks threats and offers launching and intercept function. It's got several sensors including flat-panel radars placed at strategic locations around the vehicle so—
CYNTHIA: It protects 360 degrees around the vehicle?
GENE: That's it.
CYNTHIA: No way.
GENE: That's what they claim. Once an incoming threat is identified, a countermeasure device is launched into a ballistic trajectory to intercept it at a relatively long distance. Defense says it forms a beam of fragments that'll intercept any incoming heat threat, including RPG rockets, at a

range of 10-30 meters.
CYNTHIA: Our guys need those.
GENE: The Army's got Raytheon working on it.

(Long pause.)

ALICE: (*to CYNTHIA*) You ready for your Calculus test tomorrow?
CYNTHIA: I could pass that test in my sleep. I haven't practiced today though, so . . .

(CYNTHIA stands and starts to gather up trash from the table.)

ALICE: I'll get that, Cynthia.
CYNTHIA: I don't mind.

(She puts a pile of empty food cartons and paper plates in the trash. Gene retrieves an open bottle of wine from the refrigerator and holds it out toward ALICE.)

ALICE: (*to GENE, about the wine*) Please.

CYNTHIA: Okay. Practice. See you guys later.

(CYNTHIA exits.)

ALICE: Israel's using the system now. What are we waiting for?
GENE: Pre-existing contract with Raytheon. You know, buy American. I'm thinking of applying for the research team. The work's being done in Massachusetts so it wouldn't be as big a move.
ALICE: You don't think the product will be up and running by the time your appointment ends?
GENE: Doesn't sound like it. Right now, the group's mostly physicists and electrical engineers, but there's hardware development involved, so I'd have a shot, especially with my experience on the committee. I don't know. It's something to think about. (*pause*) I'm beat. I think a couple of presses and then bed.
ALICE: You exercised two hours ago.
GENE: It relaxes me. Helps me sleep better. (*beat*) You know that.
ALICE: Can it wait a minute? I have a couple things I want to talk to you about.

GENE: I'm up at 5:30 tomorrow, Alice.
ALICE: It's important.
GENE: (*he's staying*) Shoot.
ALICE: Have you read this? (*reading*) "Retired Army Colonel John D. Norwood, former head of the Army office responsible for purchasing body armor, is under criminal investigation for alleged violations of federal law related to his taking a position with one of the major providers of Interceptor body armor to the Army. Federal law enforcement agencies are gathering evidence that the U.S. Attorney will present to a federal grand jury."
GENE: Alice, I have to get up early.

(*pause, then cello music starts*)

GENE: What are we talking about here, Alice? (*pause*) You want me to guess? (*beat*) You want to at least tell me where you read that?
ALICE: Probably the same place your daughter read it.
GENE: There's a corrupt guy in the army. That's not exactly news.
ALICE: It's news to Cynthia that your committee defended Interceptor when Dragon Skin has proved to be—
GENE: It has not proved to be anything.
ALICE: (*reading again*) "In a hearing before a House subcommittee, the Defense Department's own medical examiner testified that a study by his office has concluded that up to 80% of Marines killed in Iraq from upper-torso injuries could have survived if they had been wearing body armor with side plates such as those provided by Dragon Skin."
GENE: I'm sure the committee's going to call for a side-by-side test at this point.
ALICE: What else could the committee do, now that everybody's being investigated or indicted? You know what? I'm going to make a copy of that article for Mary Lou.
GENE: She's an idiot.
ALICE: You think so?
GENE: My job has nothing to do with these things.
ALICE: You were hired because of your scientific expertise. You're on the damn committee. If it's not your job to apply your scientific expertise to issues taken up by the committee, then, tell me, what's your job?
GENE: I'm a professional staffer. I can't influence the Committee to—
ALICE: You can't? Then why did you move your family across the country?

Why did you uproot your daughter in the middle of her junior year of high school? The idea was it was going to be worth it because you were going to help make our troops safer.

GENE: I did make them safer. I went to Iraq to teach them how to use truck armor I designed and that has saved lives.

ALICE: But when you sat around quietly during this body armor debacle, you were also party to making them less safe.

GENE: (*getting up from his chair angrily*) That's it. This conversation's over.

ALICE: You decree that this conversation is over? (*beat*) Gene. Your children adore you. I believed following you here was the right thing to do for our family. I think you owed it to all three of us to suggest the committee entertain the possibility that there might be better protection for our soldiers available, and I think you owed it to us to do that before investigations started happening.

GENE: Alice. (*She waits.*) I am not in the army. I am not a member of Congress. I'm a guy who was lucky enough to get a chance to help design tank armor that has succeeded in protecting our soldiers. I'm proud of that, and nothing army colonels or corporate CEOs or NBC or even you do or say is going to take that away from me. I'm not going to allow that to happen. That's it. That's all. That's the end.

ALICE: I understand.

GENE: Good. I'm glad.

ALICE: Now you understand me. Your family gave up a life all of us loved in California. Thank God Cynthia found a boy she likes because so far her life here has been about nothing except her schoolwork and the cello. I haven't seen her over here with a girlfriend, have you? Peter's been miserable every day since we got here.

GENE: Families move. He'll adjust.

ALICE: After he gets done adjusting to being in the hospital? He was depressed. He was distracted. He got hit by a car.

GENE: You're blaming me for that?

ALICE: My work as a pianist was finally beginning to—

GENE: YOU ARE NOT A PIANIST. YOU'RE A FUCKING PIANO TEACHER.

(*Cello stops abruptly.*)

GENE: I realize it's unpleasant for me to raise my voice.

ALICE: Yes, that is fucking unpleasant.

GENE: And to use that language, but Alice, for Christ's sake, you're a piano teacher.
ALICE: And that's nothing compared to sitting on a congressional committee with your head in the sand. Well, I no longer care whether you think what I do when I'm not raising our children is nothing. I teach people to play music. You think that's nothing, Gene?
GENE: I didn't say it was nothing. I—just—families move.
ALICE: They do. We did. For a good reason. But it sounds like you're helpless to do anything further to protect our soldiers. So, your job here is done, and since Peter's going to have to repeat the sixth grade, he's going to repeat it in California.
GENE: What are you talking about?
ALICE: I'm taking Peter back to California. I'm going to be a piano teacher. Peter's going to be a sixth grader. When he gets out of the hospital, I'm going to try to help him catch up, do the Alice Kastakis version of home schooling. So—I don't know—maybe he's going to be a seventh grader. Sixth grader or seventh grader, he'll be in California.
GENE: Alice, you're talking like a crazy person. You're leaving me, and you're going to support Peter by giving piano lessons?
ALICE: If I were leaving you, I wouldn't be supporting Peter by giving piano lessons. I'd be supporting Peter with income from piano lessons, along with income from alimony and child support. But that's moot because I'm not leaving you.

(The doorbell rings. Pause. The doorbell rings again.)

GENE: That's Tony Bixby, I think. Cynthia wanted to say good-bye to him.
ALICE: Good. I can't tell you how relieved I was when she told me she invited Jeremy Gunderson to the Sadie Hawkins dance.

(GENE opens the door. It is indeed ANTON.)

ALICE: Hello, Tony.
ANTON: I hope I'm not intruding.
ALICE: Not at all. *(to GENE)* What I'm saying is, your appointment is temporary. Since you have to look for another job, look for a job in California. Tony, I have to say good night. I have to find a dress pattern that will please Cynthia. There's no telling how long it'll take. Cynthia has high standards.

ANTON: (*extending his hand*) It's been a pleasure.
ALICE: (*taking it*) That's sweet. Have a good trip home.

(*ALICE exits.*)

ANTON: Your wife is very gracious, but I think I've come at a bad time.
GENE: No. We were talking about something I really didn't want to talk about. Sometimes just shutting up is the best solution. Not solution.
ANTON: Respite.
GENE: Respite. That's more like it.
ANTON: I'm sorry I'm so late. I hope I haven't missed Cynthia.
GENE: No, she was just practicing. I don't think she's gone to bed yet.
CYNTHIA: (*entering, in a bathrobe*) I'm here. (*to ANTON*) You're getting a late start.
ANTON: I went back to the wall today. I stayed until evening. As the night wore on, there were more and more moments I could spend with Virgil.
CYNTHIA: That's cool. I'm happy for that. (*She hands him a piece of paper.*) This is a list of several recordings of the cello piece I played for you. Buy them because it's fun to compare different musicians' interpretations.
ANTON: Yours will stay with me, no matter how good these are.
CYNTHIA: Good doesn't begin to describe them, Anton. You have no idea how beautiful music can sound. I put my e-mail address there too. I want you to let me know what you think when you hear them.
ANTON: All right.
CYNTHIA: I mean it. Otherwise, I'll be very unhappy, and you'll have blown your chance with the greatest girl in the world.
ANTON: I wouldn't dare.

(*CYNTHIA crosses to ANTON. They hug.*)

CYNTHIA: I hope you'll come see us again soon.
ANTON: Maybe not soon, but . . . maybe sometime.
CYNTHIA: Or I'll come see you. Once I know what college I'm going to and I'm on my own.
ANTON: As your father said to me yesterday, who knows what's right around the corner? (*to GENE*) Good-bye.
GENE: Drive safe.

(*ANTON exits.*)

CYNTHIA: Dad? I really believe if I'd met Anton when I was a grown woman, I would have instantly fallen in love with him and married him immediately.
GENE: And vice-versa it looks like.
CYNTHIA: I know. Cool, huh? Well. From my perspective.
GENE: You probably heard me yell at your mother.
CYNTHIA: Probably.
GENE: I know I shouldn't do that.
CYNTHIA: I guess you were really mad. I know she still trusts you, Dad. I'm sure of it, because that's all she's told me the last few days. Trust. Just trust. So, Dad. I applied to Julliard.
GENE: Without telling us?
CYNTHIA: Obviously.
GENE: You know, I spoke to Jeff up at Cornell.
CYNTHIA: Oh my God, Dad, don't do that. I don't want you to do that. I can get in on my own. Or if I can't, I'd rather go someplace else.
GENE: It wouldn't matter what I said, if his department didn't want you, they wouldn't take you. So, where's the harm?

(pause)

CYNTHIA: I guess that's true. *(beat)* I applied to Julliard, Dad.
GENE: So you said.
CYNTHIA: I'll find out soon if they want me for an audition. If I get one, it'll be scary and really exciting because they determine all the pieces you have to play and it's formidable, but I'm excited to see if I'm up to the challenge. If I get invited for an audition, and then if I get in—well, if I got in it would be a miracle.

(GENE takes her hand and kisses it.)

GENE: Good luck.
CYNTHIA: Thanks, Dad.
GENE: You know what I'm trying to do here, don't you?
CYNTHIA: Of course I do. *(beat)* You're protecting our soldiers.
GENE I have to stay focused on that.
CYNTHIA: Isn't this fight between the two body armor manufacturers part of that?

GENE: It is. I'm just not sure I can make a difference there.

(pause)

CYNTHIA: Hey, Dad? For my research paper—you know, for my honors seminar? I decided to do Jesse Lazear. The guy who figured out mosquitoes carry yellow fever? *(beat)* By dying? *(beat)* Since he's one of the original pioneers of bacteriology, if I do wind up pursuing bio-terrorism defense, he'd be someone whose footsteps I'd be following in. He worked for the U.S. Army Yellow Fever Commission, and I figure I'll probably wind up working for the government too. Not that I'd dream of injecting myself with something that'd kill me like he did.
GENE: Research strategies have improved considerably since the 19th century.
CYNTHIA: Thank heaven. I mean, how idiotic is it to inject yourself with something that you're trying to prove kills people? On the other hand, I admire him. *(beat)* I'm going to bed now.

(pause)

GENE: *(this is a very hard question for him)* Have I lost your respect?
CYNTHIA: You taught me half of everything I know, Dad. *(She starts to exit, then turns back to him.)* I have faith in you.

(GENE watches her exit. Then he pours himself some more wine, and sits at the table, lost in thought.)

END OF PLAY

STAND

For the sake of one's children, in order to minimize the bill they must pay, one must be careful not to take refuge in any delusion . . . . in our time, as in every time, the impossible is the least one can demand and one is, after all, emboldened by the spectacle of human history in general, and American Negro history in particular, for it testifies to nothing less than the perpetual achievement of the impossible.

> James Baldwin
> *The Fire Next Time*

He says that when he arrived with sheriff's deputies there in the cane field to identify his son, he had knelt by his boy—"laying down there with his two little eyes sticking out like bullets," and prayed the Our Father. And when he came to the words "Forgive us our trespasses as we forgive those who trespass against us," he had not halted or equivocated, and he said, "Whoever did this, I forgive them." But he acknowledges that it's a struggle to overcome the feelings of bitterness and revenge that well up, especially as he remembers David's birthday year by year and loses him all over again . . . . . Forgiveness is never going to be easy. Each day it must be prayed for and struggled for and won.

> Helen Prejean, C.S.J. writing about Lloyd LeBlanc and his murdered son David.
> *Dead Man Walking*

CHARACTERS:

ELIZABETH JONES, a sports broadcaster, 30s

DEMETRIUS WASHINGTON, African American, late 30s, Elizabeth's co-worker

RANDALL WASHINGTON, Demetrius' son, 14

CASSANDRA FREDERICK, Randall's best friend, 13

COURTNEY KAUFMAN, a kidnap victim, 12

ARNOLD ANDERSON, a career criminal, late, 30s to late 40s

SEVERAL RADIO/AUDIO VOICES

The play takes place in a suburban Michigan town just before Thanksgiving, 1999.

<u>A note on the news, traffic and weather broadcasts</u>:
The places in the script where pieces of a broadcast are written are places that the broadcast should be heard, for the sake of both rhythm and content. The sound of broadcasting can continue at a low level throughout appropriate sections of dialogue; the playwright can provide the text for complete news, weather and traffic broadcasts.

Words in parentheses should be spoken if the following line does not come in quickly enough.

ACT I

(In darkness we hear Sly and the Family Stone singing "Stand," loudly. Then lights up.)

ELIZABETH sits at a microphone at the WBZZ radio station, both a multi-line and single line phone near it. DEMETRIUS sits at a desk surrounded by the sound equipment necessary to run the radio show, a multi-line phone within easy reach. There is a very large clock with black numbers on it in plain view. DEMETRIUS is on the telephone; ELIZABETH is speaking into the microphone.)

ELIZABETH: Someone's given you bad information, guy. There is no way on God's good earth Mississippi State wins that game. NO WAY. I don't care who's got a broken hip, for Mississippi State to win that game, Auburn's whole damn team's gonna have to call in sick, buddy. Who told you that, or did you come up with this Mississippi State's going to surprise Auburn and maybe even make it to the Sugar Bowl theory all by yourself?

DEMETRIUS: *(into phone)* Okay, the Stanley Cup. Hold the line, Steve.

(DEMETRIUS writes as he speaks to callers.)

ELIZABETH: Joe in Richmondville, you're on WBZZ, stand up for Liz.

(Phone rings. DEMETRIUS answers.)

DEMETRIUS: *(into phone)* Stand. *(beat)* Yeah, that's right, you've reached—. *(beat)* Yup, this is Stand. What's on your mind? *(beat)* You tell me, I'll decide whether you tell her.

ELIZABETH: Come on, that was a long time ago. You're telling me Notre Dame's gonna win Saturday because Montana played there once? A long time ago?

(Phone rings.)

ELIZABETH: That has nothing to do with tradition, buddy, in my country we call that addiction. You're sick, Joseph. You need a 12-step program.

DEMETRIUS: (*into phone*) Stand. Hold the line. (*to he first person*) Okay, you call back when— (He gets interrupted.) You know what? DON'T CALL HERE AGAIN.

(*ELIZABETH looks over at him sharply.*)

DEMETRIUS: News, stand by. (*to the person on hold*) Now what can we do for you?
ELIZABETH: (*comes in on "stand by"*) Let me leave you with this thought, Joseph.

(*ELIZABETH covers the mic with her hand and speaks quickly to DEMETRIUS.*)

ELIZABETH: Is Jack here?
DEMETRIUS: He's here.
ELIZABETH: (*still to Demetrius*) And what is all that yelling about? Hold it down. (*into mic*) I'm not interested in their glorious past. What have they done lately? (*beat*) Jeff in Downington, if you can hang in, I'll be with you right after the news. This is Liz Jones on Stand, the Peninsula's only sports talk show. You're listening to WBZZ. It's six o'clock.

(*ELIZABETH turns the mic off.*)

ELIZABETH: (*to Demetrius*) What have we got?

(*As the scene progresses, we hear the news broadcast by someone we can't see. DEMETRIUS looks through his notes.*)

NEWS BROADCAST: A gathering of the heads of seven Arab nations took place today—(in Cairo).
DEMETRIUS: (*overlap*) Let's see. Steve wants to talk—(about)
ELIZABETH: (*comes in on "Steve"*) Could that man once in his wretched life inform me that he's here and ready to do the news?
DEMETRIUS: Steve wants to talk about (the Redwings)
ELIZABETH: (*comes in on "wants"*) Would it kill him, Demetrius, to set my mind at ease, let me know he's in the building, for God's sake?
NEWS BROADCAST: . . . of North Korea. The President warns the United States will not—(tolerate)

DEMETRIUS: (*overlap, pointedly*) Lizzie?
ELIZABETH: (*She doesn't like to be called Lizzie—she's told him a million times*) Lizzie. That's hilarious. I'm so amused, I can hardly speak.
DEMETRIUS: That'll be the day. Elizabeth. Try to comprehend this. When Jack gets here, he tells me, I take care of you. He's the news guy, I'm the producer, you're the talent. See what I mean?
ELIZABETH: I just asked him a couple days ago, just as a courtesy, you know, to poke his head in here and wave when he arrives.

(*The phone rings.*)

DEMETRIUS: (*into phone*) Stand, hold please. (*beat*) Hang on, Randall. (*to ELIZABETH*) Do I look like a man who has nothing to do?
ELIZABETH: (*is this the right answer?*) No?
DEMETRIUS: Then please believe me when I tell you I don't have time to discuss this with you three times a week. He'll wave if he remembers to wave. Otherwise, trust me.
ELIZABETH: Oh, for God's sake, I trust you.
DEMETRIUS: In that case, do you want to hear who's holding?
NEWS BROADCAST: Locally, a twelve-year old girl named Courtney Kaufman was abducted (from her kitchen in Port Huron . . .)
ELIZABETH: (*sees he is waiting for her undivided attention*) Yes. Tell me who's holding.
DEMETRIUS: Steve thinks he's got an incredible insight about the Redwings. He's on six. Some weirdo's called about a dozen times.
NEWS BROADCAST: . . . police have been looking for the girl since early this morning.
ELIZABETH: (*overlap news*) The same weirdo you were yelling at? Loudly? While I was on the air?
DEMETRIUS: That's the one.

(*The phone rings. DEMETRIUS picks up.*)

DEMETRIUS: (*into phone*) Stand. Hold please. (*to ELIZABETH*) There's a Packers fan on (line 4)
ELIZABETH: (*comes in on "Packers"*) Honestly, Demetrius, couldn't Jack be persuaded to just peek in? Couldn't he? Would you ask him?
DEMETRIUS: You're the star. There's a Packers fan on 4—Jim? (*He looks through his notes.*) Yeah. Jim on 4. (*points to her mic*) Here we go.

ELIZABETH: (*reminding him*) Your child's on hold. (*as she turns to the mic*) Put on some nice music.

(*A second, then "Badge" (Cream) starts to play.*)

DEMETRIUS: (*into phone*) Another couple seconds, then I'm with you, son.
ELIZABETH: (*getting a sign from DEMETRIUS, into mic*) They don't make bands like that anymore.

(*The music fades.*)

DEMETRIUS: (*into phone*) Stand, thanks for waiting.
ELIZABETH: Now don't all you boys be calling and begging me for heavy metal. Demetrius and I don't approve of heavy metal, do we, Demetrius?
DEMETRIUS: (*into phone*) Baseball's fine with us any time of the year.

(*DEMETRIUS writes.*)

ELIZABETH: Stand up, Jim, you're on WBZZ. (*beat*) Yeah, talk to me.
DEMETRIUS: (*into phone*) Randall, what's up?
ELIZABETH: Listen, hon—you mind me calling you that? The thing you have to worry about is consistency, right? He's impulsive, he's like a teenager, he's an adolescent playing a man's game. Like Favre at the beginning of his career.
DEMETRIUS: (*into phone*) I don't think so, Randall.
ELIZABETH: (*into mic*) With Favre, the premature ejaculation was confined to the field, but it's pretty much the same dynamic.
DEMETRIUS: (*into phone*) Because I want some time with you myself tonight.
ELIZABETH: The difference is Favre's a white boy. No off the field criminal activity for Favre.

(*DEMETRIUS looks at ELIZABETH for a clear couple seconds. The phone rings. It rings again.*)

DEMETRIUS: (*into phone*) Son, I've got to go. I'll see you later. (*beat*) I promise, by 9.

(*The phone rings again. He picks up.*)

DEMETRIUS: (*into phone*) Stand.
ELIZABETH: Yes, when he's on, he's brilliant, but if you were watching closely, you'd realize how often he suddenly starts making one mistake after another, and I mean stupid mistakes, rookie mistakes. Hey, the guy's not a rookie anymore. Face it, fella, I'm right about this. You're wrong.

(*ELIZABETH disconnects him with a flourish.*)

(*Lights up on RANDALL and CASSANDRA in RANDALL's bedroom, as lights dim on ELIZABETH and DEMETRIUS. We can still see them, but we can't hear them.*)

RANDALL: He says no.
CASSANDRA: Your father hates me.
RANDALL: He does not hate you.
CASSANDRA: He hates me because I'm white.
RANDALL: Don't talk ridiculous.
CASSANDRA: I saw a movie where this guy worked in like a Black Liberation bookstore, and he had a white girlfriend and everything, and the bookstore owner would tell him (*imitating him*) "if our race meant something to you, you'd be shootin' that white bitch."
RANDALL: Cassie. (*beat*) You're not my girlfriend.
CASSANDRA: You don't think your father thinks I'm a white bitch, do you?
RANDALL: My father doesn't talk like that.
CASSANDRA: He never lets you stay over at my house.
RANDALL: That's cause you're a female. He wouldn't let me stay over *any* girl's house. My dad wants to protect me, you know? I think it's like he's trying to protect me from myself or something like that. And anyway, my dad doesn't understand us. He doesn't have a best friend, Cassandra, he doesn't have any kind of friend. He's got buddies, not friends. They play cards and they laugh and have a few beers.
CASSANDRA: We laugh.
RANDALL: I know, that's not what I'm saying. Just look, my dad does not hate you. C'mon, call your mom and say you're staying for dinner.
CASSANDRA: Can't. My father's getting home today.
RANDALL: That's it then. You have to stay here for dinner. Call your mom and say I'll walk you home at ten.
CASSANDRA: She won't let me. He's home for Thanksgiving—big deal,

big celebration. Anyway, don't worry, he's usually okay when he first gets back in town.
RANDALL: Four days till Thanksgiving—that won't last.
CASSANDRA: I know.
RANDALL: I hate him.
CASSANDRA: I love him, I guess.
RANDALL: I keep tellin' you, that's crazy. How come you love a drunk?
CASSANDRA: (*a shrug*) I just do.
RANDALL: Well, he does not like me as much as I do not like him.
CASSANDRA: (*dramatic*) Randy?
RANDALL: (*making a little bit of fun of her*) Yes?
CASSANDRA: We've been friends since we were four or something, right?
RANDALL: (*this girl has lost her mind*) Right.
CASSANDRA: Do you think it would ever happen that we'd fall in love?
RANDALL: No.
CASSANDRA: You could never fall in love with me?
RANDALL: No. Never.
CASSANDRA: Do you think I'm pretty at least?
RANDALL: What are you talking about? I don't know.
CASSANDRA: Well thanks a lot.
RANDALL: Let me put on some music, all right?
CASSANDRA: No, I'm gonna go. I'll meet you at the pond tomorrow after school.
RANDALL: Cassie, what is it with you today? You are acting really weird.

(*CASSANDRA watches RANDALL look through his CDs for a few seconds.*)

CASSANDRA: Randy?
RANDALL: (*looking at her incredulously*) What is *up*, Cassie? Why are you not just sayin' what you got to say but instead you're sayin' my name with a big question mark? What's *up*?
CASSANDRA: (*pissed*) God, I'm sorry. For*give* me.
RANDALL: Now you're pissin' me off.

(*She picks up a CD.*)

CASSANDRA: Explain to me why you have a CD called "Bitch Better Have My Money."
RANDALL: That one of my friends gave me—

CASSANDRA: (*overlap*) Curt probably.
RANDALL: Yes, Curt, which I already told you and which I don't like much and which my daddy would kill me if he saw it so I don't even know why I keep it.
CASSANDRA: Yeah, that's what I mean, why—(*do you keep it*)
RANDALL: HOWEVER. (*pause*) This is not the first time you have seen that CD. You and I, we've already had this discussion, so I am asking you for the third time WHAT IS UP?
CASSANDRA: I started my period.
RANDALL: You mean you're bleeding?

(*CASSANDRA shakes her head "yes."*)

RANDALL: Does it hurt or something?
CASSANDRA: No. It's just messy.
RANDALL: I believe that. (*beat*) So, exactly how much blood we talkin' about?
CASSANDRA: I don't know. It's my first time.
RANDALL: Like a quart?
CASSANDRA: God, I hope not.
RANDALL: A tablespoonful—like every day?
CASSANDRA: Add one tablespoon blood to one cup orange juice, stir, start the day off right.
RANDALL: That's sick.
CASSANDRA: I don't know how much blood. All I know is I woke up this morning and it was in my underpants and all over my sheets.
RANDALL: That's disgusting.
CASSANDRA: No it's not. It's—natural.
RANDALL: I'm glad I don't have to do that bleeding.
CASSANDRA: Yeah, well. (*She can't think of anything. A beat, then—*) I'm glad I don't have to go to war.
RANDALL: That's a little different.
CASSANDRA: I guess. Different kind of blood.
RANDALL: Yeah. (*beat*) My dad did.
CASSANDRA: Yeah, I know.
RANDALL: He got shot, he got a big ol' scar.
CASSANDRA: Have you seen it?
RANDALL: Yes. It's big.
CASSANDRA: (*after a pause*) Randy? (*quickly*) Sorry.

RANDAL: That's all right. I didn't realize you were bleeding and all. It's no wonder you're behavin' so strange.

CASSANDRA: You think you could walk me home before your father comes? I know it's still early but with you know who home, and with the state my body's in, and you know, that girl got kidnapped. I'd just rather not walk home alone.

RANDALL: Certainly. That's no problem whatsoever. You want to go now, or should we have some music first? How about we have a couple of tunes, then we'll go?

(As RANDALL looks through his CDs, we hear ELIZABETH, still in dim light.)

ELIZABETH: Folks, I love our Lions as much as you do, but let's face it. They stink. Why pull punches—you think that's going to help them put points on the scoreboard? But hey, in a mere six weeks it's gonna be a new century and then who knows what could happen? World peace? The Lions sign some guys who can actually play football?

(A DMX song comes up from RANDALL's bedroom. Lights up full on ELIZABETH and DEMETRIUS. They remain up on RANDALL and CASSANDRA.)

ELIZABETH: You know, Henry, you are absolutely right. Don't ask me why, but I wasn't even thinking about how few points they've given up. Henry, I'll be damned. This may be a WBZZ first. You just may have changed Liz's mind.

(DEMETRIUS plays a tape of wild applause for a few seconds. He stops the tape, buzzes the traffic guy.)

DEMETRIUS: *(into phone)* Stand by, Chris.

ELIZABETH: Henry, West Coast fans are suffering their own tragedy. There's no question in my mind that the 49ers are over, because their fabulous and very very cute quarterback suffered still another concussion. I mean, how much of a beating can one quarterback take? *(beat)* Uh oh. Demetrius, I'm distraught. I've lost Henry's respect. Aw, Henry, what's a girl to do? Honestly, have you gotten a good look at those buns? I'm not blind for God's sake. *(beat)* I understand, Henry. Some of you callers are so so sensitive, I'll try to keep that in mind. Thanks for the call, guy, now you're going to have to go whine someplace else. This is WBZZ, you're listening to Stand with Liz Jones every evening from 5 to 8. Hey, we've got Chris Cutler with traffic coming up and then—

(*The phone rings.*)

DEMETRIUS: (*into phone*) Stand. Uh huh, well she's got an interview coming up.
ELIZABETH: (*continuing*)—an interview with one of the scariest defensive tackles in the business, so stay tuned folks.
DEMETRIUS: (*into phone, overlap*) She'll be taking calls again in about 20. (*beat*) Hey, buddy, how about you shut the fuck up? (*he buzzes*) Go, Traffic.
ELIZABETH: (*overlap, looking at DEMETRIUS*):Here's Chris Cutler.
TRAFFIC: Traffic is unusually light this evening (including at the 84/97 junction, where—)
DEMETRIUS: (*into phone*) Yes, you do have to go through me to get to her. (*beat*) Sir, you call here again, I'll call the police.

(*ELIZABETH gets up, crosses to him.*)

DEMETRIUS: I guarantee it.

(*DEMETRIUS hangs up. Music keeps playing in RANDALL's room.*)

CASSANDRA: Let's hear this bitch one, Randall.
RANDALL: What for?
CASSANDRA: Just I want to hear it. You heard it, right?
RANDALL: If you want it so bad, I'll play it when this one's over. But you are not gonna like it.

ELIZABETH: (*to Demetrius*) Same weirdo?
TRAFFIC: The threatened strike seems to have been averted—(so the busses continue to run)
DEMETRIUS: (*overlap, upset*) He keeps calling and I keep explaining that I won't put him through unless he tells me what subject he wishes to discuss, whereupon he starts in with—a whole lot of bullshit.

(*ELIZABETH touches his shoulder.*)

ELIZABETH: Who is this person, Demetrius? He's getting to you.

(DEMETRIUS pulls away from her.)

DEMETRIUS: Do you mind?
ELIZABETH: Do I mind? Yes, I mind. Demetrius. Dear.
DEMETRIUS: Tell me that was not "dear" I just heard you call me.
ELIZABETH: We've worked together for two years. Surely you can tell me what's wrong.
DEMETRIUS: Where does it say in my contract that you may put your hands on me?
ELIZABETH: Put my hands on you? Demetrius, for heaven's sake. *(beat)* Oh. OH.

RANDALL: *(putting on the other tape, to CASSANDRA)* Okay, here it goes.

ELIZABETH: I've seen you like this before. This person made a racist remark? Is that what's up your butt?
DEMETRIUS: I thought you reserved that earthy repartee for your loyal listeners.
ELIZABETH: Well, I guess you're upsetting me.

("Bitch Better Have My Money" (AMG) comes up in RANDALL's room.)

DEMETRIUS: Come to think of it, I should have put him on, the two of you could have had a nice chat about the off the field crime rate among black athletes.
ELIZABETH: What?
DEMETRIUS: What about Bret Favre's over-the-counter drug abuse? That wasn't criminal activity?
ELIZABETH: I'm not following you.
DEMETRIUS: Forget it.
ELIZABETH: Forget what? *(pause, sigh)*: Okay, have it your way. But I'm right, he called you - (some racist name, didn't he?)
DEMETRIUS: You're always right, yeah.
ELIZABETH: *(another tack)* So. How does he know you're black?
DEMETRIUS: I don't know.
ELIZABETH: What did he say?
DEMETRIUS: None of your business.
ELIZABETH: I beg to differ.

DEMETRIUS: You can beg and plead all you want. (*chuckles*) My racial slurs are mine. You can't have 'em.

CASSANDRA: (*to RANDALL*) This song is disgusting.
RANDALL: Yeah, I know. How 'bout I turn it off?
CASSANDRA: No, I want to hear it. (*beat*) So I can know what I'm up against.
RANDALL: You know they're singing about black girls.
CASSANDRA: So?
RANDALL: So nothin'. So I'm just tellin' you, I'm just remindin' you. Cassie, you are in a bad mood, you know?
CASSANDRA: I guess. (*She turns off "Bitch Better Have My Money."*) What else have you got?

(*She opens his CD drawer. He starts to protest, but too late.*)

CASSANDRA: (*beat*) Randy?
RANDALL: Don't start with me now.
CASSANDRA: There's a gun in here.

(*Silence.*)

CASSANDRA: Randy, did you hear me? I found a gun.
RANDALL: What about it?
CASSANDRA: What do you mean, what about it? Are you nuts? Is this your gun?
RANDALL: Yeah, it's mine.
CASSANDRA: Where'd you get it?

DEMETRIUS: (*to ELIZABETH*) Your interview's on line two.
ELIZABETH: I have two commercials before the interview. What did the caller say?
DEMETRIUS: He's an asshole. Let's leave it at that.
ELIZABETH: What did the asshole say?

(*The phone rings.*)

DEMETRIUS: (*answering*) Stand.

CASSANDRA: Did you steal it?
RANDALL: Come on, you know I don't steal.

DEMETRIUS (*into phone, overlap*): She'll be back on in about 20 minutes. (*beat*) 20 minutes, yeah.

(*CASSANDRA takes the gun out of the drawer.*)

CASSANDRA: I'm taking it to your father.
RANDALL: What are you talking about? Cassie, put that down, it's loaded.

(*CASSANDRA drops the gun on the bed.*)

CASSANDRA: It's LOADED?
RANDALL: Don't be throwin' that around.

(*DEMETRIUS hangs up, works with the tape player.*)

(*RANDALL picks up the gun and puts it away.*)

RANDALL: (*after a beat*) I didn't steal it. I bought it. I need the gun, all right? Let it go.
CASSANDRA: (*overlap*) What for?
RANDALL: For protection. Come on, Cassie, you know everybody's got 'em. Luke's had one since he was 10.
CASSANDRA: Luke's a gangster, Luke's sick.
RANDALL: You're not in high school yet, you don't understand what it's like, all right? Kids carry 'em at school. If there's an argument, they bring 'em out. I've seen 'em. Look, you can't tell my dad.

(*Silence. ELIZABETH still stands looking at DEMETRIUS, her arms folded, then a big sigh and she approaches him.*)

ELIZABETH: Demetrius. Whatever I said, you took it the wrong way.
DEMETRIUS: Get ready.

CASSANDRA: It's not like we live in the city, Randy. You don't need it.
RANDALL: I need it. Curt got robbed on the way home first day of school, dude put a gun in his face. Some psycho comes into school firing, I'm not

laying down, I'm protecting myself. I don't know about you, but I want to do my best to get older.

(A couple beats, then CASSANDRA sits down on his bed, upset.)

CASSANDRA: But there's not really anything we can do about that. Don't you know that?

(RANDALL sits beside her.)

RANDALL: Yeah, but I don't want to think that. (*beat*) I do think it, but I don't want to think it. So that's why I have the gun, see?

(ELIZABETH continues to stand beside DEMETRIUS and not sit at her microphone.)

DEMETRIUS: The man and I have had the same conversation four times today. The guy claims he's got something he can say only to you and I tell him he's not getting on the air unless he tells me what he wants, and then he starts making unkind remarks about my skin color. You know I have no sense of humor.
ELIZABETH: What the hell, put him on the air.
DEMETRIUS: No.
ELIZABETH: I can handle this jerk off, put him through.
DEMETRIUS: Absolutely not.
ELIZABETH: If he starts in with that crap on the air—(he'll be sorry)
DEMETRIUS: He won't. I'm not putting him through.
ELIZABETH: Come on, let me have a crack at him.
DEMETRIUS: Did I tell you to get ready?
ELIZABETH: I'm ready. Look, maybe if I talk to him, he'll cease and desist.
DEMETRIUS: Then you talk to him off the air. I make it a policy to refuse to give certain kinds of assholes a public forum.
ELIZABETH: It would make a great show. Come on, you know I'll murder him.
DEMETRIUS: Whose decision is this?
ELIZABETH: You are being unreasonable.
DEMETRIUS: Whose decision?
ELIZABETH: You better stay on my good side. One day I am going to have a nationally syndicated television show and if you're nice to me—

DEMETRIUS: (*overlap*) I don't doubt it.
ELIZABETH: And if you are very, very nice to me, I'll take you with me.
DEMETRIUS: If you're smart you'll take me with you, and you're smart, so I'm not going to give it another thought.
ELIZABETH: You are so damn stubborn, you know that?

CASSANDRA: (*to RANDALL*) I'm ready to go.

ELIZABETH: All right, the next time he calls, tell him to hold. I'll take him during a commercial.
DEMETRIUS: (*to ELIZABETH*) You've got it.

CASSANDRA: You said you'd walk me home.

(*RANDALL stops the tape as DEMETRIUS brings up the Beatles' "Run For Your Life" and ELIZABETH sits at the microphone.*)

(*RANDALL and CASSANDRA exit. Lights fade.*)

(*Music up—"She's No Lady, She's My Wife" (Lyle Lovett). Then lights up on ELIZABETH and DEMETRIUS.*)

ELIZABETH: This is Liz Jones back with you on the Peninsula's ONLY sports talk show. That was a beautiful sentiment from Lyle Lovett to start this segment—she's my wife, that's why I hate her. Thank you, Demetrius.

(*Phone rings.*)

ELIZABETH: Let's go to Jerry on line 4.
DEMETRIUS: (*answering the phone*) Stand.
ELIZABETH: How 'bout it, Jerry? How'd you like that lovely Lyle Lovett snippet?
DEMETRIUS: (*into phone*) She wants you to hold. (*beat*) Yeah, that's what she said. (*pause*) Is there a word in there you don't understand? She wants you to hold.

(*DEMETRIUS puts the caller on hold.*)

ELIZABETH: (*to DEMETRIUS*) Jerry says who the hell's Lyle Lovett and furthermore, he called to talk sports, not music, have I got that right, Jer? He's only got a few working brain cells so he has to save them all up and spend them on one and only one subject. (*beat, then repeating what he just said*) And he hates that country music. Jerry, you know what happens to callers who criticize my Demetrius' taste in music, don't you? Flush this guy, Demetrius.

(*Phone rings. DEMETRIUS plays the "flush" tape.*)

DEMETRIUS: Your wish is my command. (*answering*) Stand. (*to ELIZABETH*) Go to commercial. (*into phone*) What can I do for you?

(*DEMETRIUS writes.*)

ELIZABETH: (*into mic*) Folks, please refrain from calling unless all your cylinders are firing. Is that too much to ask? I'll be right back with you, but stay tuned, especially if you have a special occasion coming up because believe me, trust me, Common Ground bakes the best cakes in the Western hemisphere.

(*ELIZABETH is off the air. She stands up, stretches.*)

DEMETRIUS: (*into phone*) I'll put you through now. (*beat*) Hello? Hello?

(*The caller's gone. DEMETRIUS hangs up.*)

ELIZABETH: (*begins snapping, then singing*)
With a pink hotel
A boutique
And a swinging hot spot.
Don't it always seem to go
That you don't what you've got till it's gone?

(*Wrong note. She looks at DEMETRIUS. He shakes his head.*)

ELIZABETH: (*singing*) Gone. (*wrong note*) Gone. (*wrong note*)
DEMETRIUS: Give it up.
ELIZABETH: Who asked you? (*pause*) I was going to be a singer once you know.

DEMETRIUS: Whatever you say.
ELIZABETH: I can sing. Anyway, I could deliver a song. I had a lot of personality.
DEMETRIUS: Uh huh. Let's see a little of that personality. In about a minute.

(The phone rings.)

DEMETRIUS: *(into phone)* Stand. *(beat)* I thought I had you on hold someplace. Oh, it's an emergency. Yeah, I understand, uh huh, you urgently need to speak to her.
ELIZABETH: I'll take it.
DEMETRIUS: *(into phone)* Hold the line. *(to ELIZABETH)* Take it fast.

(ARNOLD enters and stands very near her—he is not at the radio station. He's on the phone.)

ELIZABETH: *(into phone)* This is Liz Jones.
ARNOLD: Hello. Liz?
ELIZABETH: That's what I said. What the hell do you want?
ARNOLD: Do you mind that I called?
ELIZABETH: I mind that you've been insulting my producer all evening.
ARNOLD: *(pissed)* I was going to talk to you about Courtney Kaufman.
ELIZABETH: Who's that?
ARNOLD: Forget it.

(ARNOLD hangs up and exits.)

ELIZABETH *(to DEMETRIUS)*: He's gone.
DEMETRIUS: Forever, I hope. Get ready.

(ELIZABETH sits at the microphone. DEMETRIUS points to her.)

ELIZABETH: *(into mic)* Okay, we have another half hour to take your phone calls. Liz will talk about anything that tickles your sports lovers' fancy. The basketball season's in full swing. Our Pistons have won as many as they've lost. Hey, it's been worse. We had a couple of terrific upsets in the NFL last weekend.

(The phone rings.)

DEMETRIUS: Stand.
ELIZABETH: I'll even talk baseball as long as I don't have to listen to anybody whine about those poor taken advantage of billionaire owners. And hey, here's tomorrow's question. Name a super bowl championship team with a so-so quarterback. The lines are open.

(She glances at DEMETRIUS.)

DEMETRIUS: Rich on one. Umpires' strike.
ELIZABETH: We're going to Rich on line one, and we all know he's had a lot of experience standing up to Liz. Rich, you're on WBZZ. Go ahead, tell me I told you so.

(RANDALL enters quickly.)

RANDALL: Hey, Dad.
DEMETRIUS: What're you doin' here, Randall? You got your homework done?
RANDALL: I don't have any homework.
DEMETRIUS: Don't you try to get over on me.
RANDALL: I wouldn't, Daddy.
DEMETRIUS: You mean you know you couldn't so you're smart enough not to push your luck. (*buzzes*) Jack, stand by.
RANDALL: (*overlap*) Yeah. I had to walk Cassie home cause her daddy's back in town.
DEMETRIUS: Too bad.
RANDALL: Yeah. So, I figured you get off soon, I'll come on over, we can get us some pizza.
DEMETRIUS: That's a definite possibility.
ELIZABETH: (*in the middle of a harangue*) YOU HAVE SERIOUSLY GOT TO BE KIDDING. You repeat that opinion around town, they're going to haul you off and lock you up in a padded room.
RANDALL: How come she gets so excited?
DEMETRIUS: That's her job.

(RANDALL crosses to ELIZABETH.)

RANDALL: Hi, Lizzie.

(*ELIZABETH waves to him; she is listening to her caller. RANDALL crosses back to DEMETRIUS.*)

ELIZABETH: Yeah, you better change the subject. Players have the right to strike, but umpires don't? Rich, what are you thinking? (*She listens.*) Uh huh.
RANDALL: I've got to ask you a favor.
DEMETRIUS: Go on.
RANDALL: It's a big one.
ELIZABETH: (*overlap*) You are just full of idiotic opinions today, Rich. One guy's got his nose between another guy's legs, if that's not encroachment, what is it? Love?
DEMETRIUS: (*to RANDALL*) Well?
RANDALL: Would you show Cassie your scar from the war?

(*The phone rings. DEMETRIUS buzzes.*)

DEMETRIUS: (*into phone*) Go News. Stand. Uh huh. What's on your mind?
ELIZABETH: (*to DEMETRIUS*) Have you seen my United Airlines copy? Hi, Randall.
NEWS BROADCAST: . . . search continues for Courtney—(Kaufman)
ELIZABETH: (*overlap*) I know your father told you I don't like to be called Lizzie.
RANDALL: No, he didn't.
ELIZABETH: No, he probably didn't.
RANDALL: Why don't you?
NEWS BROADCAST: . . . of cocaine confiscated from a seventh grader's locker at Chippewa Middle School—(in the second such seizure)
ELIZABETH: You know the way your father becomes unglued if I call you Randy?
RANDALL: If anybody calls me Randy.
ELIZABETH: My father felt the same way about my name because he named me Elizabeth, the most beautiful name in the world.
RANDALL: What about your mom?
ELIZABETH: My mother?
RANDALL: You said your daddy named you, and I'm sayin' what about your mother?

ELIZABETH: My mother named me too.
RANDALL: My mother's dead.
ELIZABETH: Mine is too.
NEWS BROADCAST: . . . Dow Jones Industrial closed up 110 points making this the third day in a row the Dow has enjoyed an increase of over 100 points.
RANDALL: (*overlap*) I was three, daddy says.
ELIZABETH: I was seven.
DEMETRIUS: (*handing it to her*) United Airlines.
ELIZABETH: Thank you.
RANDALL: I don't remember mine. Do you?
ELIZABETH: Yes. (*changing the subject*) What are you guys up to for Thanksgiving?
RANDALL: Pies. My dad always makes pies. You should come. He makes good pies.
ELIZABETH: I honor a long-standing Thanksgiving tradition at my house. The Lions on national television.
RANDALL: Bet Chicago kills them.

(*The phone rings.*)

ELIZABETH: Bite your tongue. (*to DEMETRIUS*) Are you not teaching this child anything important, such as we stick with our lousy football team come hell or high water?
DEMETRIUS: (*into phone*) Stand.
RANDALL: My dad says you were a basketball player.
ELIZABETH: Yup. I was a basketball player with a beautiful name.
DEMETRIUS: (*to ELIZABETH*) He's back on the line.
RANDALL: I play volleyball.
ELIZABETH: I know. (*pointing to DEMETRIUS*) He told me.
RANDALL: And I coach it. I coach girls.
ELIZABETH: That's admirable, Randall. Good for you.
DEMETRIUS: (*to ELIZABETH*) You taking this call and getting this guy off my back?
ELIZABETH: Excuse me, Randall.

(*She picks up the phone. ARNOLD enters and stands very near her, as before.*)

ELIZABETH: (*into phone*) You spend most of the evening trying to get

through to me, then you hang up. I've got to tell you, that's not the way to Liz's heart.
ARNOLD: I'm sorry, but I don't want you to defend him. He's been rude to me.
ELIZABETH: Exactly what is it you do want?
ARNOLD: I want to talk about Courtney Kaufman.
ELIZABETH: (*into phone*) And who the hell is that? Let me guess, some Division 2 basketball player, right?
ARNOLD: (*don't be silly*) No. She's only 12.
ELIZABETH: (*into phone*) Look, guy, I've had a long day, who the hell is Courtney Kaufman?
ARNOLD: (*beat, confused*) You're joking with me, right?
DEMETRIUS: (*overlap*) Courtney Kaufman?
ELIZABETH: (*overlap, into phone*) You're boring me. What's your name?
ARNOLD: It's all over the news.
DEMETRIUS: Elizabeth, who is that?
ELIZABETH: (*into phone*): What's your name?
DEMETRIUS: Elizabeth—(*tell me who that is*)
ELIZABETH: (*into phone*) Hold the line. (*to Demetrius, as in "what the hell do you want"*) WHAT?
DEMETRIUS: Courtney Kaufman's the kid who was kidnapped this morning.
ARNOLD: (*overlap*) She's the girl who was abducted this morning.
ELIZABETH: (*into phone*) Who is this?
DEMETRIUS: (*overlap*) Who is that?

(*ARNOLD hangs up. He exits.*)

DEMETRIUS: What was that about?
ELIZABETH: He wanted to talk about Courtney Kaufman.
DEMETRIUS: He didn't say why?
ELIZABETH: He hung up when he heard your voice. I don't think he likes you.
DEMETRIUS: You're breaking my heart.
ELIZABETH: Play some pretty music for me, will you, Demetrius?

(*As she walks to the microphone, he puts on "No One in the World" (Anita Baker). After a couple measures, Elizabeth sings along, prettily. Once she starts to sing, the phone rings. DEMETRIUS picks it up, and it rings again immediately.*)

DEMETRIUS: (*answering*): Stand, hold the line. (*He picks up the other line.*) Stand. Yeah, she'll be taking calls in a minute. Right now she's singing.
ELIZABETH: (*into mic*) Anita Baker. Isn't that pretty? Welcome back to Stand.

(*DEMETRIUS plays a couple of measures of "Stand".*)

ELIZABETH:—with Liz Jones. Let's go to John in Mt. Vernon. Stand up, John.
RANDALL: Dad, you haven't answered my question.
DEMETRIUS: (*covering the mouthpiece, to RANDALL*) I'm on the phone.
ELIZABETH: (*into mic*) So, what's your point, John? Oh, women don't belong—that's a favorite word of mine, John, don't you love that word, BE - LONG? John, I'm getting literary on you, forgive me. You were saying? (*beat*) Oh, yes, women don't BELONG in the old football locker room. Or in sports journalism at all because—(*beat, then repeating what the caller said*) Women don't play sports. (*pause*) John, has your IQ been tested recently? I'm only asking because I realize how many Americans struggle through life with a learning disability. (*beat*) Oh. I see. Demetrius, my caller wonders whether I have a boyfriend.
DEMETRIUS: Don't we all?
ELIZABETH: (*into mic*) Oh. Pardon me. John doesn't wonder. He's certain I could not possibly have a boyfriend, because if I did, I'd have a different attitude.
DEMETRIUS: Fat chance.

(*Sound of a big flush. ELIZABETH looks in surprise at DEMETRIUS, who shrugs.*)

ELIZABETH: What can I say, folks?

(*Phone rings.*)

DEMETRIUS: (*into phone*) Stand, what's up?
ELIZABETH: There are certain things my producer will not stand for.

(*DEMETRIUS plays "Stand" for a couple measures.*)

ELIZABETH: I can take one more before we call it a night.

(She looks at DEMETRIUS.)

DEMETRIUS: Clint. College football death threat.
ELIZABETH: Clint, you're on WBZZ, talk to me.

(Phone rings. ARNOLD enters.)

DEMETRIUS: *(into phone)* Stand.
ARNOLD: Do you know who that guy was?
DEMETRIUS: *(into phone)* No, I do not know who—that guy was.
ARNOLD: Do you know why he asked her about her boyfriend?
DEMETRIUS: *(into phone)* No, I do not know why he asked about her boyfriend. Don't you listen to the show?
ELIZABETH: *(into mic)* Yeah, did you <u>hear</u> about that?
ARNOLD: *(overlap)* I listen to the show every day.
DEMETRIUS: *(into phone)* Well, then, you heard what he said.
ARNOLD: Don't let people talk to her like that.
DEMETRIUS: Hey, he was just some weird guy. You know what I'm sayin'? Some weird guy?

(ARNOLD hangs up and exits.)

DEMETRIUS: Good talking to you.
ELIZABETH: *(into mic)* Clint, I know it. You are so right.
RANDALL: *(overlap)* Dad!
DEMETRIUS: Randall, why do you think Cassandra, in her wildest young lady dreams, would want to see my scar?
ELIZABETH: *(turning to them, covering the mic)* SHHH!
DEMETRIUS: What makes you think a little girl wants to see a big man's scar?
RANDALL: It's just that—she thinks you hate her.

(Phone rings.)

DEMETRIUS *(to RANDALL)*: I see. Showing her my scar will appear to her to be a sign of affection. *(into phone)* Stand. *(beat)* No, we're done for today.

(DEMETRIUS starts up "Mr. Wendell" (Arrested Development).)

ELIZABETH: *(into mic)* There is nobody, I mean nobody on this green earth, who loves and adores sports more than Liz Jones but, Clint, you tell me, a coach loses a game and his wife and child receive a death threat? What is that? Would you mind telling me, what is that?
RANDALL: *(referring to the music, delighted)* Hey, daddy.
DEMETRIUS: *(into phone)* The game's Thursday afternoon. Uh huh.
ELIZABETH: This guy's got to put his family in hiding, Clint. Hey, everybody, listen up, Liz has something to tell you.
DEMETRIUS: *(into phone)* Yeah, you call tomorrow. She'll be here.
ELIZABETH: IT'S JUST A GAME. *(beat)* With any luck at all, the Feds'll apprehend this crazy person. Death threats against the families of college football coaches. Would somebody out there tell me, what does that mean?
DEMETRIUS: *(he's late for the traffic report)* Shit.

(He fades out Arrested Development, fades in "Stand". Buzzes.)

DEMETRIUS: *(into phone)* Stand by, 10 seconds. *(couple beats)* Hey, Don't bust my balls. *(beat)* Yeah? Well, buy yourself a watch.
ELIZABETH: Thanks for the call, Clint, and that's it from Liz Jones and Stand. Come on, boys, get up off those tushes.
RANDALL: Dad?
ELIZABETH: *(a half-shout)* You've been sitting much too long.

(DEMETRIUS increases volume. A few more measures of "Stand" play.)

RANDALL: Dad?

(DEMETRIUS buzzes.)

DEMETRIUS: Go, Traffic.
ELIZABETH: Demetrius, you flushed of your own volition.
TRAFFIC: A big rig overturned on—(the Springville Road overpass)
ELIZABETH: Aren't you the one who keeps telling me to stop this flushing thing, it's not dignified, it's beneath us.
DEMETRIUS: Yeah. Well, you set a terrible example.
ELIZABETH: Are we still in a snit?

DEMETRIUS: We?
RANDALL: C'mon, Dad, I think it would mean a lot to her.
DEMETRIUS: Randall, I am not going to show your little girlfriend my scar.
RANDALL: She's not my girlfriend.
ELIZABETH: (*overlap*) Your father is particularly touchy about his body today, Randall.
DEMETRIUS: You want to wait for me outside, son?
RANDALL: No.
DEMETRIUS: Now. I'll be right there.
TRAFFIC: . . . 2-car injury accident—(blocking lane 2)
RANDALL: C'mon, Dad, don't bust my balls.
DEMETRIUS: (*scolding*) Hey!
RANDALL: Cassie's not my girlfriend.
DEMETRIUS: Go on.
RANDALL: (*as he exits*) She's not my girlfriend.
TRAFFIC: . . . 7-mile back-up on northbound I 94—(since about an hour ago)
ELIZABETH: (*to DEMETRIUS*) My turn to be scolded?
DEMETRIUS: Let me explain something to you if you don't mind.
ELIZABETH: Explain. Please.
DEMETRIUS: We are not friends.
ELIZABETH: Oh. (*beat*) I thought we were.
DEMETRIUS: We're not. We're co-workers. You're the host. I'm the producer. I'm the producer on both the morning show and your show—as opposed to being your personal property. Do we understand each other?
ELIZABETH: I think not. I merely put my hand on your shoulder. You became entirely undone. Demetrius, I apologized, for what I don't know. How on earth can a remark I don't even remember constitute "we're not friends?"
DEMETRIUS: I don't want to cuddle with you, all right?

(*The phone rings.*)

ELIZABETH: Cuddle?
DEMETRIUS: (*into phone*) Stand. (*beat*) Yeah. (*He puts the caller on hold; to ELIZABETH, pointing to phone*) That's him.

(*ARNOLD enters and stands near her, as before.*)

ELIZABETH: First of all, I placed my hand gingerly on your shoulder. Secondly, how could you use the word (*disgusted*) "cuddle" in reference to me?

(*DEMETRIUS starts to shut down the sound board.*)

ELIZABETH: I touch. I make flailing attempts to reassure. I even hug occasionally.
DEMETRIUS: You might give some thought to what comes out of your mouth instead of saying whatever pops into your head. That way, you might remember what you say on the air.

(*ELIZABETH picks up the phone.*)

ELIZABETH: Your point notwithstanding, I do not "cuddle." (*into phone*) The show's over. You want to talk about Courtney Kaufman. I don't. Does that settle that?
ARNOLD: The reason for my call is to find out if you want to help this little girl.
ELIZABETH: (*into phone*) What are you talking about?
ARNOLD: I know where she is.
ELIZABETH: (*into phone*) Then you want to talk to the police.
ARNOLD: No, Liz, I want to talk to you. Don't you want to help this little girl?
ELIZABETH: (*into phone*) How do you know where she is?
ARNOLD: I took her.

(*ELIZABETH puts her hand over the receiver, speaks to Demetrius.*)

ELIZABETH: He says he took her.

(*DEMETRIUS dials out on the 1-line phone on ELIZABETH's desk.*)

ARNOLD: She's sitting beside me. Would you like to speak to her?
ELIZABETH: (*into phone, quickly*) No.
ARNOLD: I'm saying you can speak to her if you like.
DEMETRIUS: (*into phone*) I need to talk to somebody about Courtney Kaufman.
ELIZABETH: (*into phone, overlap*) What am I going to say to her?

ARNOLD: Never mind then. I thought you might like to speak to her.
ELIZABETH: (*into phone*) It's not that I don't want to speak to her.
RANDALL: (*entering*) Dad?
ARNOLD: I'll put her on.
DEMETRIUS: (*into phone*) Yeah, I need to speak to somebody about—. Yes, I'll hold. (*to RANDALL*) Wait outside, Randall. Not outside the building. In the green room.

(*ARNOLD brings COURTNEY onstage.*)

RANDALL: (*as COURTNEY enters*) Daddy, let's go, I'm hungry.
DEMETRIUS: Randall, wait in the goddamn green room.
ARNOLD: (*to COURTNEY*) Say hello.
RANDALL: (*overlap, as he exits*) You don't have to yell.

(*COURTNEY starts to cry.*)

ARNOLD: Don't cry. Say hello.
COURTNEY: Hello.
ELIZABETH: (*into phone*):Hello. (*beat*) Is this Courtney?
COURTNEY: Yes.
DEMETRIUS: I'm at WBZZ radio station, we have a guy on the phone says he's got Courtney Kaufman.
COURTNEY: Can I talk to my mom?
ELIZABETH: Um. Courtney, your mom's not here.
COURTNEY: Can you help me?
ELIZABETH: I don't—. (*She doesn't know what to say.*) Courtney—.

(*Pause. COURTNEY starts to cry again.*)

ELIZABETH: Yes, I can. I can help you.

(*ELIZABETH puts down the phone, turns to ARNOLD. They are both still on the phone, but they face each other and speak directly to one another.*)

DEMETRIUS: I'm telling you, he's been calling here all day.
ELIZABETH: Courtney?
ARNOLD: Hello. Liz?
ELIZABETH: Where did she go?

ARNOLD: She's sitting right beside me here. I can't stay on long because I have to give her some dinner.
ELIZABETH: Why did you call me?
ARNOLD: I wanted to ask about the Eagles chances in the playoffs. (*Long pause.*) Well? (*Another long pause.*) The Eagles chances in the playoffs?
ELIZABETH: Good. I think they're good.
ARNOLD: You think a new quarterback can take them to the playoffs?
ELIZABETH: (*not knowing what he wants to hear*) That depends.
DEMETRIUS: (*into phone*) Yes, fine, I'll hold.
ELIZABETH: They've got some great rookies and—
ARNOLD: You don't hold it against me that I'm still an Eagles fan, right? You understand about fans if anyone does. I grew up in Philadelphia so of course my heart's still there. And why should I root for the Lions when they do nothing but let me down year after year. Right?
ELIZABETH: Absolutely right.
ARNOLD: When Cunningham was there? Man, he had the most brittle bones in all of football. Injury. Injury. Injury. INJURY. It was so disheartening, and then what's he do? He takes the Vikings to the Super Bowl. (*pretty angry*) He never took the Eagles to the Super Bowl. (*calming down*) He had to do what was best for him. That's understandable. That's what we all do. (*beat*) So I start thinking I'll call you, but I don't because—well, you're famous and I figured I'd be tongue-tied, and then there's the other problem, the problem of your co-worker. But then I'm thinking it over and I'm—you know, I'm arguing with myself. I'm sayin' after all, she's awfully smart, she knows things, get her opinion. That might really put your mind at ease. (*beat*) And then earlier today it came to me, because I've got a third problem. I've got Courtney. If I kill her, that's one solution. That would be my only choice if you involve that nigger or the cops. (*beat*) Or if she cries too much, because then I can't think. (*beat*) But then I realized I could solve both my problems at one time. We'll arrange a place to meet and talk about the Eagles' chances. And then I'll give you Courtney. (*couple beats*) Will you come? (*beat*) Liz? Will you come? (*beat*) You have to come. If you don't come, I'll kill Courtney.
DEMETRIUS: (*into phone*) Look, how many people am I gonna have to tell this? We have a guy on the phone—(*for the 10th time*) Demetrius Washington. I'm a producer at WBZZ radio.
ARNOLD: I'll call you tomorrow, Liz, and we'll arrange a meeting. Right now, I'll give Courtney dinner and then we'll find a place to stay tonight.
ELIZABETH: Wait.

ARNOLD: It's no good to trace the call because number one, we'll be leaving here and number two, if you do, I'll kill Courtney.
ELIZABETH: No, I have a question.
ARNOLD: Go ahead.
ELIZABETH: Is this the first time you've—
ARNOLD: Yes. Today. First time caller.
ELIZABETH: No. (*beat*) Have you ever killed a person?
ARNOLD: Yes.
ELIZABETH: A child?
ARNOLD: That depends. People have different ideas about how long childhood lasts.

(*ARNOLD hangs up. ELIZABETH hangs up. ARNOLD and COURTNEY exit. DEMETRIUS hangs up.*)

DEMETRIUS: They've received hundreds of calls. If we want to make a statement, we have to go down to the station.
ELIZABETH: He wants me to meet him. He says he'll turn Courtney over to me.
DEMETRIUS: We'll tell it all to the cops.
ELIZABETH: I don't know. I have to think about . . . (*She is shaking.*) If we involve the police, he'll kill that kid.
DEMETRIUS: This is a crazy fucked up guy, Elizabeth, you cannot—(try to handle this situation on your own.)
ELIZABETH: I think if the police get involved, it will make her situation worse.
DEMETRIUS: How do you figure that?
ELIZABETH: That's what he said. He wants to meet me. He'll keep her alive so he can meet me.
DEMETRIUS: What are you telling me? You're considering going to meet this lunatic? (*beat*) Elizabeth? Tell me you are not considering—(going to meet him.)
ELIZABETH: This is not your call, Demetrius.
DEMETRIUS: You're not umpiring a baseball game.
ELIZABETH: Please. He's trying to put this child's life in my hands.
DEMETRIUS: Don't let him. I'm going to the police station. You can come with me or not.
ELIZABETH: No, Demetrius. He referred to you specifically. Stay out of it.
DEMETRIUS: Forget that.

ELIZABETH: Demetrius, he's been baiting you all day, he warned me on the phone to keep you out of it. The guy's not just an asshole, he's a racist asshole.
RANDALL: (*entering*) Dad, we goin'?
ELIZABETH: I think you should take Randall home.
DEMETRIUS: I will go to the police station. Then I will take my son home.
RANDALL: Police station?
DEMETRIUS: Son, come on over here.

(*RANDALL goes to him. DEMETRIUS pulls RANDALL to him, keeps his arms around him.*)

RANDALL: Daddy, what's goin' on?
DEMETRIUS: We've got a situation here, Randall. We got a strange phone call, and we have to—(go down to the police station.)
ELIZABETH: How can I get this across to you? The man said if you involve that nigger, I'll kill—

(*DEMETRIUS and RANDALL both look hard at her. She stops abruptly.*)

ELIZABETH: Don't look at me like that. That's exactly what he said, so why don't you take your kid home? (*beat*) An hour. Give me an hour.
RANDALL: (*scared*) Daddy, let's go. Let's go home.
DEMETRIUS: (*to ELIZABETH*) This guy's not one of your run of the mill callers, you can't just flush him when he gets on your nerves. Don't you make a bad decision and hurt that little girl.
ELIZABETH: Likewise I'm sure, so get the hell out of here because guess what? I think this guy might really kill people, and guess what else? He doesn't like black folks.
RANDALL: Daddy.
ELIZABETH: He said he would kill her if you were involved, so I'm not endangering her right now, you're endangering her right now, so get out.

(*Long pause*)

DEMETRIUS: I'll talk to you in one hour.
ELIZABETH: Go.
DEMETRIUS: One hour, or I'll go down there myself.
ELIZABETH: Go.

(DEMETRIUS and RANDALL exit. ELIZABETH stands still for a moment, then turns out the lights. After a couple beats, COURTNEY appears.)

COURTNEY: *(a sob)* Can you help me?

BLACKOUT

ACT II

(The stage is dark. Lights come up dim on the radio station. ELIZABETH sits in semi-darkness. The clock reads 9:45.

On another part of the stage, RANDELL and DEMETRIUS at home, watching TV. DEMETRIUS dials a phone.)

DEMETRIUS: *(on the phone)* Elizabeth, pick up if you're there.
RANDALL: Dad? *(beat)* Dad?

(DEMETRIUS hangs up.)

RANDALL: Can we try it? 'Cause I really hate that taste. It reminds me of that nasty egg nog.
DEMETRIUS: If it doesn't have nutmeg, it's not an apple pie.
RANDALL: Let's experiment just this once. Okay?
DEMETRIUS: I'll think it over.

(Loud knocking on their door. RANDALL gets up to answer it.)

DEMETRIUS: I'll get it.

(He exits. COURTNEY enters the radio station, her hands tied behind her back.)

COURTNEY: *(a whisper)* Can you help me?

(Several beats, then COURTNEY exits. DEMETRIUS returns.)

DEMETRIUS: It's your friend Cassandra.

RANDALL: Where is she?
DEMETRIUS: She won't come in. I told her you couldn't go outside this time of night and she said could you just stand inside the kitchen and talk to her. No mention of the scar.

(RANDALL gets up and walks to the edge of the stage. DEMETRIUS watches the news.)

RANDALL: *(to CASSANDRA, who is off)* Cassie? What's up? *(beat)* Cassie, come on in here. *(beat)* Come on, is this about that whole do I think you're pretty thing? Because if you knew how some of the dudes talk about you, you wouldn't bring up that kind of question. *(beat)* Like, they all want to know am I porkin' you and if not, then why do I want to be spendin' time with you? 'Cause with you and me it's not about pretty, Cassie, and you know, sex isn't much anyhow. It goes by so fast you hardly know you had it.

(CASSANDRA flies into the room.)

CASSANDRA: You've had sex?

(pause)

RANDALL: Just one time.
CASSANDRA: I can't believe you didn't tell me.
RANDALL: Well. It's a little bit personal.

(CASSANDRA shoves him.)

CASSANDRA: I'm your best friend.
RANDALL: Yeah you are. So what are you doing standing outside acting like an idiot?
CASSANDRA: I'm afraid your father's mad.
RANDALL: Mad about what?
CASSANDRA: I don't know. It's late.
RANDALL: You got to stop mixing up my father with your father, all right?

(CASSANDRA and RANDALL enter the room where DEMETRIUS sits.)

NEWS ON TV: Police have received dozens of calls from—(people who believe they've seen Courtney Kaufman)—
RANDALL: Standing outside my door. Cassie, sometimes you're just ridiculous.
NEWS ON TV:—but so far no leads have panned out. At this point, the authorities have no clear picture of the kidnapper, and the possibility that they will be able to find the white car described by Courtney Kaufman's neighbors grows more remote.
CASSANDRA: That girl who got kidnapped. She's dead.
RANDALL: You don't know that.
CASSANDRA: Sure. She's dead, or else she'd be back by now or somebody would have found her or something.

(DEMETRIUS turns off the TV.)

DEMETRIUS: Why are you talking like that?
CASSANDRA: I just don't think everyone should get their hopes all up. They're always dead.
DEMETRIUS: That is a very defeatist attitude for someone so young.
CASSANDRA: Sorry.
RANDALL: Daddy—(you just don't understand Cassie.)
DEMETRIUS: Have you ever seen anybody dead?
CASSANDRA: No.
DEMETRIUS: Never?
CASSANDRA: No.
DEMETRIUS: Think about it. How about at a funeral?
CASSANDRA: No.
RANDALL: Daddy, we're gonna go on into my room.
DEMETRIUS: I've seen a lot of people dead.
CASSANDRA: I know.
DEMETRIUS: You don't want to wish somebody dead.
RANDALL: Daddy, she's not.
CASSANDRA: (*overlap*) No, I don't. (*beat*) I guess I better go home.
DEMETRIUS: Why'd you come here tonight?
CASSANDRA: Not to wish anybody dead, Mr. Washington.
DEMETRIUS: I know that was not your intention. (*beat*) I believe the more positive our thoughts, the better it will be for that kidnapped child. If she's already dead, our thoughts can only lift her spirit higher. If she's not, the more positive, the more joyful, our thoughts, the better.

CASSANDRA: Joyful?
DEMETRIUS: It only stands to reason. Which might be better for her, thousands of people thinking and saying she's dead, or thousands of people thinking there's hope?
CASSANDRA: Did you think that way in the war?
DEMETRIUS: No. Only the rarest, luckiest of us had hope there.
CASSANDRA: Then you changed your mind?
DEMETRIUS: Then I changed my mind.
CASSANDRA: But then, if we think positive—(*She waits, collects her thoughts.*) Then our hearts might get broken.
DEMETRIUS: That's the trick.
CASSANDRA: It's a good one.
RANDALL: (*seeing Dad and CASSANDRA hitting it off*) Can Cassie stay here tonight?
DEMETRIUS: (*to CASSANDRA*) Do your parents know where you are?
CASSANDRA: I told them I was staying over a girlfriend's house. They don't like Randall that much. They pretend they don't mind that we hang out together, but I can tell they do.
RANDALL: They don't fool me. I can tell.
CASSANDRA: Let's face it. I'm white, Randall's black.
DEMETRIUS: Your parents are somewhat narrow minded then.
CASSANDRA: Yeah, they're bigots. So that's why I thought you didn't like me either, because I'm white.
RANDALL: Cassie, you're demented. Shut up.
CASSANDRA: But Randall says you do.
DEMETRIUS: (*a smile*) I see. That doesn't explain what you're doing out at this hour.
CASSANDRA: See, I saw my father was going to be okay tonight. Sometimes he gets on a kick. (*imitating*) "I'm not EVER taking another drink," and then he doesn't for a couple days. So I thought it'd be okay to leave my sister and come over here—so I could just get away from him. That's what makes me sick about my father. He's such a phony. In another day or two he'll be sloshed.
DEMETRIUS: Tonight, he believes he'll never take another drink.
CASSANDRA: Yeah. Probably. But I think if a person just fools himself over and over again, then you can't really trust him.
DEMETRIUS: You're right.
CASSANDRA: My mom says I should give him the benefit of the doubt, but I don't want to. Why should I? He doesn't deserve it.

DEMETRIUS: She wants you to have some hope.

CASSANDRA: I told you, Mr. Washington. Hope is dangerous. See, adults don't listen.

DEMETRIUS: Sometimes we don't listen to you. Other times, we have something so important to tell you, we feel compelled to repeat ourselves. Otherwise, we would be irresponsible.

CASSANDRA: (*after a beat, not a question*) You're not a phony.

RANDALL: Don't mind her, Dad. You know Cassie. That's just the way she talks.

CASSANDRA: (*to DEMETRIUS*) Can I ask you a personal question?

DEMETRIUS: All right.

CASSANDRA: Would you be upset if Randall and I fell in love?

RANDALL: Cut that, Cassie. Come on.

DEMETRIUS: I will not be upset when Randall falls in love. (*to RANDALL*) I have to make a phone call. Get your friend something to drink.

(*DEMETRIUS moves to another part of the stage, to the phone.*)

CASSANDRA: (*to RANDALL*) The real reason I came over here is because I'm worried about that gun.

RANDALL: Shut up.

CASSANDRA: It's dangerous. You have to get rid of it.

RANDALL: I'm not getting rid of it, now shut your mouth.

CASSANDRA: I'm not shutting my mouth.

RANDALL: At least come on into my room.

CASSANDRA: (*as they exit*) Your dad said get me something to drink.

(*RANDALL and CASSANDRA exit. Lights up full on ELIZABETH at the radio station. DEMETRIUS dials a phone.*)

DEMETRIUS: Elizabeth, your hour is up. (*beat*) Dammit, pick up. (*beat*) I'm going to try at the studio. (*beat*) If I don't hear from you in 15 minutes, I'm going down to the police station.

(*DEMETRIUS hangs up, dials again. The phone at the radio station rings. ELIZABETH looks over at it. It rings several times. DEMETRIUS hangs up; the phone stops ringing. After a few beats, COURTNEY enters.*)

COURTNEY: You don't know my mother. I'm very worried about her.

Because—well, cause she's always worried about me. I don't think she can take this. What if I die and she's so torn up about it she can't take care of my little sister anymore.

ELIZABETH: You're not going to die.

COURTNEY: He pretended he worked for one of my teachers, that's why I opened the door. I only opened it a little ways, and then he broke the chain. I wanted you to know I didn't go with him on purpose or anything. My mom's always telling me not to do that. Do you think you can help me? Because the only thing is I have a try-out in two days for a show at school and I don't want to miss it, because I don't think that one teacher will let me make it up. I'm going to sing "Apple Blossom Time".

ELIZABETH: You sing?

COURTNEY: Not really. But my friend Alicia? She says singing's all about style anyhow and you don't actually have to have a good voice.

ELIZABETH: That's true.

COURTNEY: She thought it would help me because I'm so shy, so we got dressed up for Halloween as the Andrews Sisters. Do you know who they are?

ELIZABETH: Yes. There are three of them.

COURTNEY: Yes. Becky came too and she's a very good singer.

ELIZABETH: (*a beat*) I sing. I did when I was younger.

COURTNEY: Did you sing on Halloween?

ELIZABETH: No. The last year I went trick or treating, I dressed up as a flapper and every time someone opened the door, I did the Charleston.

(COURTNEY laughs.)

COURTNEY: Do you think you could untie me? Or do you think this man will?

ELIZABETH: I don't know.

COURTNEY: I hope I'm on a poster. Do you think if I am that will help?

ELIZABETH: I'm not sure.

COURTNEY: Did this ever happen to you?

ELIZABETH: An old man came in halfway through a movie at the Jerome Theater once and sat next to me. My mother was still alive so I couldn't have been more than six. He was all dressed up with a fancy hat and white gloves and he leaned over and whispered, "Good movie."

COURTNEY: That scared you?

ELIZABETH: I didn't even stay for the end of the movie. It was the dead

of winter, but I ran out into the freezing afternoon without my coat and ran home so fast, I couldn't speak for a few minutes once I got there. My mother kept saying, "What's wrong, Lizzie? What happened?"
COURTNEY: This man gives me food. (*beat*) I hope he brings me someplace I recognize because then at least I'll know where I am.
ELIZABETH: All that old man did was whisper to me. If he had touched me, or tried to take me away from my mother and father . . .
COURTNEY: I know. I'm scared. (*She starts to cry.*) Can you help me? Can you help me?

(*ARNOLD enters.*)

ARNOLD: Don't you want to help this little girl?
COURTNEY: Can you help me?
ARNOLD: You could help this little girl. After all, I'm not asking you to do anything you don't do every day.
COURTNEY: Elizabeth?

(*ARNOLD exits. COURTNEY exits. ELIZABETH does not move for a couple of beats. Then she dials her phone. Lights up on DEMETRIUS as his phone rings. He answers it.*)

DEMETRIUS: (*into phone*) Hello. (*beat*) Hello.
ELIZABETH: (*into phone*) Demetrius?
DEMETRIUS: (*into phone*) Elizabeth? You're late.
ELIZABETH: (*into phone*) You didn't talk to the police, did you?
DEMETRIUS: (*into phone*) No, I did not.

(*DEMETRIUS and ELIZABETH put down phones and face each other. They are still talking on their phones, but not holding them. They can move physically very close to one another during the rest of this scene.*)

DEMETRIUS: Are you ready to go down to the station?
ELIZABETH: He said if I involve the police, he'll kill that kid: I can't get that out of my head. How do I know he's not watching me? How do I know he hasn't been watching us come and go at the studio? How do I know he's not gaping at me through the window right now?
DEMETRIUS: (*quietly*) Calm down. You must think clearly. This man kidnapped a young girl and then called you to discuss Randall

Cunningham's football injuries. He's crazy. You cannot control him.

ELIZABETH: God, I don't know what to do. (*a tiny brainstorm*) Maybe I should contact her family or—(someone who knows her.)

DEMETRIUS: (comes in on "family") No.

ELIZABETH: Maybe they can tell me what to do.

DEMETRIUS: Don't you fucking do that, Elizabeth. (*pause*) Let me tell you what I know. I know that if it were my son, I would not want a radio talk show personality to try to effect his rescue.

ELIZABETH: But what if I can help her?

DEMETRIUS: God.

ELIZABETH: Because listen. Either way he's crazy, but he wants to meet me, so maybe I can—(do something the police can't.)

DEMETRIUS: What is it with your ego, Elizabeth? What's the scenario you're envisioning? You meet this motherfucker, you shoot the shit about his fantasy super bowl for a while, then he hands Courtney over and waves and says (*he's infuriated*) "SEE YOU GIRLS, THANKS FOR DROPPING BY?" Okay, now listen to me. This child is not any more or less your responsibility than she is mine.

ELIZABETH: (*fierce, very upset*) You know that's not true. Because if he murders her it will be on my head, not yours. You didn't talk to him.

DEMETRIUS: (*overlap*) I talked to him several times.

(*she just keeps talking*) He didn't talk to you about Courtney.

DEMETRIUS: Right, he just talked to me about kicking my black ass if I didn't put him through.

ELIZABETH: (*she just keeps talking*) You didn't hear him say if you do THIS I'll kill her and if you do THAT I'll kill her, so it's easy for you to wash your hands of it and—(expect me to do the same.)

DEMETRIUS: (*comes in on "easy"*) Easy? You think you're the only one who feels for this kid? You think I'm washing my hands of something here? Are you calling me a coward, Elizabeth?

ELIZABETH: No, for God's sake, I'm not calling you anything. Stop telling me all the time I'm insulting you. I'm not insulting you.

DEMETRIUS: (*a deep breath*) Sorry.

ELIZABETH: I'm terrified for her. I want to rescue her.

DEMETRIUS: You can't.

ELIZABETH: Because it's not fair. Because she's just a little girl. Because I can't bear to think of her with that man and how scared she is and what might be happening to her. I need to do something.

DEMETRIUS: You have to separate what you need from what's best for

Courtney.

ELIZABETH: I don't know if I can, Demetrius. (*beat*) I'm not you. You're so sure you know what's best for her, but I'm not. (*pause*) There's no possibility he'll turn her over to me?

DEMETRIUS: I don't think so.

ELIZABETH: There's no possibility the police will screw it up?

DEMETRIUS: That is not the point. You cannot save her life without some help. This is a job that some particular people are already trained to do. In the army, I learned that if you let the guys in charge do the job they're trained to do, and this is no matter what you think about them, your opinion about what kind of people they are doesn't count for jackshit. Just if you let them do their jobs, maybe they'll save your life. Please believe me, I don't like it any better than you do, but right at this moment, you and I are powerless. (*very long pause*) Did you hear what I said?

ELIZABETH: (*flat*) Powerless.

(*Long pause.*)

DEMETRIUS: Elizabeth? (*beat*) Elizabeth?

(*They pick up their phones again.*)

DEMETRIUS: Talk to me, Elizabeth.
ELIZABETH: I can't.

(*She hangs up. DEMETRIUS hangs up. He turns out the lights and exits. Dim light on ELIZABETH in the radio station. After a couple beats, ARNOLD enters.*)

ARNOLD: I thought I would never be able to get through to you, Liz. (*beat*) Liz? (*beat*) I never talked to someone as famous as you before.
ELIZABETH: Where's Courtney?
ARNOLD: Courtney has to sleep. If you were a mother, you'd realize that.
ELIZABETH: How do you know I'm not a mother?
ARNOLD: You're not a mother, you're not a wife, you're better than those things. You're brilliant, you know things, you put our minds at ease, you help us understand what athletes are up against. Children need to sleep, that's not the kind of thing I would expect you to know about. I don't

hold it against you.
ELIZABETH: What makes you think I care about your opinion of me?
ARNOLD: Listening to your show. If you didn't care what people thought of you, you wouldn't do the show. Would you? (*beat*) Courtney will be awake by the time you get here. She's not dead yet.
ELIZABETH: Did you hurt her?
ARNOLD: I told you I would turn her over to you.
ELIZABETH: But will you? Is she already gone?
ARNOLD: All I want from you is a conversation, Liz. All I want is reassurance.
ELIZABETH: You killed her.
ARNOLD: No.
ELIZABETH: You killed her because of me.
ARNOLD: No. Don't think all things are about you. That's not true.
ELIZABETH: I don't think that.
ARNOLD: Courtney is here with me. Courtney is sleeping.
ELIZABETH: I don't think all things are about me.
ARNOLD: Courtney is a child with her own life, separate from you. It would be better if you could think about someone else. Think about me. Don't think about Courtney. Think about me.
ELIZABETH: I want to help Courtney.
ARNOLD: That's the way to help her. Think about me, then you'll be able to help her.

(*Sound of someone at the door.*)

ARNOLD: That's your co-worker. He has a child, so he should be careful.
DEMETRIUS: (*off*) Elizabeth?
ARNOLD: Keep him away from me.

(*DEMETRIUS enters. ELIZABETH keeps her eyes on ARNOLD.*)

ARNOLD: The Eagles have come close so often. When I watch them, the knot in my stomach stays there for the rest of the game and I can't eat. I try to imagine how I'll feel when they finally win it. I'll tell you the truth. I can't imagine it. It's that feeling when you want something so badly, you won't let yourself imagine it, because you don't want to jinx it.

(*ARNOLD exits. DEMETRIUS turns on the lights.*)

ELIZABETH: You left Randall alone?
DEMETRIUS: Don't worry about Randall.

(ELIZABETH stares in the direction of ARNOLDs exit. Several beats.)

DEMETRIUS: Elizabeth?
ELIZABETH: (*still looking in the direction ARNOLD exited*) That creep was just here.

(DEMETRIUS looks around and then at ELIZABETH warily.)

DEMETRIUS: Nobody's here.
ELIZABETH: You know how many creeps I talk to in a day? (*beat*) I was a tough kid, you know? I could beat anybody at any sport you want to name.
DEMETRIUS: I imagine.
ELIZABETH: And the boys on the block didn't like it, and they came after me just like some of these guys come after me on the radio now. I only lost one fight—ever—when fucking Clifford Hepner knocked me down from behind, then sat on my stomach and punched me until a policeman stopped him. The cop was really nice, helped me up, gave me a handkerchief, but I couldn't stop crying. Not because I was hurt. Because I knew I could kill Clifford in a fair fight. (*beat*) I wish I could meet this guy and say hand her over, you creep and no, the Eagles aren't going to win shit, and have that kid put her arms around my neck and see her mother smile and thank me.
DEMETRIUS: I wish that too.
ELIZABETH: I feel the way I felt when my mother was dying. (*pause*) I couldn't stop life from taking the course it was going to take. (*beat*) I don't want to give up on Courtney, but I realize. . . . Maybe she's already. . . . (*She can't bring herself to say it.*)
DEMETRIUS: We haven't lost Courtney yet. If we give the police a chance, maybe they'll save her life. Will you let them try? Please, Elizabeth.
ELIZABETH: (*no affect*) Yes. (*more affect*) I'll call the police right now. (*even more*) I promise, Demetrius. I'll call them. (*a little of her radio personality seeping in*) I'll tell them every tiny detail of what the asshole said. I'll go down there. I'll answer all their questions.
DEMETRIUS: (*exhausted*) Don't fuck with me. Are you going to do this?
ELIZABETH: Yes.

DEMETRIUS: Are you going to go to the police?
ELIZABETH: What do you want from me, Demetrius? I said I'd go down there.
DEMETRIUS: (*beat*) Good. I'll go with you.
ELIZABETH: (*quickly, urgently*) No. Go home to Randall. (*beat*) I don't want you involved.
DEMETRIUS: I'm involved.
ELIZABETH: I don't want you any more involved than you already are.
DEMETRIUS: I can take care of myself.
ELIZABETH: Who said you couldn't? Just, please, go home to Randall. I'm going to contact the police, Demetrius. Trust me.

(*A pause.*)

DEMETRIUS: All right.
ELIZABETH: Thank you.
DEMETRIUS: I'll see you tomorrow.
ELIZABETH: Tomorrow's a big day. Super bowl championship team with only a so-so quarterback day.

(*DEMETRIUS exits. A couple beats, then ELIZABETH picks up the phone and dials. Blackout.*)

(*Sound of "You're Only Lonely" (J.D. Souther), which plays for a few measures, then off. Sound of "Urgent" (Foreigner) which plays for a few measures, then off. Sound of "Caravan" (Van Morrison). Lights up on DEMETRIUS in the studio, working with the music. He's wearing jeans and a white t-shirt. His jeans jacket hangs on the back of his chair. He turns Van Morrison off. A beat, then he puts on "U Will Know" (Black Men United). As soon as he does, the phone rings.*)

DEMETRIUS: WBZZ.
ARNOLD: (*entering as he speaks*) Put her on.
DEMETRIUS: This show doesn't start for half an hour.
ARNOLD: Let me speak to her.
DEMETRIUS: She's not here yet.
ARNOLD: Give me a direct answer to a direct question.

(*Silence.*)

ARNOLD: Why do you try to protect her from me?

DEMETRIUS: She is not here, man.

ARNOLD: No, here's the question. Do the two of you have sex together? (*Silence.*) I'll take your silence to mean yes.

DEMETRIUS: I thought you wanted to talk to her about the Eagles, man. What's this sex thing, you ever heard her talk about sex on this show?

ARNOLD: I didn't want her to discuss our conversation with you. Did she tell you everything?

DEMETRIUS: Yeah.

ARNOLD: (*furious*) Then tell her the deal's off. The deal's off.

DEMETRIUS: She told me you were an Eagles fan and you were trying to get her to meet you somewhere to talk about it. (*beat*) So I'll tell her it's off.

ARNOLD: She's going to meet me?

DEMETRIUS: I advised her against it.

ARNOLD: If you don't want her, why'd you tell her not to meet me?

DEMETRIUS: She and I are not even friends.

ARNOLD: That's a lie. I know you all want white women.

DEMETRIUS: (*steady, trying to contain his fury*) No. (*calm*) They all want us.

ARNOLD: Why don't you mind your own business? You don't know what's at stake for me with this meeting. If I could meet this woman—(everything would be all right.)

DEMETRIUS: Talk to her on the phone like everybody else. She meets one listener she's got to meet more listeners. It'll never end.

ARNOLD: SHE TOLD ME SHE'D SPEAK TO ME TODAY TO SET UP A MEETING. I want to hear that woman tell me the Eagles have a legitimate shot at the whole thing. Then I'll be happy.

DEMETRIUS: Well, she's not in yet, but I'll give her the message. What's your name?

ARNOLD: She knows my name.

DEMETRIUS: Yeah, well, I'll give her the message. (*beat*) I know all you white guys want to be back quarterbacks.

(*ARNOLD hangs up, exits. DEMETRIUS stops the music. Puts on "Love Lies Bleeding In My Hand" (Elton John) starting with the upbeat part. The one-line phone rings as Elizabeth enters. She wears jeans, a sleeveless white blouse and a lightweight white silk jacket.*)

DEMETRIUS: He just hung up.

ELIZABETH: I detest that song.

(Her desk hone rings. ELIZABETH picks it up.)

ELIZABETH: *(into phone)* Liz Jones.

(DEMETRIUS turns off the song.)

ELIZABETH: *(into phone)* Uh huh. *(to DEMETRIUS)* It's the police.

(DEMETRIUS starts up "Don't Dream It's Over" (Crowded House).)

ELIZABETH: *(into phone)* Because I just arrived. My show doesn't start until five.

(She turns to DEMETRIUS.)

ELIZABETH: He says you didn't keep him on long enough.
DEMETRIUS: Keep him on? Have I been deputized?
ELIZABETH: He says you made incendiary remarks. *(about the song)* I like that. *(she sings)* Don't dream it's over. *(or she sings along with whatever lyric is playing at this point)*
DEMETRIUS: *(overlap) I* made incendiary remarks?
ELIZABETH: *(into phone)* Yes, I do understand.

(She listens. The music plays.)

ELIZABETH: *(into phone)* To the letter, officer.

(She hangs up. DEMETRIUS turns off the music, starts to do a sound check.)

ELIZABETH: Our instructions are to proceed with the show as usual. It wouldn't do to alarm our Eagles fan.
DEMETRIUS: Did you sleep?
ELIZABETH: I fell asleep at 9:45 this morning. Thankfully, I did not awaken until 4. What'd he say?
DEMETRIUS: Nothing. *(into her mic)* Testing. Testing. Alpha. Beta. Gamma. Testing.

(It squeals. He goes to the sound board.)

DEMETRIUS: So, the phone's tapped?
ELIZABETH: That's what you wanted, right?
DEMETRIUS: What I wanted was for you not to allow your big, fat ego to get you involved in something crazy.
ELIZABETH: What did he say, Demetrius?
DEMETRIUS: Nothing. Bullshit. *(beat)* He wants to meet you.
ELIZABETH: The police haven't decided whether I will actually go to the meeting place.
DEMETRIUS: Then they're crazy too. I'm the only sane person in the joint.
ELIZABETH: Perhaps fighting in a war sobers one up.
DEMETRIUS: No doubt.
ELIZABETH: Was it not you who suggested I tell the police everything and then follow their lead?
DEMETRIUS: Yeah, that was me. *(into her mic)* Testing. Alpha. Beta.
ELIZABETH: Stop it. My microphone's fine.
DEMETRIUS: Tell me you do not know this guy's name.
ELIZABETH: I don't know his name.
DEMETRIUS: He said you did.
ELIZABETH: Oh, yes? Well, he's a sociopath, isn't he? *(beat)* Now what? You think the asshole and I are keeping secrets from you?
DEMETRIUS: The guy's got me strung out, all right?
ELIZABETH: You? I'm the one he's expecting to make his screwy dreams of football glory come true.
DEMETRIUS: All I'm saying is I just had a conversation with the guy so I'm a little on edge. *(beat)* He says if you can convince him the Eagles have a legitimate chance to go to the super bowl, he'll be happy.
ELIZABETH: I can. *(She slips into her chair disconsolately.)* Shit.

(After a couple seconds, DEMETRIUS puts his hand on the chair and kneels down beside it.)

DEMETRIUS: I believe you are doing the best thing for that kid.

(A beat, then he puts his hand lightly on her leg.)

DEMETRIUS: It's that time. You ready?
ELIZABETH: *(about to cry)* Uh huh.

(He looks at her; he doubts it.)

ELIZABETH: I'm a performer if I'm anything. On with the show.

(Split second blackout. Lights up as "Stand" comes up very loudly. ARNOLD and COURTNEY enter.

The music recedes.)

ELIZABETH: *(brightly)* Good evening, fellow sports junkies. This is Liz Jones back with you this evening on Stand, the Peninsula's ONLY sports talk show. You're tuned in to WBZZ, where Stand is brought to you by United Airlines, Common Ground Bakery and Mancusi Brothers Moving Company, serving the entire Peninsula. Today's question is about mediocre quarterbacks and the super bowl. I don't want to hear about so-so quarterbacks who <u>lost</u> the big game, anybody can do that, even I can do that. No, you have a mediocre quarterback who <u>won</u> the Super Bowl, call me, fill me in, enlighten me, listeners, because Liz depends on you. The lines are open at 808-4111. You don't have to answer today's question, I'll talk any sports you want.

(Phone rings. She looks over at it.)

DEMETRIUS: *(into phone)* Stand. *(to ELIZABETH)* Hey, you're on the air.
ELIZABETH: Who saw the Pistons and Knicks on TV last night?
DEMETRIUS: *(into phone)* Yeah, Ted, what's on your mind?
ELIZABETH: Your observations about that game would be welcome.
DEMETRIUS: *(to ELIZABETH)* Ted on 1.

(The phone rings. Another line rings.)

DEMETRIUS: He's got an answer. *(into phone)* Stand.
ELIZABETH: Ted, you're on WBZZ, stand up for Liz. What's the skinny?
DEMETRIUS: All right, she'll get you next. *(into phone)* Stand.
ELIZABETH: No, no, no, Ted. Jeff Hostettler is not a mediocre quarterback.
DEMETRIUS: *(to ELIZABETH)* Another answer on two. Harry.
ELIZABETH: You're on the air with Liz Jones. Talk to me, Harry.
DEMETRIUS: Wolverines recruiting. Uh huh. You hang on, Lawrence.

ELIZABETH: Earl Morral, '72 Dolphins. I'll be damned. Good answer, guy. But, sadly, wrong. Griese came back just in time for the AFC championship game—

(The phone rings. It rings again.)

ELIZABETH:—and then went on to win the whole enchilada.
DEMETRIUS: *(overlap)* Stand.
ELIZABETH: But Morral had 10 wins. Good run for an old guy.
DEMETRIUS: *(to ELIZABETH)* Lawrence. *(into phone)* Stand.
ELIZABETH: *(overlap)* Lawrence, you're on WBZZ.
ARNOLD: *(overlap)* It's me. Put her on.
DEMETRIUS: She's on the air.
ARNOLD: I'm next.
ELIZABETH: I have a lot of hope for this Blanchard kid, Lawrence. He was the National High School Player of the Year last year. We were lucky to get him, don't you think?
DEMETRIUS: You're next. *(to ELIZABETH)* Go to the news. *(to ARNOLD)* I'm putting you through. *(to ELIZABETH)* He's on four.
ELIZABETH: *(into phone)* Thank you, Lawrence. Time for the news, and then we have an interview I recently taped with former college and NBA coach, Jerry Tarkanian.
DEMETRIUS: *(overlap, buzzes)* You ready for the news? *(beat)* Yes, now.
ELIZABETH: This is Liz Jones.
DEMETRIUS: *(overlap)* NOW.

(ARNOLD and ELIZABETH do not hold phones, although they are both speaking on the phone.)

ARNOLD: Your nigger's trying to horn in on our meeting you know.
NEWS BROADCAST: A Gallup taken yesterday reveals that the American public is fed up with hearing about the Monica Lewinsky scandal.
ELIZABETH: *(at the same time as the news starts)* I want to speak to Courtney.
ARNOLD: I've decided where you should meet us.
ELIZABET: I'm not meeting you unless I speak to Courtney.
ARNOLD: How about you speak to her when you get here?
ELIZABETH: *(a scream; she's scared)* PUT COURTNEY ON THE FUCKING PHONE.

(DEMETRIUS goes to ELIZABETH puts a hand on her arm, which is shaking.)

ARNOLD: Hold on.
ELIZABETH: *(to DEMETRIUS)* He's putting her on.

(A pause. Phone rings.)

ELIZABETH: Shit.
DEMETRIUS: Let it ring, who gives a shit?
COURTNEY: Hello.
ELIZABETH: Courtney?
COURTNEY: Yes.
ELIZABETH: *(to DEMETRIUS, about to burst into tears from relief)* She's all right. *(to COURTNEY)* This is Elizabeth Jones.
COURTNEY: Elizabeth Jones?

(Phone rings.)

NEWS BROADCAST:—unusual sight of a seal flapping around near—(the dock.)
ELIZABETH: I'm a radio show host.
COURTNEY: Oh.
ELIZABETH: I host a sports show. Do you like sports?
COURTNEY: Not really. My dad does. *(beat)* Are you the one who's coming to get me?
ELIZABETH: Yes. I am. Courtney, are you all right?
COURTNEY: Yes. Arnold says you'll be coming to get me soon.
ELIZABETH: Arnold?
COURTNEY: Yes.
ELIZABETH: Tell Arnold I'm on my way.

(COURTNEY exits. More than one line is ringing. ELIZABETH returns to her phone, puts the receiver to her ear.)

ARNOLD: You're coming alone, you must not bring that—(nigger you work with.)
NEWS BROADCAST: No new leads in the Courtney Kaufman kidnapping case.
ELIZABETH: *(overlap)* I'll come alone.

(As we hear phones ringing and ringing, DEMETRIUS turns the multi-line phone's ringer off. Sudden silence.)

ARNOLD: It's the work you do that makes you so harsh, you know. For instance, your concern about Courtney, your suspicion. You yell. It's because you're fighting to keep the place you've won for yourself in a man's world. I know that. I realize that and believe me, I respect what you've accomplished.

ELIZABETH: *(into phone)* Where do you want me to meet you?

ARNOLD: You know the hotel right where 94 ends?

DEMETRIUS: *(overlap, on phone)* Jack, calm down. I'm running an interview right now. When I'm finished, we'll talk.

ELIZABETH: *(into phone)* I'll be there in 15 minutes. *(She hangs up.)*

DEMETRIUS: Jack's pissed.

ELIZABETH: *(to DEMETRIUS)* What do I do now?

DEMETRIUS: Wait.

(ELIZABETH's phone rings. She answers.)

ELIZABETH: *(into phone)* Hello? *(beat)* Don't worry about it. The interview's a half hour and there's 18 minutes of commercials. *(beat)* Take your concern and shove it up your ass, Jack, so you did the news ten minutes early. So what?

(She hangs up.)

ELIZABETH: *(to DEMETRIUS)* Can we fire him?

(ELIZABETH's phone rings again. She answers it.)

ELIZABETH: *(into phone, thinks its Jack again)* WHAT? *(It's the police.)* No, wait a minute. I have to go with you. *(beat)* That's a bad idea. If I go with you, she'll have a better chance.

(The police have hung up. She hangs up.)

ELIZABETH: They've got it. They're on their way. *(beat)* They want me to stay here. *(beat)* They hung up on me.

CASSANDRA: (*off, banging on the door*) MR. WASHINGTON?

(*CASSANDRA enters. She pulls RANDALL's arm trying to get him to enter. In a second, he does, carrying his jacket, blood covering his shirt and arms. He drops his jacket on the floor. They are both out of breath.*)

DEMETRIUS: Randall. (*He runs to RANDALL, frantic. He pulls RANDALL's arms down away from his face, feels different places on his body.*) Jesus, where are you hurt? (*DEMETRIUS pulls his T-shirt up over his head and off.*)
CASSANDRA: He's not hurt. (*DEMETRIUS is not listening.*) HE'S NOT HURT. (*beat*) That's not his blood.

(*DEMETRIUS uses his shirt to wipe blood off RANDALL, still feeling for a wound. ELIZABETH moves to them, unbuttons RANDALL's shirt and takes it off him. DEMETRIUS keeps wiping RANDALLs body. ElLIZABETH moves away from them, toward her phone.*)

DEMETRIUS: Son, what happened to you? Whose blood is this?
RANDALL: (*upset*) The swan.
DEMETRIUS: I don't understand.
RANDALL: The swan's blood.
DEMETRIUS: Son, I can't make sense of what you're saying.
RANDALL: (*overlap*) Okay. (*He pulls himself together.*) Okay, see. You know we got a pond by our school.
DEMETRIUS: Yeah.
RANDALL: It's nothin' much, it's a little pond and we call it the swan pond, see, because we got one swan, and he swims in this pond all alone and I guess he's old now cause he's been swimming in that pond since I was, you know, about in the fifth grade. I'm not sure where he came from, and I'm not sure if he's a he, and it's not the *school's* swan, you understand, he's the whole community's swan. Everybody goes down there and feeds him and all. Now sometime me and Cassie meet together after school at that pond and today I was early for her and I see these two dudes, they're sticking the swan.
ELIZABETH: What? They were stabbing it?
RANDALL: (*overlap*) They're sticking it over and over and he's bleeding bad. I know these guys, they go to my school, they're 15 maybe or 16, and soon Cassie comes by and I'm so mad. She says they're just gangsters and they're drunk, and then . . . one of them picks the swan up out of the

water, and just like that cuts its head off. Just cuts that swan's head off and blood gushing everywhere and I'm so mad I start yelling I'm gonna kill them. I'm gonna kill them for what they did. Cassie's yelling stop it, shut up, but I couldn't. She's grabbin' my arm, she's yelling stop, stop.

CASSANDRA: (*warning him not to say too much*) Randall.

RANDALL: So, they ran away. So, I go over there and pick up that swan and stand there with him in my arms. I'm so embarrassed because I'm crying so loud, and suddenly people come running and Cassie says we got to go, we got to run. I just ran here to you, daddy, and now I'm thinkin', I was so mad and upset, when I ran away. I let the swan go and I don't know where he is or who's gonna bury him.

(*DEMETRIUS pulls RANDALL to him, holds him. Silence for several beats, then RANDALL steps back. ELIZABETH puts her jacket around Randall's shoulders.*)

ELIZABETH: How is this possible? (*She crosses to her phone, picks up the receiver, slams it down.*) This is not possible. (*beat, to DEMETRIUS*) I can't just wait here.

(*ELIZABETH stares at her phone. We see lights from the multi-line phone blinking. ELIZABETH moves agitatedly around the room. She steps on RANDALL's jacket, picks it up off the floor, feels its heaviness, looks in its pockets.*)

CASSANDRA: (*to ELIZABETH*) Give me that.

(*ELIZABETH pulls the jacket away from CASSANDRA, pulls out the gun.*)

ELIZABETH: (*to RANDALL*) My God, is this your jacket? (*pause*) I understand. When you see that kind of violence, you want to retaliate.
DEMETRIUS: Don't speak to my son that way.
RANDALL: She's right. I want to kill those dudes.
DEMETRIUS: (*trying to remain calm*) I am not listening to you talk about killing people.
RANDALL: I hope they get expelled out of school.

(*DEMETRIUS stands up. We can see a wide, ugly scar that stretches from his navel to six or seven inches above it.)*

CASSANDRA: Oh, my God. What a humungous wound.

(ELIZABETH looks at him—first at his scar, then his face. DEMETRIUS puts on his jacket before he speaks.)

DEMETRIUS: (*to ELIZABETH*) I'll take that please.

(She gives him the gun.)

DEMETRIUS: (*to RANDALL*) Does this belong to you?
RANDALL: Yes.
DEMETRIUS: You want to kill those boys?
RANDALL: Yes.
DEMETRIUS: Alternatively, you hope they get expelled from school?

(RANDALL says nothing.)

DEMETRIUS: I have used these, Randall, do you know that?
RANDALL: I know, but daddy, you don't know, you don't know how ugly those kids are.
DEMETRIUS: (*an explosion*) Stuff that, you shut your mouth. Don't talk to me about ugly.

(Silence, during which ELIZABETH thinks to touch DEMETRIUS, finally does, tentatively. A beat, then he covers her hand with his for a moment.)

DEMETRIUS: You watch those boys, you see something ugly, and how would you like to feel that ugliness inside yourself, Randall? How do you think that's going to feel? (*beat*) Answer me.
RANDALL: I can't, Daddy.
DEMETRIUS: Why can't you?
RANDAL: Because I don't know.
DEMETRIUS: That's right. You don't know. I know. If I could cause the men I shot to become alive again, do you know how much I would give to do that? (*pause, then to CASSANDRA*) When Randall says you "grabbed his arm" and shouted stop, stop, am I to understand that you prevented him from using this?

CASSANDRA: (*near tears*) Mr. Washington, Randall would never hurt anyone.
DEMETRIUS: I understand.
CASSANDRA: He only has that gun because he's scared.
DEMETRIUS: (*to RANDALL*) I sympathize. But you may not have this.

(*Throughout the last several lines, ELIZABETH has moved closer to her phone. She stares intently at it.*)

CASSANDRA: Mr. Washington? I'm afraid Randall will get blamed, because he was all covered with blood and because he had the gun.
DEMETRIUS: Nobody will blame Randall. (*DEMETRIUS moves to CASSANDRA.*) We'll take care of that. (*to RANDALL*) You and I will re-visit this subject, Randall. Rest assured.
RANDALL: We need the police. I want to turn those shitheads in for what they did.
DEMETRIUS: (*evenly*) We'll take care of the police when we get home.

(*DEMETRIUS hands RANDALL his jacket. RANDALL takes ELIZABETH's jacket off, and gives it to her, puts his on. ELIZABETH accepts her jacket, which is now bloodstained. She's focused on the phone.*)

ELIZABETH: (*to phone*) Come on. Come on.
CASSANDRA: What's wrong with her?
DEMETRIUS: (*to CASSANDRA*) I'm going to call your parents and ask them to come and pick you up.
CASSANDRA: I don't think that's a very good idea. If anyone is going to call them, I should call them. (*beat*) I don't want to call them. I want to take a taxi.
RANDALL: (*to DEMETRIUS*) I want Cassie to come home with us.
DEMETRIUS: I can't leave now. It would be best if Cassandra—(*called her parents*)
RANDALL: (*to DEMETRIUS*) No. You have to come home with us too.
ELIZABETH: Randall your father and I are.... (*She has no idea what to say.*) We're waiting for a phone call.
DEMETRIUS: You kids will have to wait in the green room until the show's over. Are you hungry? Do you want me to get you some food?
RANDALL: We're not waiting in the green room.
DEMETRIUS: You'll wait in the green room, Randall.

ELIZABETH: (*to DEMETRIUS*) He feels safer with you.
RANDALL: (*overlap*) I'm not going.
ELIZABETH: He's scared.
DEMETRIUS: I'm aware of that.
ELIZABETH: What are they supposed to do? We can't protect them, and we won't allow them to protect themselves. (*beat*) Our children are not safe.
DEMETRIUS: The world was not made a safer place for Courtney Kaufman or anyone else because Randall had a gun.
CASSANDRA: (*as in, "please don't fight"*) Yes, we're hungry!

(*Silence. Lights dim on the radio station but do not go out as a light comes up on ARNOLD.*)

ARNOLD: (*to COURTNEY, whom we can't see*) There's nothing for you to worry about. She'll be here. (*pause*) I don't know her that well, but I know she's not the kind of person who breaks her promises. She's coming. (*pause*) She'll be here

(*Lights up full on the radio station. Outside door buzzer. ELIZABETH jumps, lets out a surprised gasp. Then silence. Several beats.*)

DEMETRIUS: That's your food. You kids take it into the green room.
ELIZABETH: Lock the door.
CASSANDRA: What is happening here?
DEMETRIUS: You kids go.
RANDALL: I'm goin'. But then Cassie gets to make pies with us.
DEMETRIUS: Goddammit, Randall.
RANDALL: She gets to.
DEMETRIUS: Do as I say.
RANDALL: (*raising his voice*) Her father's a freak so she gets to.
DEMETRIUS (*a beat*) All right, son. Now go on and eat your dinner in the green room.

(*RANDALL starts to exit, CASSANDRA following. The phone rings.*)

ELIZABETH: Oh God.

(*CASSANDRA stops and looks at ELIZABETH. The phone keeps ringing.*)

DEMETRIUS: (*to CASSANDRA*) Go go go.

(*CASSANDRA exits. The phone keeps ringing.*)

DEMETRIUS: Elizabeth. Do you want me to answer it?

(*She shakes her head "no." Lights dim as she picks up the phone.*)

ELIZABETH: Hello? (*beat*) Yes?

(*Immediately, we hear a NEWS BROADCAST in the dim light.*)

NEWS BROADCAST: Young Courtney Kaufman was killed this evening during a police attempt to rescue her from the man who abducted her from her kitchen yesterday morning.

(*Cross-fade the rest of the broadcast with "Shadow and Light" (Joni Mitchell). The broadcast grows more and more quiet and the music finally overwhelms it as the lights fade up again until there is a soft spotlight on ELIZABETH standing perfectly still.*)

NEWS BROADCAST: Police apprehended Arnold Anderson, but not before he shot and killed the child. The authorities were led to Anderson by radio sports talk show host Elizabeth Jones. On parole following a prior kidnapping conviction, Anderson contacted Jones early yesterday evening—

(*The broadcast fades out as the lights come up full.*)

ELIZABETH: Are the kids all right?
DEMETRIUS: They're fine. They're eating their dinner. (*beat*) You do not have to finish the show.
ELIZABETH: I do. I do have to.

(*DEMETRIUS fades the music out.*)

DEMETRIUS: All right. Go.
ELIZABETH (*into mic*): Liz Jones back with you on Stand. New question. Who out there has known someone who was murdered? Call Liz on

808-4111 and tell me about it.

DEMETRIUS: You're going to lose your job.

ELIZABETH: I'm not losing anything. I'm the star. Wait till you see the ratings we're going to get. (*into mic*) I know, I know, it's a sports talk show, the Peninsula's only sports talk show, but let's face up to the sad fact of the matter, folks. These days, murder is something of a sport itself, don't you agree with me?

(Phone rings and keeps ringing.)

DEMETRIUS: (*into phone*) Stand.

ELIZABETH: (*into mic*) I'll start.

DEMETRIUS: (*into phone*) She's serious. (*beat*) All right, hold on.

ELIZABETH: I knew Courtney Kaufman. Briefly.

DEMETRIUS: (*into phone*) Stand. Please hold. (*He picks up another line.*) Stand. (*He puts someone through, then to ELIZABETH.*) Bill. Then Elaine on 2.

ELIZABETH: Bill, you're on WBZZ. Stand up for Liz.

VOICE: Terrible about that little girl.

ELIZABETH: Courtney's mine. Tell me about yours.

VOICE: Mine was a high school buddy, got hit and run by a drunk.

(The phone keeps ringing. DEMETRIUS juggles phones and people.)

ELIZABETH: Elaine, stand up for Liz.

VOICE: Um.

ELIZABETH: Go on, don't be afraid. It's the Day of the Dead here on Stand.

VOICE: My next door neighbor's son.

ELIZABETH: Was he murdered, Elaine?

VOICE: Yes. He was five. He was beaten by one of his mother's boyfriend's, I think.

DEMETRIUS: (*into phone*) Stand.

VOICE: In my dorm, a girl got killed by a guy because I think she sold him bad drugs?

ELIZABETH: Stand up for Liz.

VOICE: Kid down the street, thought he was a real tough guy, maybe ten years old. He got shot on his front lawn. I imagine him cursing out the killer with his last mean breath.

DEMETRIUS: (*into phone*) Stand.

VOICE: I know a 12-year-old who murdered an old man. Does that count?
ELIZABETH: Jennifer, you're on WBZZ. Stand up for Liz.
CHILD'S VOICE: My sister got killed on a bus because the driver got shot and ran off the road. Liz?
ELIZABETH: (*shaken*) Yes?
CHILD'S VOICE: I decided that when I grow up I'm going to become a policewoman, so I can protect people.
ELIZABETH: (*on the verge of breaking down*) First things first. First you have to grow up.
DEMETRIUS: Thomas on three. (*beat*) Elizabeth. Thomas on three.
ELIZABETH: (*into mic*) Thomas?
VOICE: Liz, did you hear about the swan? I understand some children down by the pond stabbed it more than 40 times. Who would do a crazy thing like that?

(*ELIZABETH stands up abruptly.*)

VOICE: I hear they cut the swan's head off.
DEMETRIUS: (*overlap*) Elizabeth. (*quickly, to phone*) The show is over. (*He picks up another line.*) That's it for today.
VOICE: Man, that must have been a bloody sight.
DEMETRIUS: (*to ELIZABETH*) Say you're going to the weather. (*buzzes*) Weather, stand by.

(*ELIZABETH leans over to the mic.*)

ELIZABETH: (*she can barely get it out*) Thanks for the call, Thomas. Now it's time for—

(*ELIZABETH stands unsteadily and then, with a sob, falls, grabbing for her chair as she goes down. DEMETRIUS buzzes.*)

DEMETRIUS: (*into phone*) Weather go.

(*DEMETRIUS hangs up, disconnects the phone.*)

ELIZABETH: I want to go to the jail. Will the police let me see him?
DEMETRIUS: I imagine yes, they will.
ELIZABETH: I want to visit Arnold Anderson in jail. (*beat*) I want to witness

his execution.
WEATHER:—no sign of it letting up.

(DEMETRIUS reaches down for her. He kneels beside her.)

DEMETRIUS: Come on, let's get you up off this floor.
ELIZABETH: Why don't we attend his execution together? No. *(beat)* We don't execute people in this state. Crazy. That's crazy.
DEMETRIUS: You are not—. I am not in the right frame of mind to discuss executions today. *(soft)* All right? *(beat)* Come on, Elizabeth. Stand up.
ELIZABETH: Is Randall all right?
DEMETRIUS: Randall's all right.
ELIZABETH: *(after a pause)* If I'd gone to meet Arnold Anderson, would Courtney still be alive?
DEMETRIUS: No.
ELIZABETH: Are you sure?
DEMETRIUS: No.

(Pause.)

ELIZABETH: Take care of Randall.
DEMETRIUS: You know I'm going to take care of him.
ELIZABETH: Is he all right?
DEMETRIUS: My boy is just a little shaken up. I'm gonna take real good care of him, Elizabeth.
ELIZABETH: *(finally crying)* Promise me.
DEMETRIUS: *(putting his arms around her)* Don't you worry. Randall's going to be fine.
WEATHER: Wherever you're going today, drive carefully, because the streets are slick and dangerous.

(Lights fade and go out.)

END OF PLAY

❧ **UNITED** ❧

United takes place throughout the lifetimes of the 40 passengers who were killed on United Flight 93 on September 11, 2001. Their story is told in 18 scenes, some of which occur on the plane and some of which do not.

When the piece was being developed in Tucson (through five public readings) and when it premiered at Winding Road Theater Ensemble in February 2015, the music noted in the text was played live by a violist. This worked beautifully.

In the world premiere, 20 actors played all the characters, with a lot of doubling. The only character not doubled is Mariah Mills, who also acts as the narrator, if you will.

CHARACTERS

MARIAH MILLS

PASSENGERS (age on 9/11/2001)
CHRISTIAN ADAMS (37)
TODD BEAMER (32)
ALAN BEAVEN (48)
MARK BINGHAM (31)
DEORA BODLEY (20)
MARION BRITTON (53)
TOM BURNETT (38)
WILLIAM CASHMAN (60)
GEORGINE CORRIGAN (55)
PATRICIA CUSHING (69)
JOE DELUCA (52)
JOE DRISCOLL (70)
ED FELT (41)
JANE FOLGER (73)
COLLEEN FRASER (51)
ANDREW GARCIA (62)
JEREMY GLICK (31)
KRISTIN GOULD (65)
LAUREN GRANDCOLAS (38)
DONALD GREENE (52)
LINDA GRONLAND (46)

RICHARD GUADAGNO (38)
TOSHIYA KUGE (20)
HILDA MARCIN (79)
WALESKA MARTINEZ (37)
NICOLE MILLER (21)
LOUIS NACKE (42)
DON PETERSON (66)
JEAN PETERSON (55)
MARK ROTHENBERG (52)
CHRISTINE SNYDER (32)
JOHN TALIGNANI (74)
HONOR WAINIO (27)

CREW (age on 9/11/2001))
LORRAINE BAY (Flight Attendant, 58)
SANDY BRADSHAW (Flight Attendant, 38)
JASON DAHL (Pilot, 43)
WANDA GREEN (Flight Attendant, 49)
LEROY HOMER (First Officer, 36)
CEE CEE LYLES (Slight Attendant, 33)
DEBORAH WELSH (Flight Attendant, 49)

CHORUS
All 43 characters who are not passengers or crew members on the plane (except MARIAH) are part of the CHORUS and are played by five actors. Whether they move in and out of scenes or stand together as a chorus traditionally does, I leave up to the director. Scene breaks are indicated by the CHORUS announcing the name of a new scene.

(CHORUS and MARIAH MILLS stand on the stage.)

A musician plays the viola—Telemann's Viola Concerto in G Major, third movement, starting with the 8th measure.

(When MARIAH steps forward, the music stops.)

CHORUS: OBSESSION

MARIAH: I don't know how I knew. I just knew. We were sent home from school that morning. September 11, 2001. That morning. I threw myself on my bed and couldn't stop crying. My mom kept telling me the things you're supposed to tell your kids in the face of that kind of tragedy. It's all right to be scared. It's good to get all that sadness out. I kept sobbing and having a hard time breathing. When I could finally speak, I said, "I think one of my birth parents is dead." My mom became really alarmed.

CHORUS MEMBER: How could you know that?

MARIAH: I just knew. The next day I pored over the newspaper and saw the crash site in a Pennsylvania field—a two-page photo spread with firefighters and the coroner and random onlookers. I stared and stared and stared at that photo. I was mesmerized. United Flight 93 was traveling at 563 miles an hour when it hit the ground. Causing the 44 people on board to vaporize. My adoptive parents had agreed to raise me as a Catholic and make sure I got a good education. When I reached 19, I would be allowed to see the adoption records and, if I consented, the birth parents would be allowed to meet me. I was 16 in 2001. I had two and a half years to see what I could discover about the people on that flight. I was fairly sure none of the terrorists was my birth parent. I have a recurring waking nightmare in which I hear those men praising their God while in the act of murdering 40 people. I believe Allah had a few choice words for those killers. Paradise? I don't think so. Besides those four? 40 other people. Very small number of people for a cross-country flight. Much larger number of people to gather information about. I became obsessed. How old were they? What were their families like? Where did they grow up? Did they have pets? What gave them joy? Where did they sit on the plane? Did they have faith?

CHORUS MEMBER: Faith in what?

MARIAH: What happened was this: soon after they realized their plane was being hijacked, they discovered that two planes had been flown into the

world trade center earlier that morning and another had been flown into the Pentagon, killing thousands of people. Then they decided—
CHORUS: Together.
MARIAH: Unanimously. They decided to try to overcome the terrorists and take back the plane. (*beat*) My obsession began as a search for a birth parent. I think it ended as a search for something else.

CHORUS: CREW

(*Five flight attendants enter. There's some laughter.*)

DEBBIE: I was so hot. I just couldn't stand it anymore.
WANDA: So you disrobed at a party? For heaven's sake, in front of all the guests?
CEE CEE: You ever heard of gettin' yourself a drink of water? My husband would have driven away and left me there.
WANDA: See, that's the advantage of being divorced. You can take your clothes off at a party if you want to and there's nobody to fight with about it later. Not that I've ever had the urge to take off my clothes in public.
DEBBIE: I still had my underwear on.
WANDA: Oh Lord!
LORRAINE: Hopefully, you got in the pool immediately.
DEBBIE: Yeah, I did. That's why I took my clothes off in the first place—so I could get in the pool immediately.
SANDY: (*she's from North Carolina*) I'm tryin' to imagine the look on Phil's face if I did something like that. Course I wouldn't dream of doin' it. Not a chance.
CEE CEE: Maybe if I had too much to drink.
CAPTAIN JASON DAHL: (*entering and passing by them*) You ladies thinking about getting on the plane?
LORRAINE: Debbie's telling us a story.
CEE CEE: About stripping down to her skivvies at a pool party.
JASON: None of that randy talk, ladies. I'm a married man. (*pointing behind him*) Look out. Leroy's got new photos.

(*JASON exits.*)

DEBBIE: I grabbed a towel and then I felt cool and dry and ate like a horse.
SANDY: You had a whole weekend off? How'd you wrangle that?

LORRAINE: I worked Labor Day, but that's fine because I'm planning to take a good long time at Christmas.
WANDA: I'll work Christmas as long as I get Christmas Eve. I've got responsibilities at the church.
FIRST OFFICER LEROY HOMER: (*as he enters, by way of greeting*) Lorraine! Haven't seen you in a month of Sundays.
LORRAINE: I hear you've got new pictures of Laurel.
LEROY: Sure do.

(*LEROY takes out a wallet from which he removes some photos. They pass them around.*)

LORRAINE: What is she? A year old now?
LEROY: Ten months.

(*JASON steps back in.*)

JASON: Hello? Anybody?
CEE CEE: Hush.
SANDY: (*referring to photo*) Will you look at all that beautiful hair? Neither of mine had any hair to speak of at that age.
LEROY: That's my baby.

(*Freeze.*)

(*Viola plays viola part, and maybe some clarinet part transposed, of Bruch's Eight Pieces for Clarinet, Viola, Piano: II.*)

ILSE HOMER: (*Chorus Member*) (*LEROY's mother*) August 26, 2006. Good Morning, my darling Leroy! I spoke to Laurel yesterday. Next month she will enter first grade! Such joy, such happiness she brings to all of us. Already she plays piano beautifully—she and I play together over the phone, often the same song at the same time, or else one of us plays a solo to the other. My darling, I still remember your cute round face when you were born. Daddy called you "the Pope." Tomorrow I will let balloons fly into the sky for your birthday. I hope they will reach you. I know that you are with us. I feel your spirit around me. Much, much love, my wonderful child. Your mourning Mom.

(LEROY unfreezes and enters a scene from his life.)

LEROY: About another week and we're in Germany, Mom.
ILSE: A live performance of Bruch's viola and clarinet concertos in the city of his birth. Tell me what mother has such a generous son.

(He kisses her cheek.)

ILSE: How much will Cologne have changed, I wonder?
LEROY: Well, you were—what—15 when you came here? And now you're—88?
ILSE: Now you're a bad boy.
LEROY: I'll brush up my German. You study up on Cologne.

(LEROY freezes. Viola out. ILSE speaks to MARIAH.)

ILSE: I came here from Germany in 1945. Leroy's father came here from Barbados soon after. My children say, "Fate brought you together."
MARIAH: *(to audience)* If Leroy was my father, I'd inherit a huge family. He had a brother and 7 sisters. That would be fun for me. I'm an only child.
ILSE: Leroy wanted nothing more than to fly. As a boy of 8, he was already doing odd jobs to save money for flying lessons. Air Force Academy. Desert Storm. He was a man you would be proud to have as a father. If he were your father, all of us would welcome you into the family with open arms.

JASON: *(stepping in again)* Folks? We all have to be on the plane before the passengers start boarding, right? Leroy? Put Laurel away.
DEBBIE: Wanda, you're with me and Lorraine in First Class.
SANDY: Debbie, I don't mean to pry, but what's that thing around your neck?
DEBBIE: *(taking it off to show her)* You like it? I bought it because it matches Dylan's coat, and I tied one of my scarves around his neck, so he can smell me when I'm away.
LORRAINE: And who is Dylan?
DEBBIE: *(putting the scarf back on with a flourish)* My Dalmatian.
WANDA: *(amused)* Oh, Lordy.
DEBBIE: *(addressing the universe)* Wild blue yonder? Here we come again.

CHORUS: LANGUAGE

MARIAH: My Dad told me be careful, Mariah. You're embarking on a perilous journey. Perilous. Dangerous. Dicey. Hazardous. Precarious. Treacherous. (*pause*) Vulnerable. (*beat*) There's only one word Flight Control heard Leroy say. It's his only extant communication from the cockpit.

LEROY: Mayday!

MARIAH: Growing up, my ambition was to become a sportswriter, but only if I could cover the Minnesota Twins. Starting when I first realized what it meant to be adopted—so when I was five or six—my most cherished daydream was that I'd discover my birth father was a Minnesota Twin. Harmon Kilebrew or Tony Oliva or Bert Blyleven. One of the skills I developed as a rabid baseball fan is the ability to hold hundreds of stats in my mind simultaneously and that skill is also what made it possible for me to hold so much information about so many people on a plane in my mind. Ties to Germany was one of the uncanny number of things the people on the plane had in common. Two of the 40 passengers were born in Germany, like Leroy Homer's mother. One still lived there.

CHRISTIAN: Wirklich? (Really?)
HILDA: Ja. Schwedelbach. Was ist mit Ihnen? (Yes. Schwedelbach. What about you?)
CHRISTIAN: Mainz.
HILDA: Sprecken Sie Englisch? (Do you speak English?)
CHRISTIAN: Of course. It is necessary for my business.
HILDA: What is it, your business?
CHRISTIAN: I am the Deputy Director of the German Wine Institute.
HILDA: Oh, I love the sweet German wine. The Riesling.
CHRISTIAN: Certain Riesling is not so sweet, Miss—
HILDA: Hildegarde.
CHRISTIAN: A beautiful name.
HILDA: The moment we arrived at Ellis Island people began calling me Hilda.
CHRISTIAN: Ah. Hilda is nice too. So. Now California is your home?
HILDA: New Jersey is too cold for me now, so I'm going to live with one of my daughters near San Francisco. A new life at my age. (*She laughs.*) I

resisted at first, but she convinced me by sending me photographs of the beautiful farmer's market in her town. I used to take her and her sister to the farmer's market when they were growing up. Such a wonderful place to meet people. (*out of the scene*) I thought of my family's farm on the outskirts of our town. When I was a child, we sold fresh eggs at the road. We were a tiny farmer's market of our own. The police came to take away a Jewish woman who boarded with us and my parents understood we had to leave Germany. We had better luck than many thousands of others—the luck of knowing it was time to go. You know what good luck this was? I lived for 79 years and nine months and the Jewish woman taken from our home? No such luck. In spring and summer, Schwedelbach is blanketed by rape blossoms. As we went down, visions of those wild and bright yellow flowers flooded my thoughts.

(Viola plays George Frederic Handel's Viola Concerto in B minor, III, starting at measure 10.)

(HILDA smiles broadly, maybe even a giggle.)

HILDA: As a child, I had a pet goose.
CHRISTIAN: (*drawing her back to him*) Gans?!
HILDA: Yes! I kept him on a leash! And you? Do you have children?
CHRISTIAN: A son and a daughter, yes. No goose, but a dog, yes.
HILDA: Variety is the spice of life. Perhaps you'll e-mail about the dry Riesling and I'll search for some to try.
CHRISTIAN: I know some lovely restaurants in San Francisco where you can sample a delicious glass of dry Riesling. You'll write down your e-mail for me. I'll send the information.
HILDA: How very exciting.

(Viola out.)

MARIAH: Hilda would have been 63 when I was born, Christian 18 and in college in Germany.

JEAN: I don't mean to intrude, but did I hear someone in this row speaking German? (*looking behind her*) Or this row?
CHRISTIAN: You heard correctly. It was Hildegarde and I speaking.
JEAN: I haven't heard German spoken in such a long while. I lived there for

a short time many years ago.

(Everyone freezes except MARIAH.)

MARIAH: Jean was a nurse, her husband Don an economist. They had both been married before and never expected to be divorced; they didn't believe in divorce. Then the thing happened that happens when you hold a firm belief, but your life dictates you behave in a way that undermines that belief. Each of them fell into a little bit of a funk.

JENNIFER PRICE: *(JEAN's daughter, speaking to MARIAH)* It was sort of a blind date, if you can call riding to Bible Study together a date. I was in eighth grade when Don arrived on our doorstep to meet my mother. Basically, he never left.

DAVE PETERSON: *(DON's son.)* In Jean, Dad found a kindred spirit. Dad would say, "She has three daughters, I have three sons! Kismet!" My Dad was kind of a big muckety muck in our tiny New Jersey town, but meeting them for the first time, you'd never know how well off they were. They could have afforded to fly first class but they didn't. *(beat)* Not that it would have made a difference. *(beat)* They didn't live lavishly.

JENNIFER PRICE: We had a pretty nice house though.

DAVE PETERSON: Pretty nice. Not lavish.

(Freeze. Except for JEAN and DON.)

JEAN: It wasn't the size of the house that made us choose it. It was the weather. Don loves weather.

DON: I could watch the Weather Channel for hours. At the time we got on the plane, we lived in Spring Lake, New Jersey right near the ocean. Jean's very health conscious so we'd walk on the boardwalk together regularly. More than once, a storm threatened. She'd go back to the house, but I'd stay and watch the waves. The waves, the lightning.

JEAN: Sometimes he'd even stand on the boardwalk in the rain.

DON: There's something so alive about weather. It makes me feel like God's talking to me. I realize when it storms a lot of people are hearing and seeing it, but it makes me feel like the Almighty is speaking only to me.

(DON sits in his seat. JENNIFER and DAVE resume talking to MARIAH.)

JENNIFER PRICE: Mom was much younger when she lived in Germany. She thought she might become an academic and teach German. No. Her life took another path.
DAVE PETERSON: After Dad retired, they became missionaries. They didn't try to convert people. Not that kind of missionary.
JENNIFER PRICE: They ministered to people in need overseas and—
DAVE PETERSON: And counseled people here at home too. When he died, Dad was working with men who were recovering drug addicts.
JENNIFER PRICE: Brought a couple of them home for dinner. Scary. You know. A little.

MARIAH: When I imagine the people on the plane, sometimes I try to picture what they were doing in the last moments of their lives. The Petersons must have been praying, and I'll bet they were ministering to the people sitting near them.

JEAN: Don? (*DON turns to her.*) I was right. I did hear people speaking German.

(*JEAN moves toward her seat and HILDA gets out of hers as CEE CEE approaches.*)

CEE CEE: What are you ladies doing in the aisle? (*pointing*) Seat belt sign's turned on.
JEAN: (*as she sits*) Yes. Thank you.
HILDA: I have to make a little visit to the ladies' room.
CEE CEE: You'll have to sit down and wait till the seat belt sign's turned off.
HILDA: Oh no, I don't think I can.
CEE CEE: I used to be a police officer, Ma'am. (*kidding*) You don't want me to have to make a citizen's arrest.
HILDA: I too was once a police officer.
CEE CEE: You were a police officer? How long ago was that?
HILDA: Wait a moment. (*Her idea of a joke.*) No. That was my husband.

CHORUS: GRANDPARENTS

MARIAH: I was 16 remember and it took me a couple months before I realized something: probably no one on the plane who had grandchildren was going to turn out to be my birth parent. Not Hilda. Not Jean or

Donald Peterson. But it was weird. Because even if I decided a person couldn't possibly be my mom or dad, I wanted to know all about her anyway.

GEORGINE: When my granddaughter was born I was in Las Vegas with my friend Jacque.

MARIAH: Like Georgine Corrigan.

GEORGINE: When she opened the door to the hotel room, I was suddenly shocked by the realization that—well, I blurted out—
JACQUE: (*Chorus Member*) She screamed.
GEORGINE: WE'VE BECOME OUR MOTHERS!
KEVIN MARISAY: (*GEORGINE's brother, Chorus Member*) September 11, 2007. I miss you, my sister. Today is a rough day for me. I could not go to Pennsylvania this year.

(*GEORGINE and KEVIN chase each other around, playing tag as they did as children. JACQUE runs over from her place in the chorus and tags KEVIN.*)

JACQUE: You're it!
GEORGINE'S MOTHER: (*Chorus Member*) (*as though calling to her from inside their house*): Georgine!

(*They stop and stand still, listening. GEORGINE puts her finger to her lips, indicating "shhhh" to the others.*)

GEORGINE'S MOTHER: Georgine!
GEORGINE: What??
GEORGINE'S MOTHER: Is Kevin out there with you?

(*KEVIN starts to move toward his mother's voice. GEORGINE pulls him back.*)

GEORGINE: No.
GEORGINE'S MOTHER: Go find him and come inside. It'll be dark soon.
GEORGINE: (*to JACQUE*) Let's go play at your house.
JACQUE: (*running off*) Meet you there!
KEVIN: But we gotta go home.
GEORGINE: No, Kevin. What you should do is, you should tell mom I

found you playing over at Jacque's house. (*pulling him by his hand or shirt*) C'mon, let's go.

(*She freezes.*)

KEVIN: (*to MARIAH*) The Portage River ran behind our house in Woodville, Ohio. As kids we ignored all property lines. The entire neighborhood, including the river and the woods, was our playground. Georgine was the center of excitement at our house. It got very quiet when she left for college. She was on her way home to Honolulu when the plane crashed—she'd been in New York at an antique show. We shared an interest in collecting antiques and her little girl was all grown up, so I suggested we try to make a business of it. And together, we succeeded. The day before the crash I tried again to talk her into moving back to the mainland. (*pause*) My sister lived so far away. I was used to not seeing her for long stretches at a time. So it took a while for "never again" to sink in.

(*GEORGINE unfreezes.*)

GEORGINE: Kevin! Come on!

(*KEVIN and GEORGINE run off the stage as JOE DRISCOLL and BILLY CASHMAN enter. Joe is a loud Irish guy. Billy is more soft-spoken than, and amused by, JOE. They've made this trip together many times before.*)

MARIAH: (*to audience*) Joe Driscoll had five grandchildren.

JOE: I keep telling the wife come along, climbing is a spiritual experience. At the summit, I feel as if I'm in church I tell her. She won't budge. Then I think, do we really want the wives along? (*beat*) Nah!

DON: (*as he and JEAN take their seats in the row behind JOE and BILLY*) I don't do any mountain climbing myself. Haven't been in good enough shape for a good long time. But you hear "mountaintop" as a way of describing the place where wisdom resides, and that's going to include God's wisdom.

BILLY: "Thousands of over-civilized people are beginning to find out that going to the mountain is going home."

JOE: Billy! You've been reading!

BILLY: You suggested I read it, so I read it. (*to the PETERSONS*) The man

wrote an article in 1875 that captures just how I feel about the outdoors. Little bit of a wonderful thing—capturing what somebody's going to feel a hundred and twenty-five years in the future! (*to JOE*) I memorized a couple sentences. You want to make something of it?
JOE: Give us another one.
BILLY: Not on your life.
JOE: Then I might have to sing one.

(Irish folk music played on viola—Star of the County Down.)

BILLY: Joe, it's 9 in the morning.
JOE: (*singing, accompanied by viola*)
    In Banbridge Town in the County Down
    One morning last July
    From a boreen green came a sweet colleen
    And she smiled as she passed me by.
    She looked so sweet from her two bare feet
    To the sheen of her nut brown hair—
BILLY: (*to the PETERSONS*) He comes back from Ireland with half a dozen new songs every year.
JEAN: Don? You don't think he's going to sing the whole way across the country, do you?
JOE: Everyone ready to join in? I'm comin' up to the chorus.

(Freeze.)

MARIAH: At first, all I wanted was to find out who my birth parent was. Soon, I wanted to find out who every one of those passengers was. Billy—he was an ironworker and a paratrooper in Vietnam who grew up in a tough New York neighborhood and turned into a guy whose ideas about beauty were pretty expansive.

(BILLY unfreezes and we see a blow-up of one of the works of art made by his nephew, DANIEL BELARDINELL.)

DANIEL: (Chorus Member) (*to MARIAH*) I have a slew of uncles and aunts. Uncle Billy was the only one who ever came to see my exhibitions. (*to BILLY*) Thanks for coming, Uncle Billy. What'd you think?
BILLY: Nice. That is, I can't say I'm sure what you're getting at. But the

pictures make me want to laugh. So that's nice. (*to MARIAH*) See, I liked that response because a lot of people don't get that the work's supposed to be funny.

(*BILLY returns to his seat. He hands JOE a post card.*)

BILLY: That's from Daniel's latest show.
JOE: What the hell is it?
BILLY: That one is sort of a goddess. You know, a happy goddess.
JOE: Get out of here.
SANDY: Coffee? (*JOE holds out his cup. She pours, looks at the post card.*) Isn't that interesting? Those big eyes and big red lips. I took a painting class once—watercolors. I was just terrible at it. I content myself with taking care of my garden, which is beautiful if I do say so.
BILLY: That postcard's an announcement for a show of my nephew's paintings. All these paintings—not all of them all the time—but all the ones in this show? He made them with nail polish.
SANDY: I've got to think you're pulling my leg now.
BILLY: I think he means them to be funny.
SANDY: Well, isn't that ingenious.
CEE CEE: What've you got there?
SANDY: A post card from an art exhibit. One of the passengers has a nephew who's a painter.
CEE CEE: Looks like a witch.
SANDY: He says it's a goddess.
CEE CEE: Give me some of that coffee.
SANDY: (*as she gives CEE CEE a cup*) I've never known anyone who was an artist. I've probably flown with a whole bunch of them, but I've never known one personally. Have you?
CEE CEE: No, but I bet Debbie has. Let's buzz her and see. (*picking up a phone*) Debbie, come back here, will you? We got a question for you.
DEBBIE: (*on a different part of the plane/stage*) What? I'm making coffee.
CEE CEE: Sandy and me got 27 of 'em back here, the three of you can't take care of 9 between you?
DEBBIE: We've got 10. What do you want?
CEE CEE: We want to know if you've ever known an artist. In real life I mean.
DEBBIE: If I've known an artist? You mean, like Vincent Van Gogh?
CEE CEE: No. One who's alive. (*She turns back to SANDY*) What's with the

guy singing?
SANDY: 14B asked me the same thing. We're going to have to re-seat her and her husband if he keeps it up.
CEE CEE: If he keeps it up, I'm going to have to throw him out the window.
SANDY: Cee Cee, I don't believe your bite's half as bad as your bark.
LORRAINE: (*to DEBBIE*) How's the coffee coming?
DEBBIE: (*pointing*) It's happening. Can you do me a favor and make the guy in 4D a screwdriver?

(*MARK BINGHAM—the guy in 4D—waves.*)

LORRAINE: Sure.
DEBBIE: Wanda, I'll be right back. Coach cabin has an urgent problem.
WANDA: Do tell.
DEBBIE: (*as she crosses to SANDY and CEE CEE, speaking to WANDA*) You ever known an artist?
WANDA: (*as DEBBIE moves away*) Several.
LORRAINE: Really?
DEBBIE: (*still moving toward SANDY and CEE CEE but talking to WANDA*) Sunday school kids don't count.
WANDA: Says you.

CHORUS: MURDER

(*Viola plays cha cha music—Sway.*

WANDA *extends her hand. A* MAN (*Chorus Member*)—*takes it and they cha cha.*)

WANDA: I still do a mean cha cha.

(*WANDA and the Man she's dancing with freeze.*)

MARIAH: I read a lot of memories of the people who once danced with the people on this plane. There were a lot of athletes on this plane. There were a lot of people who were police or were related to police on this plane. There were many people on the plane who did work on behalf of those less fortunate, like the Petersons. Three of the women on the plane, not counting the flight attendants, were EMTs. Whoa!, I kept thinking.

No way!, I kept thinking. My mind kept turning to ideas like "destiny" and "courage" and whether those concepts have any real meaning. And I thought about—

MARIAH and CHORUS MEMBER: Dying with dignity.

(WANDA and the MAN resume dancing.)

WANDA's HIGH SCHOOL FRIEND: (*Chorus Member*) You're Wanda, right?
WANDA: (*chuckling and dancing*) Yeah, I'm Wanda.
WANDA's HIGH SCHOOL FRIEND: You're not Sandra pretending to be Wanda.
WANDA: We don't even look so much alike now that she's put those extensions in her hair.

(WANDA and the MAN stop dancing. As he dances away, she blows him a kiss.)

WANDA: Me and Sandra loved to fool people. That's what twins do. Sandra'd have a lunch appointment—maybe with someone she worked with?—and I'd show up in her place and later she'd jump out from behind the shrubbery, cackling. My sister has the loudest, most hilarious cackle, you can't imagine, you'd have to hear it. At our birthday parties, sometimes we'd switch clothes and Sandra'd wind up saying something like, what's wrong with you, can't you tell I'm drunk and Wanda's not drunk? I'm not Wanda, I'm just drunk in Wanda's clothes. Then cackle, cackle, cackle. Lord.

MARIAH: (*looking at WANDA*) Sometimes, my thoughts were interrupted by my blurting out loud, "Oh my God, could she be my mother?" Then I'd think, she may not be my mother, but she's somebody's mother.

(JOE, Wanda's 18-year-old son and JENNIFER, her 20-year-old daughter.)

JENNIFER: (*Chorus Member*) I don't think Mom would have wanted you to do it. She wanted you to go to college.
JOE: (*Chorus Member*) You're going to college for both of us, all right? It's gonna be the police academy for me.
JENNIFER: But Mom's gone, so I have to make sure you're—

JOE: Forget that. You're not taking her place. No one is. Never. Some freak stabbed our mother to death. In the name of God. He murdered our mom in the name of God.

MARIAH: Wanda's family is convinced she's the flight attendant who was killed immediately because she wouldn't let those guys into the cockpit.
DEBBIE: Well. Her first. Me later.
MARIAH: That's what the 9/11commission report concluded. Not that anyone could know that for absolutely certain, but passengers who talked to people on the ground said—
WANDA: One of the passengers tried to help me.
DEBBIE: (*pointing to MARK [MICKEY] ROTHENBERG*) He was stabbed to death, like Wanda and me.
WANDA: Mickey Rothenberg.
DEBBIE: One of those brash Brooklyn types. Pretty funny guy, had me giggling a lot.
WANDA: When they grabbed me, he stood up. Kept yelling at those guys, like they didn't have knives. "Are you crazy?" he kept yelling.
MICKEY ROTHENBERG: (*standing up, yelling*) What are you doing? Are you crazy?? You're crazy.
WANDA: He was a brash Brooklyn type all right. And a real gentleman.

(*Viola plays It Will Stand, a rock and roll song from 1962.*)

MYRNA SINGER: (*Mickey's Childhood Friend, Chorus Member*) I grew up with Mickey. We lived in the same apartment building, on the same floor, and our families were very close, always in one another's apartments. I remember teaching him to dance the lindy when we were kids.

MARIAH: See? Dancing.

MYRNA: (*12 or 13*) C'mon, Mickey, you can learn this.
MICKEY: (*also 12 or 13*) I'm kind of a klutz as you know.
MYRNA: But try.
MICKEY: I'm trying. What do you think? I'm a putz who won't even try something?
MYRNA: (*counting as she shows him*) Here. One. Two. One two three. One. Two. One two three. See? Now—turn. two. One two—
MICKEY: Turn? What's that, a joke?

MYRNA: Turn. Two. One two three.

(They freeze. MICKEY steps out of the freeze.)

MICKEY: What I took to doing in college—I mean besides becoming a champion bridge player if you don't mind my pointing it out—was teaching young ladies I was dating how to dance the lindy, like I'd been dancing the lindy since birth. They'd say "Brooklyn"—that's what they called me in college. So they'd say "Brooklyn, the lindy? How old-fashioned." Which, translation? I was charming the pants off them.

(MICKEY returns to MYRNA, twirls her around. They laugh, as they fade from the scene.)

(Viola out.)

DEBBIE: I survived three bouts of melanoma. In Bali, I survived near-fatal pneumonia. Some people would call that ironic. I call it really crappy luck.
MARIAH: Destiny. Fate. Luck.
CHORUS: Same thing?
DEBBIE: It takes two seconds to slit someone's throat but those two seconds felt more like two hours. I swear to God, I thought about every single person I have ever loved in those two seconds. Every one. I swear.
WANDA: I didn't say it, but I thought it in my mind: Lord, please hear my confession.
DEBBIE: Like you have anything to confess, Wanda Green.
WANDA: Deborah, we all have things to confess.

JENNIFER: *(to her brother)* At least talk to Aunt Sandra about it.
JOE: Okay. I'll talk to Aunt Sandra. But I've made up my mind.

MARIAH: *(as JOE and JENNIFER exit)* I was able to contact Wanda's son at the Narcotics Unit, 28th precinct. In Harlem. Which is where he works.

MARK BINGHAM: *(friendly)* How's that screwdriver coming?
LORRAINE: Coming right up. *(turning to TOM BURNETT across the aisle)* Can I get you something, Mr. Burnett?
TOM: No thanks. I grew up in the Midwest. We don't drink alcohol at this hour. *(to MARK)* A screwdriver before breakfast. You're a better man than

I am.
MARK: Orange juice is good for you.
TOM: I've heard that.

CHORUS: WHAT GRIEF DOES

JASON: Lorraine, did you put my anniversary card in the mail?

MARIAH: Jason. The pilot. His wedding anniversary was coming up on the 13th. He was planning to take his wife to London.

MATT: (*JASON's 15-year-old son, Chorus Member*) Mom said he never took her to London. She said he just thought this other girl was hot, so that's why he—I mean, my mom said she was hot. I'm not saying it. My mom said it.

(*JASON holds his hand out to his wife, (Chorus Member) who takes it and they dance a fox trot. Viola accompanies with "Begin the Beguine." Kenji Bunch's version, for viola.*)

MARIAH: Inevitably, I guess, after September 11 there were disagreements—sometimes pretty nasty disagreements—in this case, about Jason's headstone, which is in a cemetery in San Jose near the neighborhood where he grew up. His family's business—Dahl's Dairy Delivery—was a neighborhood touchstone. One of those bars or greengrocers or—I don't know—pizza places—that when you drive by, you think, "almost home".
MATT: It's where my Uncle Ken got buried after he died in Vietnam. It's where my father belongs.
MARIAH: Jason's wife—this boy's stepmother—bought a headstone, had her name engraved on it next to Jason's, and put it in a plot in Colorado where she and Jason lived. His family objected.
MATT: Cause it wasn't right.

MARIAH: Jason's wife moved the headstone to his family's plot in his hometown. Jason's mother replaced it with a headstone engraved with only Jason's name.

(*JASON and his wife stop dancing.*)

(Viola out.)

SANDRA DAHL: *(JASON's wife)* I'm never going to marry again. I want to be buried with him.

MARIAH: There was a lawsuit.
CHORUS MEMBER: That's what grief does.
MARIAH: Grief creeps up in a hundred different ways. *(beat)* When the cockpit was breached, Flight 93 was still transmitting to the control tower. Jason is recorded, literally screaming—
JASON: GET OUT OF HERE! GET OUT OF HERE!!
SANDRA DAHL: I believe Jason tampered with the automatic pilot. I'm sure of it, because once the . . . by the time they took over flying the plane, the automatic pilot had stopped working.
MARIAH: Captain Dahl was lying on the cockpit floor dying. For half an hour? That's the theory.

CHORUS: HALLMARK

MARK: *(accepting a drink from Lorraine)* Thanks. *(looking at her name badge)* Lorraine.
LORRAINE: You're welcome, sir.
MARK: Do I look like a sir to you? *(extends his hand)* Mark. Bingham.

ALICE HOAGLAND: *(MARK's mother, Chorus Member)* Come on, Mark. Stop kidding around. I mean, a joke's a joke—
MARK: It's not a joke. Why would I joke about something like this, Alice?
ALICE: You want a slap? Don't call me Alice.
MARK: Mom? I'm not kidding. I'm gay.
ALICE: But—
MARK: But?
ALICE: But—
MARK: *(interrupting her sharply)* Mom. Don't make me be angry with you. *(beat)* Hey! Guess what I dressed up as for Halloween? *(beat)* A transvestite lumberjack.
ALICE: *(amused—he got her)* You have any pictures?

(MARIAH quickly moves to MARK and ALICE as she speaks.)

MARIAH: I want to see those pictures. (*beat*) There was an avalanche of publicity about this guy being gay. I eliminated him from contention because I didn't realize that his being gay didn't necessarily mean he wasn't my Dad. He was one of the passengers who telephoned people on the ground. The first thing he said was—

MARK: Mom? This is Mark Bingham.

MARIAH: So, we're talking about a very shaken up person. His parents actually named him Gerald Kendall Bingham, Jr.

MARK: (*much younger*) I'm definitely having a new name, Mom.

ALICE: You're nine years old. You don't get to choose a new name. I mean it, Gerry.

MARK: That's not my name. That's Dad's name. I want my own name.

ALICE: (*to MARIAH*) It was just Mark and me for quite a while when he was a boy, and we had some hard times. Some desperate times. Some homeless times.

MARK: My name is Mark now. Mark Bingham.

(*ALICE fades from the scene; MARK turns to LORRAINE.*)

MARK: Hey, Lorraine. What's the movie?

LORRAINE: Shrek.

MARK: Where Eddie Murphy's the donkey? Cool. How long till breakfast? (*holding his glass toward her*) Do I have time for another?

TOM: *Two* cocktails before breakfast.

MARK: Breakfast of champions.

TOM: Impressive. I tend to save drinking alcohol for the evening. Although I do like to treat my mother to a glass of wine after mass some Sundays.

LORRAINE: Oh, he's tall. He can handle it.

CEE CEE: (*on intercom*) Lorraine? My birthday's November 26. You got that written down?

LORRAINE: I got teased quite a bit about the greeting cards. Why is that so terribly funny? I don't think there's such a thing as a greeting card addict. And even if there were, think how much worse it could have been. I could have been a crack addict. I traveled a lot, so I didn't see people consistently, even people I thought the world of. What should I have done? Lost touch

with them completely? Many times, I sent cards to people who hadn't contacted me for years. My husband said—
ERICH BAY: (*Chorus Member*) Lou. You're in your 50s and the woman hasn't contacted you since you were 30. Your friendship can't mean much to her if—
LORRAINE: I think you're jumping to conclusions.
ERICH: What other conclusion could I come to? What's the point of continuing to send a card on her birthday? Tell me that.

LORRAINE: (*turning front again*) That I was thinking about someone. That was the point. And it was a way to keep track of my life. It was a way to acknowledge time passing. It was a way to bring to mind things from my past I didn't want to forget. Erich wanted to know how I knew. If I hadn't heard from someone for so many years, how I knew the cards were appreciated. Well. I didn't.
LORRAINE'S HIGH SCHOOL CLASSMATE: (*Chorus Member*) September 12, 2002. Lorraine, you would have liked the gentle words so many people spoke about you at the service tonight at the football field. All your Neshaminy High classmates miss you and love you.
LORRAINE: The cards were a kind of wonderful ritual too. It was calming to find a time every day to sit down for 15 minutes and write them out. If my schedule didn't allow it, then I did it on the plane.
ERICH: I don't know what Hallmark's going to do without her. They're going to go bankrupt.

DEBBIE: (*to SANDY and CEE CEE*) Okay, so where's this masterpiece?

(*SANDY hands DEBBIE the post card.*)

DEBBIE: Holy cow! That's fantastic! (*stepping a few steps down the aisle, asking loudly*) Who belongs to this post card?
CEE CEE: Quiet down.
SANDY: (*overlap, pointing*) Tall guy there in row 15. His nephew—
CEE CEE: (*overlap*) Why hasn't somebody fired her?

(*DEBBIE's gone, on her way to BILLY.*)

DEBBIE: Your nephew made this? Did you see it in person?
BILLY: I did.

DEBBIE It's so strange, but so wonderful. His paintings get shown a lot?
BILLY: All over the world.
DEBBIE: Can I keep this?
BILLY: Sure. I bet there's a lot more where that came from.
CEE CEE: Deborah? Dylan probably wants to get back to first class.

SANDY: (*Looking toward DEBBIE as she approaches BILLY, then out of the scene*) That's a different thing in the South. Dogs. I was raised on a farm and I don't mind sayin' I was delighted to leave the farm behind, but I did miss the dogs. At one time we had five and mostly? Outside making friends with the chickens. One of 'em was my special gardening pal. She'd help me dig up the dirt for planting. That was a sight to see.

CHORUS: CARPE DIEM!

(*HONOR WAINIO sits in row 11. LOUIS (JOEY) NACKE sits behind her. In row 12 on the other side of the aisle sits MARION BRITTON. HONOR stands and looks toward the bathroom.*)

HONOR: Should I go check on her?
LOUIS (JOEY): She was running pretty fast to the ladies.
MARION: Motion sickness. Happens fast.
LOUIS: Or you never know. Could be a bun in the oven.
HONOR: (*leaning over toward him, extending her hand*) Honor.
LOUIS: That's your name?
HONOR: Honor Elizabeth. Like Ann Marie. Or Mary Ellen.
LOUIS: Louis Joseph Nacke the second. People call me Joey, which I prefer to Junior.

(*HONOR moves out of the scene.*)

HONOR: You know what I did four days ago, Joey?

(*Viola plays Bloch's "Hébraique" for Viola and Piano": III, starting when viola part starts.*)

HONOR: I didn't say it, but it's what I wanted to say. It's what I wanted to say to everyone I bumped into on the subway, sat near in a restaurant, everyone who crossed my path after I got home from Europe. I wanted to say, "I had lunch on the Champs-Elysees." (*indicates the viola music*) Hear that? I played viola in Maryland's All-State Senior High School Orchestra. (*listening*) That was my audition piece.

(*Pause, while viola plays solo a few seconds. Then dialogue continues under.*)

HONOR: My grandmother used to tell me, "Honor! Carpe Diem!" Till I took that trip, I thought all those times she told me to seize the day she meant hooray! You made valedictorian, or congratulations on your promotion, what did I tell you? You can do anything. When I was in Paris, I realized she wasn't just talking about corporate success or making buckets of money. She also meant, "You have a friend getting married in Europe? Go to Europe!" So now? I've seen Paris! I can die happy.

(*Viola out.*)

(*LAUREN GRANDCOLAS stumbles into her seat.*)

HONOR: You all right?
LAUREN: Morning sickness.
LOUIS: What'd I tell you?
HONOR: (*overlap*) That's wonderful!
MARION: Hey, you want a bagel?
LAUREN: You mean now?
MARION: Sure, I brought the best bagels.
LOUIS: H & H?
MARION: Is there any other bagel?
LOUIS: (*to LAUREN*) She's right. Nothing like 'em. Might settle your stomach. Bagel, you know, bland but filling.
LAUREN: No thanks. I want to just sit here quietly for a minute. (*She puts her arms across her stomach.*)
HONOR: You sure you're all right? Do you want me to call the flight attendant?
LAUREN: No, I'm okay. (*beat*) I'm returning home from my Grandmother's funeral, so . . .
MARION: Hard to lose your Grandma, right? No matter how old you get, right? My father was a cop and my Grandma and I used to worry about him together. We'd cook and worry. Worry and cook.
LOUIS: Good food. Nothin' beats it. I myself make a mean lasagna. It's got

the Bolognese sauce and it's also got the béchamel. So rich you wouldn't believe.

(*LAUREN stands, her hand on her stomach.*)

LAUREN: Oh. (*beat, then a deep breath*) No. (*She sits down.*)
HONOR: Are you a chef, Joey?
LOUIS (JOEY): Don't I wish. Nah. I work for K-Bees—big toy company. You probably heard of it? I spend a lot of time moving pallets of Barbie accessories around a big warehouse.

MARIAH: Joey was a self-proclaimed tough guy.
PAULA JACOBS: (*LOUIS' sister, Chorus Member*) When some guy came speeding down our block and nearly ran over our little brother, Joey ran out into the street and punched the guy right through his car window. I said: through—a—car—window. Another time a guy cut him off, and this was when Joey was a lot older, like in his thirties. The guy cut him off and two blocks later he had to stop at a light, so my brother caught up with him and this guy flipped him off, right? So, Joey gets out of his car, and screams at the guy—
LOUIS (JOEY): You got something to say to me? I'll knock you back into your Generation X.
PAULA: Joey's most cherished possession? One of Roberto Clemente's baseball Jerseys.
LOUIS (JOEY): He was a hero, that guy.
PAULA: That's what Joey wanted to be. When he was a kid, he thought he was superman. He had a cape and he used to jump out the kitchen window pretending like he was flying. First floor window, but still. In high school he always took up for kids who were being bullied. Without fail. After he died, I got a Superman tattoo in his memory. (*rolls up one of her sleeves*) See this? I had them put mine right in the same place Joey had his.

MARIAH: Roberto Clemente was an outfielder for the Pittsburgh Pirates. He died in a plane crash bringing provisions to impoverished people in Puerto Rico.

LAUREN: (*to MARION*) Can I try one of those now? (*MARION hands her a bagel and LAUREN nibbles on it.*) I'm flying home from my grandmother's funeral. She was 100 years old. If anyone could be ready, she was ready. If

she were here, she'd say, "What are you doing worrying about me dying? You should be thinking about you living."
HONOR: Mine would say the same thing.
LOUIS (JOEY): Yeah, right. Carpe Diem.

CHORUS: SERENDIPITY

MARIAH: How wonderful to have a father like Joey. (*beat*) I adore my adoptive father. The search I embarked on has nothing to do with him or my mom and thank God I was lucky and they understood that. (*beat*) So this is what I'd do.

CHORUS MEMBER: Read and read and read—
CHORUS MEMBER: (*as the other CHORUS MEMBER continues to say "read and read and read"*) Talk and talk and talk.
MARIAH: I'd talk to people who knew one of the passengers, and then I'd think about that person—
MARIAH/CHORUS: for days on end.
MARIAH: And maybe get excited because I'd think this person could be the one. But then I couldn't know for sure. And I'd move on to someone else.

ALICE BERTORELLI: (*JOHN TALIGNANI's sister, Chorus Member*) My brother was a gourmet chef. No one could cook like John.

(*JOHN TALIGNANI sits in his house watching a baseball game. ALICE moves to him.*)

ALICE: Happy birthday, Johnny.

MARIAH: John Talignani had been a widower for four years. He could be found watching his 55-inch television most days, either a baseball game—didn't I tell you, so many things in common?—or QVC.
CHORUS: The shopping channel.

JOHN: (*pointing to the TV*) Mets at Atlanta. Already I can tell they're gonna break my heart again this year. (*He changes the channel.*) I'm looking to buy myself a birthday present. My big pot with the built-in colander? (*pointing to TV*) That's where I got it. You want a drink? Sit down, I'll get it. You can't make a decent Old Fashioned to save your life.

ALICE: Johnny, listen, I really think you should let us take you out. It's your birthday, you don't want to be cooking for all of us. (*to MARIAH*) But he'd always say the same thing.
JOHN: Not gonna happen. I'm not letting anybody pay good money to eat food I can make better at home. I argued about this with Selma for 25 years. She never won the argument and you're not gonna win it either.
ALICE: Why be retired if you can't relax? It's time to take it easy.
JOHN: Alice, serving drinks to Donald Trump was not difficult.
ALICE: (*to MARIAH*) He worked as a bartender in a fancy Manhattan restaurant most of his life.
JOHN: (*standing*) Alice! Watch me do Bobby Darin. I've been practicing.

(*JOHN stands and does his best imitation of Bobby Darin, snapping his fingers, cocking his head, being jazzy."*)

JOHN: (*singing*): Oh, the shark, babe, has such teeth, dear
And he shows them pearly white.

(*John freezes.*)

ALICE: (*to MARIAH*) He's not your father. Because, believe me, if he was, he and Selma would have raised you on Staten Island. Johnny would have given anything if they could have had a kid together, especially a daughter. As it was, he treated Selma's three boys like they were his own.

(*Viola plays bassoon part Strauss Duet Concertino for Clarinet and Bassoon: II: Andante under the following.*)

MARIAH: John was traveling to recover the body of one of his stepsons, who had been killed in a car accident in California. Encountering this kind of information—John Talignani's stepson, Jason Dahl's brother—brought home to me that—
CHORUS Member: Tragedy's not a contest.
MARIAH: I'm not saying that John Talignani's or Leroy Homer's or Billy Cashman's or Lauren Grandcolas' deaths were sadder than anyone else's. But the people on that plane were aware their deaths were imminent, and they… Somehow, they kept their wits about them.

CHORUS: THE BACK OF THE PLANE

(Loud laughter. CEE CEE and SANDY step toward it. ANDREW GARCIA is standing. PAT CUSHING is seated in the row in front of him and JANE FOLGER is sitting beside her. PAT is howling with laughter.)

SANDY: What on earth?
PAT: Listen to this. (*to ANDREW*) Do it again.
JANE: Pat. It was not that funny.
PAT: (*still trying to control her laughter*) You are so persnickety
JANE: And you are such a pushover.

(Freeze.)

MARIAH: (*pointing*) Pat Cushing was married to Jane Folger's brother. 10 grandchildren between them.

(Viola plays Chopin's Nocturne Op 15, No 1 in F Major under, soft part at the beginning or his Ballade No. 4 in F Minor, Op. 52.)

JIM MEEHAN: (*JACK FOLGER's army buddy Chorus Member*) (*to Mariah*): Jack Folger and I were good pals growing up in Bayonne. Jane had a beautiful family. Jack was the oldest of five. He was killed near Kam Ky in Quang Nam Province. He came home in a closed coffin after being listed missing for one week. I was in the Marine Corps then, and I rode in a limo in my uniform cause I was a pallbearer. The death took a toll on Jane and this is where it gets personal and I'm not sure I should get into the details . . . but I'll jump forward and say after a very hard time, Jane finally did get it together. She went back to work at the bank. She was, you know, a very brave person.

JANE: (*to a son we can't see*) Your Aunt Pat tells me it's our duty to play the cards we're dealt. For God's sake, it has nothing to do with duty. We play the cards we're dealt because we have no choice. (*beat*) Because you're dying, Terrence. Why do you think I'm here? (*beat*) This has nothing to do with Jack. Your brother died a long time ago.

(Viola out.)

JANE: And where I've been for the past several years is somewhere else being angry at you, just as you have been here being angry at me. (*beat*) Now that I've decided that Catholicism is a fraud, I realize its standards were ridiculous ones to judge you by, and it goes without saying that I regret it. (*beat*) I regret it. Now. We're not going to discuss it anymore because arguing about it weakens you. I'm going to move in with you. No arguing. I'm going to stand between you and people who might frighten you. Or upset you. Or annoy you. (*beat*) Except me.

MARIAH: Jane was in her early forties when her son Jack was killed in Vietnam and 60 something when her son Terrence died of AIDS. When Flight 93 crashed, she was 73. My search was four or five months old when I started focusing on her and Pat. I felt this . . . longing.

CHORUS Member: Piercing.

MARIAH: This piercing longing. I knew the longing couldn't possibly mean either of them was the parent I was searching for, but I wanted so badly to speak to Jane. I thought—I wondered—was she happy at the end? I mean, did she believe she would be with her boys again? But I couldn't ask her that, even in my imagination. Instead, I asked (*to JANE*), What do you mean Pat was a pushover?

JANE: I'm exaggerating. She wasn't the least bit a pushover. She was kind. The closest I ever saw her come to losing her temper was when one of her children wore blue jeans to the dinner table.

PAT: (*with a little laugh at herself*) Because that's unacceptable.

JANE: She had a wonderful laugh. I, on the other hand, had rage.

PAT: What gave Jane joy was music. We went together to the symphony and the opera and chamber music concerts at Christmas and even—

JANE: We even saw Rosemary Clooney in person once.

PAT: That was magical.

JANE: It was.

(*PAT turns back to ANDREW. JANE covers her face with her hands, as though that would block ANDREW out.*)

ANDREW: (*to CEE CEE and SANDY*) Ever see "The High and the Mighty?" (*imitating John Wayne*) I played a pilot haunted by the past.

JANE: Good grief.

ANDREW: (*back to his own voice*) I'm good at imitating other people's voices. I can still fool my wife. I call her on the phone and pretend to be a bill collector or one of the kid's teachers or something like that and I fool her. She falls for it. One time I called her and pretended to be Jimmy Stewart. (*He grins.*) She said oh, stop it, Andy. She knew it was me. I think because Jimmy Stewart had already died, which my wife knew, and I didn't.

(*JOHN walks up the aisle in the plane, passing CEE CEE.*)

JOHN: Excuse me. I need to use the—
CEE CEE: No problem. Seat belt sign's turned off.

(*HONOR walks down the aisle, returning from the bathroom to her seat. She bends down to pick something up. JOHN doesn't see her and bumps into her. He helps her up; she's holding Daniel Belardinelli's post card.*)

JOHN: Sorry, I didn't see you there. You all right?
HONOR: I'm fine. (*holding the post card toward him*) Is this yours?
JOHN: (*tilts his head to look at it*) Not mine.
HONOR: Looks like an announcement for an art exhibition.
JOHN: (*pointing to the bathroom*) Excuse me. I have to use . . .
HONOR: Sure, sorry. (*extending her hand*) Honor.
JOHN: And I'm John. Speaking of which . . .

(*JOHN hands HONOR the post card and exits. A great clattering of noise from the front of the plane. Shouts! Shouters should include JASON and LEROY and MARK ROTHENBERG. HONOR, PAT, JANE, ANDREW, CEE CEE, and SANDY look toward the front of the plane.*)

SANDY: What's going on in first class?
PAT: (*overlap*) What's going on up there?
ANDREW: Sounds like some kind of argument or—.
SANDY: I'll see what I can find out.

(*There's a bit of turbulence. HONOR falls into CEE CEE.*)

HONOR: Whoa!

CEE CEE: (*looking up*) Why didn't the Captain turn on the seatbelt sign?

HONOR: (*looking at her name tag*) Cee Cee. Cute name.

(Now HONOR and CEE CEE are both out of the scene.)

CEE CEE: Lorne said that same thing when he started trying to get me to go out with him—cute name. And I told him sure, I'll go out with you, what time you want to come by? And he said, "What? Did I ask you for a date?" And I said well, Lorne, it's now or never because I'm tired of your pussyfooting around. And a couple months later I moved myself and my two boys in with him and his two boys and that was three years before I called him from the plane and woke him up and he couldn't make out what I was saying so I had to call him back and finally I got to hear his voice. (*to HONOR*) Your mother and my mother—they live in Florida, 20 miles apart.

HONOR: 16.9 miles.

MARY WHITE: (*Honor's Mother, Chorus Member*) September 11, 2009. My baby girl, today was a beautiful sunny Florida day at CeeCee's statue overlooking the Indian River Lagoon.

HONOR: (*to CEE CEE*) You got a statue. I didn't get a statue.

CEE CEE: I was a police officer. So.

MARY WHITE: The program was very nice. Cee Cee's mother and I held hands like we do every year and thought about our two beautiful daughters. This year Lorne came and brought red roses for Cee Cee, but I brought the yellow ones you loved so much.

(HONOR continues down the aisle to her seat. As she passes, the post card falls to the floor and KRISTIN GOULD picks it up. She reads the back.)

KRISTIN: Nail polish. Fascinating.

MARIAH: Kristen Gould sat alone in row 21, although if she felt lonely there she had only to lean over toward Andy Garcia to hear him telling a joke or doing an impersonation. She started writing poetry at the age of six.

ALLISON VADHAN: (*Kristin White Gould's Daughter, Chorus Member*) Five.

(Viola plays last 8 measures of Mozart's Serenade for Winds in B flat Major, "Gran Partita,": III.)

ALLISON: She'd written 30 or 40 poems by the time she was 10. Eventually, she reverted to journalism. She wrote for magazines skewed toward the medical—*Environmental Health*, for example, *Women's Health*. My mother was brilliant. She spoke Turkish fluently and read Latin and studied ancient civilizations. She was wearing a bracelet made of Byzantine coins the day she died.

MARIAH: And she was open-minded. She loved Mozart and Michael Jackson equally.

KRISTIN: Genius is genius. And it comes in so many thrillingly different packages. I taught contredanses to many of my friends. We wore out several of my recordings of Mozart's music dancing them. Michael Jackson on the other hand. Appreciating his brand of dancing was a spectator sport. I did give it the old college try on occasion. (*a laugh*) Absurd. And then there's this. (*She holds up Daniel Belardinelli's post card.*) That's genius of a entirely different stripe.

MARIAH: I miss her.

(*ALLISON turns sharply to MARIAH.*)

ALLISON: What?

MARIAH: I didn't actually say that to Kristin's daughter. But I thought it. (*beat*) She would have been 49 when I was born. That year, exactly thirty 49-year old women in the United States had babies.

KRISTIN: I contemplated death from time to time. I read about it. I even wrote about it. (*a smile*) I thought when the time came, I'd approach it philosophically. I suppose I anticipated having more time to prepare. (*after the smallest beat, she leans into ANDREW, tapping his shoulder*) Excuse me? (*ANDREW turns to her.*) I'm wondering—

CEE CEE: (*to KRISTIN*) Ma'am?

KRISTIN: (*to ANDREW*) Can you do Michael Jackson?

CEE CEE: Ma'am? Take your seat.

ANDREW: (*to KRISTIN*) For Michael Jackson you have to be standing up. (*off Cee Cee's look*) Maybe later.

CHORUS: A PLAN

MARIAH: I was shocked by some of the things people wrote and said about the passengers' attempt to take over the plane. Like—

CHORUS MEMBER: They weren't thinking about saving other people's lives. They were just—

CHORUS MEMBER: They weren't trying to save other people.
CHORUS MEMBER: (*overlap*)—trying to save themselves.
MARIAH: Well, some passengers told people on the ground they were waiting to make their attempt over an unpopulated area so no one on the ground would get hurt. That's why they crashed in that beautiful field near Shanksville. Or I hear this a lot.
CHORUS MEMBER: Of course they tried to take over the plane.
CHORUS MEMBER: What choice did they have?
CHORUS MEMBER: (*overlap*) They had no choice.
MARIAH: Untrue. They could have panicked. They could have not made phone calls. But they did and when they did, they found out about the planes flying into the world trade center. They could have not interacted with one another and therefore not had a plan. They could have done nothing at all and hoped for the best. Here's what they did instead. One of the hijackers was standing in the aisle claiming to have a bomb. During his four conversations with her, Tom Burnett told his wife he went from one passenger to the next whispering something like—
TOM: We don't think this guy really has a bomb. We think they're planning to use this plane as a weapon. There are a couple guys on board who can fly a commercial airplane, and we're going to try to overcome the hijackers and take control of the plane. What do you think?
SANDY: Debbie? What's going on up there? Debbie? Debbie?
TOM: I told one of the flight attendants—
SANDY: Me.
TOM: —what we were planning to do and she—
SANDY: I couldn't reach the first class crew… and then the first class passengers were herded into the back and I saw the guy who claimed he had the bomb. I heard Cee Cee leaving her husband a message.
CEE CEE: I hope I see your face again.
SANDY: So I thought to call Phil. I told him we had a plan. Then I filled two coffee pots with boiling water.
MARIAH: See, they didn't just do something: they decided together to do something. They took a vote. Jane Folger and Pat Cushing voted. Hilda Marcin and Christian Adams voted. Jean and Don Peterson voted. Georgine Corrigan voted. Joe Driscoll and Billy Cashman voted. Andrew Garcia and Kristin White Gould voted. Those who could vote—because they hadn't already been killed—voted unanimously in favor of trying to take over the plane. Thirty-five minutes after they voted, they were dead.

(If there is to be an intermission, this is a good place for it. Although I prefer the show run without one, I leave this decision to the director.)

CHORUS: PEACEFUL TOMORROWS

MARIAH: I realized I was in love with all of them. I had small shocks of recognition all along the way.

(Viola plays the Main Theme from Terminator 2.)

(TOSHIYA KUGE is watching the movie on a VCR. He is in JAPAN.)

MARIAH: When I thought about Toshiya, I felt one of those shocks. He must have struggled to feel a sense of belonging because he wasn't living in his own country. He'd come here for college and I thought he must feel like I felt when I first understood what it meant to be adopted. Thinking about Toshiya made me realize that, while some of the folks on the plane were too old to be my parent, others were too young.

(Music fades out under TOSHIYA's speech).

TOSHIYA: *(imitating what he's hearing, 11 or 12 years old)* "I need your clothes, your boots, and your motorcycle." *(making sure he's pronouncing it correctly)* "Motorcycle." *(He mimics riding a motorcycle.)* "Motorcycle." *(Big grin. Very proud of himself. He fast forwards. Now he changes parts.)* "Hey, get off me! Help!" *(very carefully—this is a difficult word for him)* "Help." *(beat)* "Help! Get this psycho off me!"
YACHIYO KUGE: *(Toshiya's Mother, Chorus Member)* What's that movie?
TOSHIYA: Terminator 2. *(dramatically)* Judgment Day.
YACHIYO: You already watched that movie yesterday. Find something better to do.
TOSHIYA: Something better than learning English? It's important to know English if you want to make something of yourself in this world.
YACHIYO: Wait till you reach high school. Then learn to make something of yourself.
TOSHIYA: But this is a good way. *(pointing)* I copy the talking in this movie, then I know I am doing it right.
YACHIYO: Toshiya, do your homework.
TOSHIYA: But you know what I mean, Mama? Don't you think I make a

good point?

MARIAH: Toshiya was America's biggest fan. He loved to hike and paddle canoes. He loved American football. He was wearing a Pittsburgh Steelers shirt when he died, which was when he was 20. His mother performed a Buddhist death ritual for her son at the crash site. Incense. Flower petals. A rope tied around a tree to mark a sacred place.

YACHIYO: Thank you for joining me to wish farewell to my son. (*chanting*)
  ga-te, ga-te
  paragate
  parasamgate
  bod-hi, sva-ha!

(*Viola plays Schubert's "Fantasy in F Minor, D. 940: I." A couple measures and then MARIAH speaks. Music out after DEORA says, "I ask peace.)"*

MARIAH: Like Toshiya, Deora Bodley was a sophomore in college. Her father Derrill was a music professor and what people in the sixties used to call a peacenik. By the time she was in eighth grade, Deora was a little peacenik too. After she died, her father traveled to the Middle East encouraging people not to give up on peace.

(*DEORA at age 13, reading.*)

DEORA: "Some people ask who, what, why, where, when and how. I ask peace." (*beat*) What do you think, Dad?
MARIAH: And once she got to high school—

DEORA: C'mon. Do it with me.
ALY: (*Deora's Friend*) It's depressing, Buddha.
DEORA: The idea is to educate people so it goes away, doofus. (*with energy and a sense of humor*) Out! Out! Damned AIDS!! We will cure you! And until we cure you, we will banish you from our bodies! And listen, in a few years I'm taking my act on the road. So many kids in Africa are born with it and my Dad knows about organizations that do HIV prevention stuff over there. Come with me! We'll spend a year blanketing the continent with condoms and then we'll go on a safari!

ALY: April 22, 2006. Buddha. I don't even know where to start. We were best friends for so many years. You were my better half, my reasoning, my inspiration. Not a day goes by where I don't think of you and that horrible day. I have never met anyone quite like you and don't think I ever will. Since that morning, a piece of me has been missing and I will never be the same. I try to use the strength you left me with to motivate myself to make a difference like you did for so many people. I love you, D!!!! Forever in my heart! Love, Your Best Friend, AlyKat

MARIAH: Deora's father founded Peaceful Tomorrows, an organization for Flight 93 families who wanted to pursue peace. Many of them did and still do.

CHORUS: MATH

MARIAH: I was born in 1985 when Toshiya and Deora were four years old. For me to be her daughter, Christine Snyder would've had to have gotten pregnant at 13.

(Viola plays Brahms Sonata No. 1 in F Minor, Ops 129, I, quietly.)

(CHRISTINE SNYDER and a GIRLFRIEND [Chorus Member] at Windows on the World at the top of the World Trade Center where the music is playing. They're both a bit tipsy.)

GIRLFRIEND: So spill, Chris. How's married life?
CHRISTINE: Wonderful!
GIRLFRIEND: That's what we all say after three months. You're still in the honeymoon stage.
CHRISTINE: I wish Ian could see this. *(standing, stepping toward a window)* The city's so gorgeous from up here.

(CHRISTINE steps toward the violist as GIRLFRIEND says the next line. Christine sways her arms to the music, maybe pretend conducts.)

GIRLFRIEND: Yep. Nothing more beautiful than the Big Apple after dark, all lit up.
CHRISTINE: *(a step toward the violist)* Brahms. Sigh.
GIRLFRIEND: You ready for another drink?
CHRISTINE: Oh no.

GIRLFRIEND: Come on. We'll get you a taxi.
CHRISTINE: No no no. I have a plane to catch in the morning.
GIRLFRIEND: Don't go yet. I haven't seen you in two years.
CHRISTINE: I'm not going anywhere. Not till you tell me why you're still with that arrogant self-involved jackass.
GIRLFRIEND: Not everyone marries her high school sweetheart, Chris. Don't worry about me, okay? He's not that bad.
CHRISTINE: No no no no no. Don't be desperate. (*takes her friend's hand and says with absolute sincerity, even if her tipsiness is showing*) You are way way better than that.
GIRLFRIEND: Man, I miss you.

(*Viola Out.*)

CHORUS: It's true.
MARIAH: Yes. Christine had a drink at Windows on the World with a friend the night before she died.

(*CHRISTINE sits in the boarding area nursing a headache; GEORGINE CORRIGAN enters, wearing a lei that's a bit worse for wear. She sits down near CHRISTINE. After a beat or two—*)

GEORGINE: Hey, you okay?
CHRISTINE: Fine. Just a little bit of a headache.
GEORGINE: Too much celebrating?
CHRISTINE: I rarely drink, so.... (*beat, as she rubs her head a bit, then looks at GEORGINE*) Do you mind if I ask—where'd you get that lei?
GEORGINE: It's the same one I brought over here from Honolulu. I brought it for my brother Kevin. I told him Kevin, what you should do is, you should put it in the refrigerator and take it out when you want to wear it or else you should just put it on the table or someplace and it'll make your apartment smell nice and sweet. Well, he did put it in the refrigerator and that's where it stayed the whole week. So I'm taking it home. It looks a little ratty but it still smells good.
CHRISTINE: So you live—
GEORGINE: In Honolulu. You?
CHRISTINE: I grew up in Oahu.
GEORGINE: What're you doing in New Jersey?
CHRISTINE: Tree conference.

GEORGINE: What's a tree conference?

CHRISTINE's GIRLFRIEND (*to Mariah*): Chris was a Certified Arborist, one of only a handful of women certified in the United States. (*beat*) At her memorial service at the Ala Moana Beach Park in Honolulu, there was a soft, all-embracing breeze through the trees that at once told me she was there with us.

(At some point, RICHARD GUADAGNO enters and sits down. MARIAH points toward him.)

MARIAH: Richard Guadagno was the Manager of a wildlife refuge and Christine Snyder was an arborist, so I imagined them sitting near each other in the airport waiting for the plane.
CHORUS MEMBER: Waiting to board the plane that would carry them to their—
MARIAH: (*overlap*) Because she'd gone to the tree conference and he could easily have attended that conference, because they were both—
CHORUS: They were on their way, they were waiting to board.
MARIAH: My imagination was running wild.
JERRY GUADAGNO: (*JERRY's Father, chorus member*) Did I remember to give you the primrose?
RICHARD: Yeah, Dad.
JERRY: You got the crape myrtle, the Japanese maple, and the primrose?
RICHARD: I've got all three cuttings in my backpack wrapped real well so they'll make it to San Francisco with me. They'll be planted in my garden by the next time I talk to you.
JERRY: Then, yeah, let's get going. (*a step, and then—*) But I want to ask you, Rich. Your mother's dying to know and truthfully, I am too.
RICHARD: Okay.
JERRY: This girl, this Dique? (*DEE-KAY*)
RICHARD: Yeah?
JERRY: You mentioned her a lot, which is not like you. And you phoned her—what?—two-three times in a weekend? So, we're wondering—You know, we're wondering.
RICHARD: Yeah, we're engaged.
JERRY: What, you don't tell anybody?
RICHARD: I haven't exactly asked her yet.
JERRY: Rich. In whose world are people engaged if nobody's popped the

question?

RICHARD: We're talking a lot about what it'll be like after we're married. So, you know, we're both assuming.

JERRY: You'll want to cement that.

RICHARD: I'm on it, Dad. No worries.

JERRY: You're sure you've got the cuttings?

RICHARD: I spent ten minutes wrapping them. I've got them.

JERRY: Then we better get to the airport.

JERRY: You made your grandmother very happy by the way.

(They exit.)

MARIAH: Because he traveled to the East Coast to attend his grandmother's 100th birthday party. And I'm thinking—he's the right age, and he's handsome–not that I wouldn't love a dad who wasn't handsome. He was a nature photographer and he hiked and he played guitar and he surfed and he lifted weights, he could bench press 350 pounds, which is twice what he weighed. And the great love of his life was his German Shepherd, Raven. Who wouldn't want this guy to be her dad? I couldn't stop thinking maybe it's him, maybe it's him, maybe it's him, God, maybe it's him.

(A Tim McGraw song, "Where the Green Grass Grows," blasts suddenly.)

(Mariah, Christine, Georgine, Richard all look toward the noise.)

CHRISTINE: *(makes her head hurt)* Oh my God.

RICHARD: *(overlap)* What the hell's that?

(Music out.)

(As it goes out, NICOLE MILLER sticks her head in, holding her Walkman.)

NICOLE: Sorry. Tried to stick the little jack thingy in the wrong hole.

MARIAH: Nicole Miller. Even if she weren't so young, I couldn't conceive of having a mom who blasts Tim McGraw music. On the other hand, I told you how there were a lot of athletes on the plane. Nicole was one of them.

(*NICOLE sits on a porch in cutoffs. It's summer. Viola plays "Where the Green Grass Grows" from the "String Quartet Tribute to Tim McGraw" album. NICOLE is happily singing and dancing along. Her friend RENEE enters dressed much differently from NICOLE—in a crisp white blouse and preppy pants maybe. Viola underscores the scene, fading throughout it. At NICOLE's feet lies—*)

RENEE: Oh my God, what the hell's that?
NICOLE: It's a pig. What's it look like?
RENEE: It's black though.
NICOLE: It's a potbellied pig. Mostly all potbellied pigs are black.
RENEE: Nicole, it's huge.
NICOLE: 302 pounds. (*to pig*) Hey! Agnes, no. Stop that. (*to RENEE*) She's forever rooting in my father's flowers.
RENEE: Aren't you scared of it?
NICOLE: No. She's no different than a dog. I mean, she's different than a dog but she's still my dad's pet. She's sweet. (*affectionately, as though to a baby*) Aren't you, Agnes? (*to RENEE*) Let's go down to the creek. You have your suit?
RENEE: No, I—
NICOLE: You want to borrow one of mine?
RENEE: I thought we were going to ride.
NICOLE: Let's jump in the creek, then we'll ride. Dad keeps three horses out here. You can pick the one you like best. Race you to the creek!
RENEE: Wait, I need a bathing suit! Nicole!

(*RENEE turns and speaks to Mariah.*)

RENEE: Nicole was an all-state swimmer her senior year in high school. And she was a runner, and a horseback rider, and a softball player. And we were both Homecoming Princesses that year. We rode on a float together right through downtown San Jose. She had tons of friends—girls, boys. Pigs. I hadn't seen her in over a year when 9-11 hit. It's interesting to me, some of the information that's come out about the passengers fighting back. I know Nicole must have been one of them. She had a fire in her.
MARIAH: I thought, how would that look—that fire in her. When Tom Burnett polled her about overcoming the men in the cockpit, would she have said—
NICOLE: Fuck yeah!
MARIAH: (*a beat as she looks at Nicole standing frozen*) No. That's not Nicole.

Maybe she said—
NICOLE: (*fierce*) I'm not going down without a fight.
MARIAH: I mean. She listened to country music and you don't have to like country music to know it's got that idealism, that conviction—.
CHORUS: That fight!

(*NICOLE starts kicking ferociously at the cockpit, unintelligible sounds coming out of her.*)

MARIAH: Or maybe she rushed the cockpit with some of the others. (*NICOLE stops kicking.*) She was sitting close to the front of economy cabin, in row 10, next to the window. On the other side of the plane on the aisle was sitting the man who became Flight 93's most famous passenger.

(*TODD BEAMER sits in his seat. NICOLE picks up her carry-on and hoists it toward the overhead. TODD rises, lifts up a hand—he's really tall—gives it an extra push. NICOLE instantly turns, jumps up, and high fives him.*)

NICOLE: Thanks!

(*She sits. He sits.*)

MARIAH: Nicole was five when I was born. Todd Beamer was 16. When I thought about whether Todd Beamer might be my father, I asked myself would a teenage boy who was a devout Christian father a child out of wedlock? Much stranger things have happened, but would a person of such strong faith trust strangers to raise his child? (*beat*) I have a very special place for Todd in my heart because he too was a baseball fanatic. Different team, but still. He had a Cubs pinball machine in his family room, and a model of Wrigley Field in his office. You have to respect that.

LISA JEFFERSON: (*GTE Phone Operator, Chorus Member*) Sir? Are you there, sir?
TODD: I'm still here.
LISA: Am I understanding this correctly? Your plane has been hijacked?
TODD: Yeah. There's, I think, four guys. I, uh, I heard shouting in first class. I stood up to look, and the cockpit—
LISA: They're in the cockpit?

TODD: One's standing in the aisle. He says he has a bomb. But the others are in the cockpit. Some of us think we might be able to . . . We want to try—(*suddenly*) We're going down. (*very loudly*) WE'RE GOING DOWN! (*as though calling out to his wife*) LISA!
LISA: Yes?
TODD: No. No, we're okay. They——. I think they turned the plane around. Yeah, they——. I'm sorry. Lisa's my wife's name.
LISA: It's my name too.
TODD: It is?
LISA: Yes, it is.
TODD: Lisa? Will you pray with me?
MARIAH: They said Psalm 23 together.
LISA: The Lord is my Shepherd
LISA/TODD: I shall not want.
TOSHIYA: (*chanting quietly*) Jizo on kaka kabi sanmaei sowaka, Jizo on kaka kabi sanmaei sowaka
LISA/TODD: (*overlap*) He maketh me to lie down in green pastures.
JEAN/DON PETERSON: He leadeth me beside the still waters.
CHRISTINE: He restoreth my soul.
CHRISTIAN: Er führet mich auf rechter Strasse um seines Names willen.
LISA/TODD: Yea, though I walk through the valley of the shadow of death
TODD: I will fear no evil.

(*Freeze.*)

MARIAH: (*after two beats*) Lisa Jefferson wrote a book about this phone conversation, which ended after 13 minutes, when he said to her—
TODD: It's happening. I've got to go.
MARIAH: Then Mrs. Jefferson heard him say—
TODD: Jesus help me.
MARIAH: Then he shouted some words of encouragement to his fellow passengers. Then some of the passengers ran down the aisle following Sandy Bradshaw, who was pushing a cart carrying the pots of boiling water.

CHORUS: MARION AND WALESKA

MARIAH: Marion Britton, the bagel lady, had never been married—
CHORUS Member: So, she's not your mother.
CHORUS Member: Unmarried women have babies.

CHORUS Member: Not Marion.

(MARION's nephew, WREN BRITTON, Chorus Member, enters. He is a flamboyant, cross-dressing gay man.)

WREN: *(to MARIAH)* Aunt Marion would have been the best mommy in the world. My father was a Lutheran minister and Aunt Marion talked to him like nobody else talked to him.
MARION: He wants to wear eye make-up, let him wear eye make-up. Show me where it says in the bible boys shalt not wear eye make-up. Let's go, Wren. I'm taking you for sushi. *(to her brother)* It wouldn't hurt you to broaden your culinary horizons. He's got a better palate than you and he's only eleven.
WREN: She was like my fairy godmother. When she met my first boyfriend, she hugged him for—like—days. He said, "Wren, your aunt has very big breasts."
MARIAH: Did you ever meet Waleska?
WREN: Lots of times. Wally and her girlfriend always used to say they were going to adopt me. Aunt Marion told me they were struggling with whether to try to have a kid, which is something to which I cannot relate.

(WALESKA MARTINEZ sits petting her cat.)

(The Madonna song "Like A Prayer" is playing.)

MARIAH: Wally—Waleska Martinez—worked with Marion at the census bureau. They were traveling together to a conference.

(WALESKA picks up the cat and dances her around to the Madonna song. Two or three beats and ANGELA LOPEZ (Chorus Member), WALESKA's girlfriend, enters.)

ANGIE: Wally mama, what are you doing? You're gonna make Marlo sick.
WALESKA: Marlo loves this song.
ANGIE: She loves hearing you sing it, not dancing to it. It's a proven fact. Cats do not like to dance.

(Marlo jumps out of WALESKA's arms. WALESKA and ANGIE watch her run off.)

ANGIE: You don't watch out, you're not gonna be her favorite anymore.
WALESKA: Angie, listen. While you were at the store, something came to me. Like in a flash. It just came to me. Hal! Hal would be perfect.
ANGELA: Hal who you work with Hal? Hal who I met at Marion's holiday party?
WELESKA: He's such a smart guy. And he really likes me. Plus, look how handsome he is. Don't you think he's very dignified looking?
ANGELA: What about that lady he brought with him to the party?
WALESKA: Ay, he's married! (*disappointed*) I forgot.
ANGELA: And we decided we didn't want it to be anyone we actually know, didn't we? (*putting her arms around WALESKA*) Come on, baby, you're gonna see, we're gonna make it happen.

(*ANGELA and WALASKA dance together to what's left of the song. They freeze when WREN starts to speak.*)

WREN: Wally bought her ticket first. Aunt Marion was going to go out to the conference a day later but Wally hated flying, so Aunt Marion said she'd go out with her. Knowing Aunt Marion, what she probably said was, "You want me to take the same flight and babysit you, you big baby?" Anyhow. Aunt Marion always bought two seats because she was rather plump and there weren't two seats available in Wally's row, which was also Todd Beamer's row, so that's who Wally was sitting next to. Oh, yes. I know where every one of those passengers was sitting. I can spell all their names backwards and forwards.
MARIAH: Me too.

(*WALESKA sits next to TODD BEAMER, with one seat between them. MARION gets up, calls out to WALESKA, and comes barreling down the aisle, carrying a bag of bagels.*)

MARION: (*to TODD*) She's nervous about flying. Of all people she should know better because we work for the census bureau. We know all about statistics.
WALESKA: I took a muscle relaxant. I'll be fine.
MARION: Did you eat breakfast? I've got H & H bagels.
WALESKA: I ate, Marion. Thanks.
MARION: Suit yourself. No alcohol with that painkiller.

WALESKA: It's a muscle relaxant.

(*As MARIAH says the following, WALESKA stands.*)

MARIAH: I had waking dreams about Waleska being my mom and her and Angie and Marlo and me having dinner together—all of them coming to Minnesota with Marlo in her crate under Waleska's seat.
WALESKA: (*to MARIAH in her daydream*) Te encontré. Me siento muy feliz.
MARIAH: And her teaching me Spanish. And me saying *qué hermoso gato*. And saying *voy a venir a Nueva York*. And saying *me enseñó a bailar como usted*. (*pause*) I daydream.

(*WALESKA takes her seat.*)

MARION: (*to TODD*) You hear her order a drink, you let me know. I'm just a couple rows back in 12. All right? Is that a deal?

(*MARION turns to go back to her seat.*)

CHORUS: BABIES AND MANTRAS

(*LAUREN, returning from the bathroom still again, re-claims her seat next to HONOR.*)

HONOR: Wow. Is it like this all the time—running back and forth to the bathroom?
LAUREN: It took so long to get pregnant. It'd be worth it even if I had to spend the entire flight in the bathroom. (*out of the scene*) I'd take my temperature and call Jack at work to tell him to come home, our best chance is to make love in the next hour. It was like a scene from a romantic comedy. Except it stopped being romantic pretty quickly and it certainly wasn't funny. Month after month you're disappointed and more and more desperate. I couldn't tolerate it. I'd succeeded at pretty much everything I'd ever tried to do in my life. Good student, never a bit of trouble getting a job, never a worry about money, never a fear of trying something new—bungee jumping, white water rafting, skydiving—the scarier the better. (*beat*) So I stopped trying to get pregnant and did something I knew I could succeed at. I started writing a book about . . . (*a grin*) It was a how-to book for women—make your wildest dreams come true—which

I myself hadn't been able to do. A book's not a baby, but it was still an act of creation and I started writing it and—viola!—a few months later? Pregnant.

(LAUREN sits, holds a phone up to her ear.)

LAUREN: Jack? Jack, are you there? Pick up, honey.

(LAUREN freezes.)

JACK: *(to MARIAH)* Marin General's the hospital where our baby would have been born, and I was searching for an appropriate memorial for Lauren. I sat down with a doctor friend of mine who told me the hospital was in need of what are called these birthing rooms, where the mother gets to stay in the room and the baby is born right there and the father can be there too. Anyone you want to be there can be there. So that's what I did. I donated the money to get one of those birthing rooms off the ground in memory of her, of Lauren, and that's where I go every September 11, to Lauren's birthing room. Hundreds of babies have been born there, they've got snapshots of all of them on the wall there, and that's Lauren's legacy. *(beat)* Lauren's motto was get busy living or get busy dying. She kept that on the refrigerator to motivate her. And that's the birthing room. Babies getting busy living.

LAUREN: *(on the phone)* There's a little trouble on the plane, Jack. Pick up if you're there. *(a beat, then to HONOR)* He's not answering. *(holding out her cell phone to HONOR)* Do you want to call your people?

MARIAH: There were 29 phone calls made from Flight 93 in the 40 minutes before it crashed. The plane was teeming with life. *(pointing)* Jeremy Glick called his wife Lyz. Like Lauren and Jack, they had kind of a fairy tale life together until they started trying to conceive.

JEREMY: His-to-compatibility locus antigens? Which means what?
CHORUS: *(overlap)* What?
JEREMY: In English.
LYZ: *(JEREMY's WIFE, Chorus Member)* It means I keep miscarrying because our DNA is too similar.
JEREMY: So yeah, I'd never heard of such a thing either, but once they

figured it out they injected her with massive doses of my white blood cells and—don't ask me to explain how because even though I understand it, I can't explain it—it worked. (*beat, then on the plane's phone to LYZ*) We're thinking we're going to try it, Lyz. One of the flight attendants is boiling water and that's all we have to use as a weapon, so I don't think—. (*He's overcome for a second and then, as a cover—*) Maybe I can use my butter knife from breakfast, huh?

LYZ: I could tell he was terrified. When you've known a guy since grade school, you're pretty tuned in to what he's feeling, whether he says it out loud or not. The thing is, Jeremy's <u>body</u> was a weapon. He earned his black belt in judo when he was still in high school and he was a champion wrestler. He was one of six children so he started toughening up early in life—you can't let somebody else get the last blintz. Emmy was born a couple months before he died. We named her after Ralph Waldo Emerson because he was Jeremy's favorite writer.

JEREMY: I got no end of teasing. Transcendentalism? Whaaa? Think of it this way. Divinity is not (*pointing*) out there. It's (*pointing to his heart*) in here. Which means our souls are all a part of one massive uber-soul.

MARIAH: Uber-soul. That's what Jeremy Glick believed in. Lauren Grandcolas put the words she believed in on her refrigerator. Alan Beaven framed his and hung them on the wall behind his desk.

ALAN: Fear? Who Cares?

(*He sits in an at-rest yoga position.*)

(*Viola plays the melody from Beethoven String Quartet No 13 in B-flat major, Op. 130, II—Presto*)

(*ALAN's oldest son enters excitedly.*)

JOHN BEAVEN: (*Chorus Member*) Dad! You're not going to believe—(*He sees ALAN, thinks he's meditating.*) Shoot.
ALAN: I'm right here, son.
JOHN: Oh. Yeah, I thought it was weird for you to be meditating in the living room with that lively music playing.
ALAN: Was there something you wanted to tell me?
JOHN: Okay, so coach calls me into his office, right? And I think I'm in

trouble because he found out about the whiskey drinking on the field after Tuesday's practice, right? So I—

ALAN: Whiskey drinking on the field?

JOHN: Come on, Dad, I might as well already be 21.

ALAN: Although you're not. But you miss my point. I enjoy whiskey. I'm glad you enjoy whiskey. It's the "on the field" part that concerns me.

JOHN: Could we talk about that later? Cause, Dad! Turns out it wasn't about that. It was about the Devil Rays. The Tampa Bay Devil Rays called coach because they want to draft me!

(ALAN stands, grinning hugely, walks to JOHN arms extended, and engulfs him in a bear hug.)

A FELLOW YOGA PRACTITIONER: (*Chorus Member*) September 11, 2011. Alan, I still remember you from the Oakland Ashram. It was a great pleasure to share spiritual discovery with you. You are a dedicated Yogi. (*with Chorus*) Shanti Shanti Shanti

(Viola music fades out.)

ALAN: (*releasing JOHN from his embrace*) Son, I'm so pleased for you.

MARIAH: I was so pleased for him too, not the least because maybe he was my brother! My brother was drafted by the Devil Rays! My brother was going to be a professional baseball player! (*pause*) Fantasizing about the possibilities fueled my search. The more I imagined, the more determined I became to find my mother or maybe my father. (*beat*) Alan was a lawyer on his way to California to finish up a water rights case. The families of the passengers were allowed to listen to the plane's black box recordings. Some family members chose not to. Those who did listen heard the recording through amplified earphones. Alan Beaven's family—

JOHN: We all recognized my dad's voice. Except my little sister was only 6 when dad died so she didn't listen. In the part where there's a bunch of yelling outside the cockpit and inside the cockpit and the hijackers are trying to decide whether to bring it down? My dad was shouting something like, "keep on" or "keep up."

(Starting on, "In the part where," CHORUS begins to bang as though trying to breach the cockpit door and passengers say things like "Push now," and "Once

more" and "We've got it." They stop. We clearly hear ALAN shout the following.)

ALAN: Keep it up!

JOHN: I'm not wrong. I know my father's voice when I hear it. I heard it cheering when I got a hit and yelling in outrage when I got called out on strikes. Because according to my father, I never actually struck out in my entire college baseball career. And I heard him give lots of speeches.

ALAN: (*giving a speech*) California's rich and diverse watersheds have provided us with an exceedingly generous bounty, but there are limits to these natural systems, and we need to protect them.

MARIAH: I let my imagination get the better of me. (*turning to ALAN*) I'm applauding and waving at him and saying to myself he's so smart and committed. Maybe I won't be a sports attorney, maybe I'll be an environmental attorney like he is. "Fear. Who Cares?" From this guy I could learn courage. I could learn to do yoga. I'm clapping and clapping and thinking I'm so proud of my Dad. Then I return to sanity. He was born in New Zealand. He went to high school in New Zealand. Not that guys in New Zealand don't impregnate women too, but . . .

(*COLLEEN FRASER enters and stands on a box. MARIAH turns her attention to COLLEEN.*)

COLLEEN: (*speaking to an audience, with fire—she could have been a preacher*) Do you folks know how tall I am? I am three feet, eight and a half inches tall!!

MARIAH: Colleen Fraser also spent quite a bit of time giving speeches.

COLLEEN: And at this rally to protect the rights of disabled people there have been protesters! What are these protesters afraid of? Are they afraid that if employers can no longer discriminate against people with disabilities, they might lose their jobs? Or is it that many of us with disabilities look different from them, and we all know how much people hate people who look different from them. Well, here's the good news. If the people who are opposed to us are afraid of a woman who is three feet, eight and a half inches tall, we've got this in the bag!

MARIAH: Colleen was born with a damaged spine. As a child, she had to have more than 30 surgeries. When she died, she was Vice-Chair of the New Jersey Developmental Disabilities Council and the Director of the Progressive Center for Independent Living.

PHYLLIS MUCKS TUTTLE:(*Colleen's College Roommate, Chorus Member*) September 6, 2008. I learned only yesterday of your passing. It has been many years since we roomed together at Rutgers. Your positive attitude in spite of the pain and physical challenges you endured were inspirational to your classmates. Time and distance separated us after graduation, so I was unaware of your considerable accomplishments. I hope there are Jack-in-the-Box tacos and White Castle burgers in heaven. Rest in peace.

COLLEEN: (*in college*) Phyllis! There's this giant concert that's happening in Woodstock, man. Do you know who's going to be there? THE WHO. Roger Daltry! In person! Phyllis!! You have to come with me.

PHYLLIS: But it's outdoors. What if it rains?

COLLEEN: That's the problem with you people who've never faced adversity. You're pansies. Rain??? Who cares?

MARIAH: Women with Colleen's condition can have children, but Colleen didn't. When I got lost in thought about her, I'd imagine her mother looking down at her broken baby girl and wonder what she felt. Then I'd try to picture my birth mother looking at me and talking to my birth father, trying to make a decision. I can never put Colleen Fraser's face in that picture. I believe she would have been as unwilling to give up a baby as she was to give up championing the civil rights of people with disabilities. Her sister wrote in memoriam, "If heaven wasn't accessible before, I'm sure it is now that Colleen's there." (*pause, thinking*) Boy, I spent a lot of hours contemplating "heaven." I grew up taking it as gospel that there was such a thing. Heaven—a place where souls go? Is it their loved ones' *souls* people believe are looking down on them?

CHORUS MEMBER: All those souls in heaven? They must be indistinguishable from one another.

MARIAH: God. I hope not.

CHORUS: FIRST CLASS.

MARIAH: The people who hijacked the plane were sitting in first class where

Mark Bingham the rugby player and Mickey Rothenberg the lindy dancer sat. Linda Gronlund was sitting there too.

(LINDA GRONLUND and JOE DELUCA enter together.)

MARIAH: She was an environmental lawyer like Alan Beaven, except his focus was on water rights and hers was on clean air. Christine Snyder's was on trees. Richard Guadagno's was on nature preservation. They had it covered.

LINDA: From your lips to God's ears.

PAUL: (*LINDA's Ex-boyfriend, Chorus Member*) From the moment we met in 1979 it was clear she was unique.

LINDA: Who isn't?

PAUL: I was a volunteer EMT. She was always curious about the car wrecks, heart attacks—all the injuries I worked with. Later she became an EMT herself. One time she set her own kneecap while she was waiting for an ambulance. She had a pretty fiery temper. It was never directed toward me, but I saw it directed toward other people now and then.

LINDA: Bite me.

PAUL: We dated for a fairly long time and split with no anger. We just moved in separate directions. So it's April 2005. The Flight 93 story's on TV. At the end, they roll the names of the passengers on the flight and I happen to look up at the moment her name appears. I go to a 9/11 website and read all about her life in something like a state of shock. Some things I knew. Other things were new to me. Like I didn't know she'd become a competitive racecar driver. Although it didn't surprise me.

LINDA: That's how I met Joe. DeLuca. The guy who was sitting next to me when the thing happened on the plane.

(In a scene now, with JOE.)

JOE: I'm not going to get married that way again.

LINDA: Not to me you're not. Getting married on the racetrack? Wearing your racing gear?

JOE: I was young. I thought it'd be cool.

KAREN: (*SCHETLICK CRECCO, Joey's childhood friend, Chorus Member*) Joey was a slightly overweight handsome Italian-American boy, tall, with black hair and big, Cocker Spaniel brown eyes. He was always tender-hearted, and very careful not to hurt other children's feelings. His grandpa called me "Bella Bambina," which Joey thought was so funny.

JOE: (*imitating grandpa*) Mangia, Bella Bambina! Mangia! Mangia!

(Viola plays a few measures of The Wedding March.)

KAREN: We'd play wedding. My brother would play the priest and Joey and I would pretend to get married in my backyard. I'd use my Mom's white chenille bedspread as a train.

(As KAREN says the previous line, JOE pretends to walk down the aisle.)

JOE: (*pretending to take the vow*) I do.

(Viola out.)

JOE: (*good-naturedly*) Come on, let's play Red Light Green Light 1-2-3.
KAREN: I believe that I was in love with Joey as only a little girl in the 1950s could be. I moved away from Newark when I was 14, but I still have a special place in my heart for that sweet-natured Italian boy.

TOM KOTINSKY: (*Racing friend of Joe DeLuca, Chorus Member*) (*to MARIAH*) I always think of him in his auto gear standing next to his 4/4 bright yellow Morgan roadster, handmade in England. That car was his pride and joy. That and Raymond. This cartoon Joe drew. Raymond the cat, who was as big a racecar fan as Joe was.

JOE: Raymond, tell Linda I love her. Tell her if she marries me, she'll—
LINDA: Stop.
JOE (*as RAYMOND*): Linda, if you marry Joe, he promises you'll never regret it.

(JOE leans over to kiss LINDA's cheek. Freeze.)

TOM KOTINSKY: Things are still a little unsettled for many of us down here. Please watch over us, Joe.

(JOE and LINDA unfreeze.)

WANDA: Can I ask you to fasten your seatbelts?
DEBBIE: Give them a minute, Wanda. They're having a smooch.
WANDA: They can smooch with their seatbelts buckled.
LINDA: We'll smooch in California. Joe. Seatbelt.

ELSE: (*Linda's Sister, Chorus Member*) She called me from the plane. She said hi, Else, this is Lin. I just wanted to tell you how much I love you. Please tell mom and dad how much I love them. Then she said,
LINDA: Now my will is in my safe and my safe is in my closet.
ELSE: And she just told me the combination of her safe. And then she just said—
LINDA/ELSE: I'm really gonna miss you.
ELSE: And she said good-bye.

MARIAH: Sitting in front of Linda and Joe—Mark Bingham drinking his second screwdriver and Tom Burnett—the guy who didn't drink alcohol in the morning, the guy who polled the passengers about whether to try to break into the cockpit—across from him. On Tom's first date with his future wife Deena at Applebee's, they sat together over coffee talking for six hours. She knew she was going to marry him after he unscrewed the light bulb above the table and tossed it over his shoulder, shattering it on the floor.

TOM: I'm trying to create a mood here, and this light's not helping.

MARIAH: He too had a motivating mantra prominently displayed in his office: "In all things, speed." Soon after the crash, Tom's widow spoke about him having had a premonition.

DEENA: (*Tom's Wife, Chorus Member*) I don't object to your wanting to reconcile with God.
TOM: Yeah, it's been a long time coming.
DEENA: But Mass every day?
TOM: That's the fastest way to find out His plan for me.
DEENA: Because you had a premonition.
TOM: Yeah.
DEENA: What kind of premonition?
TOM: It's not clear yet. I think it might be something to do with politics.

MARIAH: And behind Tom Burnett, Ed Felt.

SANDY FELT: (*Ed's Wife*) I met Ed at Freshman Orientation at Colgate but we didn't start dating till our senior year. My friends all thought he was too "science nerd" for me. And his friends all thought I was too "city girl" for him. Ed grew up in a small town in upstate New York. He had kind of a purr-y voice, this sweet country lilt. One of my friends used to tell me, "You can't marry him."

CHORUS: He talks like Jim Nabors.

(Viola plays Kenji Bunch's Suite for Viola and Piano: III.)

SANDY: (*to Ed*) I'll give you a hundred bucks if you let me poach your Probability and Statistics assignment.

ED: (*teasing awkwardly*) I suspected you were only dating me to get your hands on my Probability and Statistics assignments. My question to you is this: if I grant you access to my mathematics assignments, what will you grant me in return?

SANDY: Edward! I thought you'd never ask.

JULIE DUMLAO: (*Ed's Colleague, Chorus Member, to MARIAH*) You know that guy in your college classes that was the smartest one in the room? Ed was brilliant in ways normal humans couldn't understand. Everyone we worked with was in awe of his mental prowess but never intimidated, because his sweetness—well, he was just so gentle and sweet. When he died, his office voice mail message was left running for many months-so people could call and listen to his voice. It's hard to envision the Ed Felt I knew on that plane. He was a peaceful person—he abhorred violence. I never even heard him raise his voice.

SANDY FELT: Our girls adored him. Like all sisters, they argued, which made Ed almost physically ill. He'd tell them in an almost frighteningly quiet voice—

ED: Adrienne. Kathryn. Stop.

MARIAH: He made a phone call to a 911 dispatcher from one of the plane's lavatories.

ED: (*quietly, but fearfully, near tears*) We're being hijacked. We are being hijacked.

MARIAH: After 78 seconds, the cell phone signal was lost. Right before that

happened, Ed said—
ED: We're going down.

(Viola out.)

MARIAH: I loved the thought of that sweet man being my father. But.
CHORUS: He's not.
MARIAH: His oldest daughter was born the same year as me. I *knew* him and I knew he wasn't the kind of guy who impregnated two women in one year. That sounds—maybe—odd. But it's true. I knew him.

(Silence for several beats.)

MARIAH: I often tried to imagine the terrible struggle at the front of the plane. Mickey Rothenberg dying trying to protect Wanda Green.

MARK (MICKEY) ROTHENBERG: ARE YOU CRAZY?

MARIAH: I imagined Linda Gronlund trying to help him.

(LINDA is in EMT mode, trying to help MICKEY. It's no use.)

LINDA: *(furious, to a person we can't see)* He's dead. What else do you want from him?

MARIAH: The pilot. His co-pilot.

JASON: GET OUT OF HERE!
LEROY: *(overlap)* MAYDAY!

CHORUS: GUYS WHO COULD FLY THE PLANE

MARIAH: Once the hijacking started, once Wanda Green and Mickey Rothenberg and Debbie Welsh and Jason Dahl and Leroy Homer had been killed, one of the hijackers—the one who pretended he had a bomb—forced all the people in first class to the back of the plane. *(beat)* At first, the plan was simply to break into the cockpit and prevent the hijackers from doing whatever they were going to do. But as Tom Burnett took the vote, he discovered two passengers who could fly a commercial airplane. One was Donald Greene.

CLAUDETTE: (*Donald Greene's Wife*) I'm positive. My husband could have landed a Boeing 757 with relative ease.

MARIAH: Donald Greene's father invented the Stall Warning Indicator, a device that gives pilots a warning if their planes encounter conditions that might cause them to stall. Today, it's standard equipment on all airplanes. At the time of the crash, Don was the Safe Flight Instrument Company's Executive Vice President. With an engineering degree from Brown and having learned to fly a plane at the age of ten—

CLAUDETTE: (*to MARIAH*) Don and the others couldn't get into the cockpit in time to prevent the hijackers from putting the plane down, but if they had (*to the audience, raising her voice a bit*) Donald could have flown the plane.

DONALD: It didn't take me long to fall in love with her.

(Viola plays Brandenburg Concerto No. 6 in B-Flat: 1, under, starting 12 measures in.)

DONALD: We met at a black tie event—a fundraiser for a museum, held in an airplane hangar with small planes parked in a semi-circle to create a more intimate space—except they turned up one plane short. My father asked me to fly in the final plane. In return, he gave me a ticket to the dinner and dance. I was happy to help What's more fun than flying a plane? I was seated next to Claudette. She's beautiful, she's a firebrand, she's smarter than I am, and she told me within ten minutes that she loved opera—which sealed the deal. As I remember it, we got married that night. Claudette swore I'd drunk too much champagne and that we didn't actually get married till a couple years later. So, yeah, the circumstances on the plane were adverse, and yeah, we didn't have much of a shot, but we had a shot. Because (*to Tom Burnett*) I can fly this plane.

MARIAH: The other was Andrew Garcia, the guy who was keeping them laughing at the back of the plane.

ANDREW: I'd only flown a commercial plane once or twice, but I knew everything about airplane controls by the time I was eight. That was the year the Stall Warning Indicator was invented. Genius. Till about ten years before the crash I worked for United. I didn't fly for United but knowing how all the controls worked and having flown smaller planes, and since all

my life I wished I'd become a pilot—
DONALD: Not the same thing.
ANDREW: Still, I think I could have done it.
DONALD: Maybe.
ANDREW: I'll admit I was relieved to realize there was someone aboard who knew for sure he could fly the plane. (*with utter honesty*) I had something more important to do. The woman sitting in front of me—her name was Pat and she'd never flown before. She was trying to stay calm, and when somebody asked her what she thought about making a stand, she said,
PAT: Yes. Of course we should.
JANE: How many of them are there?
ANDREW: I thought Patricia's companion was wavering but—
JANE: Few enough so we can kill every one of them?

(Music out.)

MARIAH: My daydream about Andrew Garcia being my Dad involved a lot of laughing. I imagined him as one of those dads who couldn't help turning everything into a pun. A Dad who could imitate both voices in a love scene.
ANDREW: (*ala Humphrey Bogart*) You played it for her, now play it for me. Play it, Sam.

(Chaotic sounds. We can hear the Stahl Warning Indicator. And the following overlapping lines, the chaos of which should continue until the crash. Each line should be spoken separately and then repeated, overlapping.)

LYZ GLICK: DAD! It's Jeremy. He's calling from the plane.
ALICE HOAGLAND: Mark? Mark. Honey. It's your Mom.
WREN BRITTON: Aunt Marion? Shhh, darling. Shhh. Shhh.
SANDY FELT: Oh my God, is that Ed's plane?
PHIL BRADSHAW): What do you mean you have a plan? Sandy? What do you mean? What kind of plan?

(THE CRASH HAPPENS)

CHORUS: MARIAH'S DAD

MARIAH: I kept having waking dreams about the people I thought might be my birth parent and then I started dreaming about them at night. And then I just dreamt about one of them over and over again. My mom called me at school one day soon after my nineteenth birthday and said, "We got the birth certificate." I said, "Well? Who are they? Tell me who they are." My mom said, "Mariah, come home." I felt panic, but I held an image of the man I'd become certain was my father in my mind's eye and that calmed me down. When mom handed me the birth certificate, she held my hand as I read it.

(MARIAH turns to look at TOM BURNETT as LORRAINE BAY speaks to him.)

LORRAINE: Can I get you something Mr. Burnett?
TOM: I'm from the Midwest. We don't drink alcohol at this hour.
MARIAH: A devout Catholic.
TOM: You know one of the best things about Catholicism? Wine's part of the ritual. Any time I can get back home, I take my mother to mass and then out for lunch and a glass of good wine. Of course, that happens in the afternoon.
MARIAH: A Minnesota Twins fan.
TOM: *(speaking to MARK BINGHAM)* You play rugby? That's what? Like football? I played football in high school, but to my current way of thinking it's all baseball all the time. You know why? Baseball takes patience. I have very little patience, which has gotten me in some trouble in my life, so when I watch those guys with their bats, waiting, waiting, waiting, and those guys in the field, waiting with them? That, my friend, is impressive.

DEENA BURNETT: *(to MARIAH)* He told me about you before we got married.
MARIAH: At Applebee's?
DEENA: Sometime after Applebee's. He told me it happened when he was in college. He told me the time was going to come when you two were going to meet and he wanted to make sure I could accept that when it happened. *(beat)* He told me he had a premonition.
MARIAH: My happiness was about much more than finding out that this brave man who spoke in a whisper to one person after another on a plane under siege was my father. I could envision him there, among those extraordinary people. I asked Deena—
DEENA: *(as in "huh"?)* Did he like to dance?

(*Sound here. Is it music? Is it viola music? Is it pop music? Whatever it is—everybody's dancing.*)

TOSHIYA: (*doing a crazy jumping up and down dance and singing in his best English*): Everybody dance now! Boom. Boom. (*beat*) Boom Boom Boom. Boom. Was that good? I'll try again. Everybody dance now!

LEROY: (*holding his hand out to ILSE*) Mom? May I have the pleasure?

(*She takes his hand. WANDA dances on doing the cha cha cha with a MAN. They turn two three four. She addresses the rest of the flight attendants.*)

WANDA: Okay, ladies, you ready?

(*She demonstrates. LORRAINE, DEBBIE, CEE CEE, SANDY follow.*)

WANDA: One, two, cha-cha-cha. Two, two, cha-cha-cha.
CEE CEE: Good grief, Debbie! You can't count to two?
WANDA: Start over. One, two—
SANDY: I can do this.
WANDA: Cha-cha-cha.
SANDY: This is a snap. Come on, Lorraine, do it with me. You go forward, I'll go backwards.
DEBBIE: Do you teach every flight crew how to cha cha? Or are we special?
WANDA: Debbie, you are special. No doubt.

MARK ROTHENBERG: Come on, try it with me. Honey, if your father can do it, anybody can do it. It's that old fashioned lindy. It's like swing dancing but without all the sliding under the legs. I learned it a long time ago, when I was a kid your age.

(*JASON DAHL takes his wife's hand and sweeps her into a dip, and then she's up with a laugh.*)

WREN BRITTON: (*singing and doing a funky dance*)
    What you find—ah!
    (*calling to her*) Aunt Marion!
    What you feel now!

(*calling to her*) Come on!
What you know—ah!

(MARION's *there, singing a line as she twirls around funkily.*)

MARION: To be real!

DONALD GREENE: That first night in the airplane hangar, music started playing and she said, "I don't suppose you can tango." (*cheerfully, striking a tango posture*) I showed her who she was dealing with.

(*They tango.*)

(*Everyone who is dancing freezes.*)

(*Viola reprises Brahms Sonata No. 1 in F Minor, Opus 120:II*)

CHRISTINE: (*dreamily, twirling around*) Brahms. When I think, there's too much work to be done, when I feel self-pity and think how can I know the work I do will mean something in the end? The answer? Brahms.

MARIAH: Deena said my Dad had two left feet. Which explains a lot about my total inability to keep a beat.

(SANDY *pushes the cart down the plane's aisle. In addition to the dialogue below, there is other encouraging yelling as the passengers attempt to breach the cockpit.*)

NICOLE: We're right behind you.
MARK BINGHAM: GO! KEEP GOING!! KEEP GOING!!
TOM: (*overlap*) PUSH!
JANE: (*from further back on the plane*) Keep going!
JANE/PAT: Keep going!!
NICOLE: C'mon, push! PUSH HARDER!!
ALAN: KEEP IT UP!
NICOLE: WE CAN DO THIS.
SANDY: Oh My God, OH MY GOD! Almost!
JOE DeLUCA: AGAIN!
LINDA: (*overlap*) GO GO GO GO!

(Freeze.)

MARIAH: My father wasn't around to teach me anything in person. But the thing I learned from him that I couldn't have learned from anyone else, I learned from the very last thing he said to Deena, four or five minutes before he died.

(MARIAH steps toward TOM. She looks at him, and he at her.)

TOM: We're over a rural area now. It's time. We're going to do something.

END OF PLAY

AFTERWORD

I wrote these plays between 1986 (*Unconditional War*) and 2014 (*United*). They are five of more than 20 plays I've written throughout my life and I believe the concerns of these five represent the foundational concerns of every play I've written, from *John* in 1978, about five women who meet in a department store's ladies' room, to *Consolation* in 2017, about the attempt of ten little known first ladies who preceded her, to console Hillary Clinton following her loss in the 2016 presidential election.

When I was asked, as a much younger playwright, to speak to the "goals" of my writing, I would say something like, "to explore dramatically my most closely held belief about how to succeed at the business of being a human being, which is that we are all here together."

As I and my work grew older, I expressed this in myriad ways: "Context is everything," for example. Recently, I saw a movie in which a character, speaking at the funeral of a gang member and drug dealer, asked one attendee after another, "What will you remember about him?" A half a dozen spoke, each expressing a different, sometimes antithetical, memory of him.

In anguish, the speaker summed it up: "You see?" he said, "No one is just one thing."

This outcry speaks precisely to the profound obstacles that separate us from one another. In *Trucker Rhapsody*, Damian cries out, "I'm telling you, there's a life inside me." In talk-backs, many audience members said that Damian was nothing more than a violent gang-banging criminal and wondered why I expected them to care about him, stating flatly that they refused to do so.

In the plays in this book, every character—from the forty people who met their deaths in United, to Damian in *Trucker Rhapsody*, to Cynthia and her father in *Armor*, even to Arnold in *Stand*, has an inner life, often buried far beneath the surface. Without a commitment to understanding this, it's impossible to accomplish what we must for all of our goods: be it by realizing what we have in common with the person who threw a concrete block at someone's head during a riot; by recognizing the need of soldiers who are fighting in a war we don't believe in for equipment that could save their lives; by understanding the need of a president for acknowledgment of not just his failures and successes but also his humanity; by acknowledging the willingness of two vastly different people who work together to call on both their sets of experiences in order to save a child; by recognizing the ability of forty "ordinary" people—just like us—to overcome the fear of their own deaths to save the lives of hundreds of others.

Today I'd say that I write plays about the multitude of gestures, large and small, swirling constantly around us and moving us toward real and resilient community.

ACKNOWLEDGMENTS

Neither the specific plays in this book nor its publication would have been possible without help from many quarters; neither would my creative life have thrived over so many years without it.

Unconditional War was written at the Ucross Foundation and further developed at the Eureka Theatre. *Stand*, too, was written at the Ucross Foundation a decade later and further developed at the O'Neill Playwrights Conference, by the Arizona Theatre Company, and by Jeff Daniels' Purple Rose Theatre, which later produced it under Tony Caselli's direction. *Trucker Rhapsody* was written at a many-years-long artist residency at Indianapolis' Phoenix Theatre and further developed through correspondence with Damian Williams—from prison—and Ben Velazquez, a graffiti artist in Queens, and at the Playwrights Center under the direction of the gifted Benny Ambush. *Armor* was commissioned by the Sloan Foundation and further developed and produced by Winding Road Theatre Ensemble, directed by Eva Tessler. *United* was also developed by Winding Road Theatre Ensemble, of which I was a founding member and Playwright in Residence, through five readings at various stages and where it received its first production. These represent only a few of the artist residencies, theaters and organizations committed to developing and producing new work and to whom I owe a great debt.

I owe an equally large debt of gratitude to people outside the theater, who have supported my work—some for many years, who encouraged me, who believed in me and the work, and who talked me down from more than a few emotional ledges. These include Mike Blau and Efraim Velazquez, friends since childhood, and their partners, Sharon Weinberg and Ivette Velazquez; Pat and Jackie Leo; Ruth Romer and Ron Bernstein; Angela and Carmine Mangino; Ann Manheimer and Art Swislocki; Keith, Kiley, Mo, Nora and Anthony DeGreen; David Johnston and Kevin Justus; and Alida Gunn, a beautiful actor and even more beautiful friend, and my children, Jessica Mischkot and Andy Press, who inspire me to do work that matches their great senses of humor, their brilliance, their generosity, and their commitment to social justice. What mother could ask for more?

Acknowledgments

Special thanks to Bryan Fonseca, artistic director of the Phoenix Theatre for more than thirty-five years and, subsequently, of the Fonseca Theatre. Bryan produced several of my plays and many, many other new plays in English and Spanish. He was in love with plays and playwrights—with all artists, really. A dear friend with an oversized heart, he died of COVID in September 2020 at age sixty-five.

Finally, thanks to Heather Tosteson and Charles Brockett, who worked long and hard to get this book out. I deeply appreciate this great gift.

Author photo is from my performance in *Wit*. Photo by Christopher Johnson.

Photo by Abril Castillo from a Winding Road Theatre Ensemble production of *United*, 2015 includes the following cast members: front, left to right: Albert Riesgo, Jill Baker, T Loving; behind them: Roger Owen, Carly Preston, Tony Caprile; back: Leslie Miller, Steve Mckee, Glen Coffman.

The cover photo is a variation of a photo by Duro'ng Nhân from Pexels.

PLAYS BY TONI PRESS-COFFMAN

FULL LENGTH

Psycho Sarah (2020)
Consolation (2017)
United (2011)
Armor (2009)
New House, New Dog (2007)
Holy Spirit (2004)
Dean the Sublime (2003)
Trucker Rhapsody (2002)
That Slut! (2000)
Touch (1999)
Two Days of Grace at Middleham (1998)
Good Soldiers, Brave Comrades, Loyal Citizens (1994)
Stand (1991)
Unconditional War (1986)
Moonlight Serenade (1985)
Patsy's Legacy (1983)
All Ye Faithful (1982)
Appleton Manor (1981)
Carolyn (1980)
Vera, With Kate (1979)
Tremont (1978)
The Feast (1976)
Children of the Land (1975)

SHORT

Pretty Ruth (2007)
Virginia Street (1994)
Patty and Josh (1980)
We're Here to Help (1979)
John (1977)

Toni Press-Coffman has written twenty-seven plays that have been produced in cities throughout the United States. She frequently writes about real people or events such as the people who died when Flight 93 crashed in a Pennsylvania field (*United*); the 1992 L.A. Riots (*Trucker Rhapsody*); Lyndon Johnson's presidency (*Unconditional War*); Dean Martin (*Dean the Sublime*); and Richard III (*Two Days of Grace at Middleham*); and dramatizes social issues impacting the lives of women and children (*Psycho Sarah, That Slut!, Stand, Holy Spirit*) or the consequences of the rampant racism that continues to plague American society (*Stand, Trucker Rhapsody*). The recipient of several playwriting awards, she is also an actress, dramaturg, and co-founder of Winding Road Theater Ensemble in Tucson, where she served as company manager for ten years. She now lives in Connecticut with her husband Glen, dog Mareeba, and cats Augie and JJ.

BOOKS FROM WISING UP PRESS

FICTION
Only Beautiful & Other Stories
Live Your Life & Other Stories
My Name Is Your Name & Other Stories
Kerry Langan

Germs of Truth
The Philosophical Transactions of Maria van Leeuwenhoek
Visible Signs
Heather Tosteson

Not Native: Short Stories of Immigrant Life in an In-Between World
Murali Kamma

Something Like Hope & Other Stories
William Cass

MEMOIRS
Journeys with a Thousand Heroes: A Child Oncologist's Story
John Graham-Pole

Keys to the Kingdom: Reflections on Music and the Mind
Kathleen L. Housley

Last Flight Out: Living, Loving & Leaving
Phyllis A. Langton

Green Card & Other Essays
Áine Greaney

POETRY
Source Notes: Seventh Decade
Heather Tosteson

A Hymn that Meanders
Maria Nazos

Epiphanies
Kathleen L. Housley

WISING UP ANTHOLOGIES

ILLNESS & GRACE: TERROR & TRANSFORMATION

FAMILIES: *The Frontline of Pluralism*

LOVE AFTER 70

DOUBLE LIVES, REINVENTION & THOSE WE LEAVE BEHIND

VIEW FROM THE BED: VIEW FROM THE BEDSIDE

SHIFTING BALANCE SHEETS:
Women's Stories of Naturalized Citizenship & Cultural Attachment

COMPLEX ALLEGIANCES:
Constellations of Immigration, Citizenship, & Belonging

DARING TO REPAIR: *What Is It, Who Does It & Why?*

CONNECTED: *What Remains As We All Change*

CREATIVITY & CONSTRAINT

SIBLINGS: *Our First Macrocosm*

THE KINDNESS OF STRANGERS

SURPRISED BY JOY

CROSSING CLASS: *The Invisible Wall*

RE-CREATING OUR COMMON CHORD

GOODNESS

FLIP SIDES

Learn more about Universal Table/Wising Up Press:
www.universaltable.org
wisingup@universaltable.org
P.O. Box 2122, Decatur, GA 30031-2122